Growth Champions

The Battle for Sustained Innovation Leadership

The Growth Agenda

Edited by Tim Jones, Dave McCormick
and Caroline Dewing

WILEY

A John Wiley & Sons, Ltd., Publication

This edition first published 2012

© 2012 Growth Agenda Limited

Registered office
John Wiley & Sons Ltd, The Atrium, Southern Gate, Chichester, West Sussex, PO19 8SQ, United Kingdom

For details of our global editorial offices, for customer services and for information about how to apply for permission to reuse the copyright material in this book please see our website at www.wiley.com.

Wiley publishes in a variety of print and electronic formats and by print-on-demand. Some material included with standard print versions of this book may not be included in e-books or in print-on-demand. If this book refers to media such as a CD or DVD that is not included in the version you purchased, you may download this material at http://booksupport.wiley.com. For more information about Wiley products, visit www.wiley.com.

Library of Congress Cataloging-in-Publication Data

Growth champions : the battle for sustained innovation leadership : the growth agenda / edited by Tim Jones, Dave McCormick, and Caroline Dewing. – 2nd ed.
    p. cm.
   ISBN 978-1-119-95413-2 (pbk.)
1. Economic development. 2. Corporate culture. 3. Creative ability in business. I. Jones, Tim. II. McCormick, Dave. III. Dewing, Caroline.
  HD87.G765 2012
  658.4'063–dc23

                       2012001523

A catalogue record for this book is available from the British Library.

ISBN 978-1-119-95413-2 (pbk) ISBN 978-1-119-96121-5 (ebk)
ISBN 978-1-119-96122-2 (ebk) ISBN 978-1-119-96123-9 (ebk)

Set in 9/14 pt BookmanITCbyBT-Light by Toppan Best-set Premedia Limited
Printed in Great Britain by TJ International Ltd, Padstow, Cornwall, UK

Contents

About The Growth Agenda

The Growth Agenda is a global network of leading-edge expertise that helps organizations identify and exploit major new growth opportunities.

We enable companies to better understand emerging changes and develop growth strategies to create and capture value from innovation. Using proven approaches that have delivered tangible, sustainable impact, we provide a unique combination of global expertise that leading organizations are engaging to help them build distinctive competences and jump ahead of their peers.

With global insights on the big challenges for the next decade, supported by leading-edge views on how growth and innovation are changing, The Growth Agenda draws together bespoke teams of experts from a wide range of organizations to help companies identify, scope, and deliver major growth platforms.

Our experts include: prominent academics; experienced individuals who have led major strategic change within organizations to deliver growth; and principal advisors who have designed, led, and supported major growth programs around the world. The network includes professors from key business schools; chief technology officers, chief marketing officers, and strategy directors from leading companies; senior consultants; and a number of influential government policy advisors.

About the Contributors

James Alexander

James is a Partner at The Foundation – a consultancy that helps businesses grow more quickly into new areas, or to fend off threats to their top line. He is also a trustee of GreenThing and the RSPB, and was previously Co-founder of ZOPA, the leading peer-to-peer landing company. Prior to this he was Strategy Director at Egg and an LEK consultant.

David Coates

David was most recently Head of Knowledge Exchange at the Technology Strategy Board in the UK working across multiple sectors. He has an extensive background in technology, innovation, and strategy consulting and is part of the Future Agenda program team.

Peter Bryant

Peter is a Senior Fellow at the Kellogg Innovation Network and Partner at Clareo Partners based in Denver. He has extensive experience in helping companies in the IT, aerospace, and materials sectors to identify and exploit new opportunities.

Charlie Dawson

Charlie is Founding Partner of The Foundation, which he established in 1999, and arose from the insight that long-term sustainable growth needed an approach that brought together different worlds – customers and business, creativity and rigour, strategy and practicality. Previously he was MD of the advertising agency that launched Daewoo Cars.

Cliff Dennett

Cliff is Commercial & Design Director at SOSHI Games creating game-based music discovery. He was previously a Senior Strategist at Orange, Innovation Director at EDS, and an independent trainer and innovation coach.

Roger Dennis

Roger is a specialist in futures thinking and the link via strategy to innovation. Previously Future Technology Specialist at Egg Bank in Europe, he is Founder of Innovation Matters based in New Zealand.

Caroline Dewing

Caroline is a communications consultant. She was previously with Vodafone where she ran the Future Agenda program and led communications on issues such as the environment, sustainability, M-health, privacy, and freedom of expression.

Mariah Hartman

Mariah is a cultural and communications strategist at Space Doctors in the UK. A seasoned marketer, she specializes in applying semiotic findings to specific marketing initiatives or issues across various sectors, from brands to corporate, from communications to product innovations.

Lucy Hooberman

Lucy is Professor and Director of Digital Media and Innovation at the University of Warwick. Her background is in TV, film production, and executive television management prior to joining the BBC's innovation team formed to take the BBC from being an analogue to digital organization.

Stephen Johnston

Stephen is CEO of Fordcastle in New York and a leading thinker on the application of new technologies. He was previously Senior Manager in Business Development for Nokia where he led corporate strategy programs to identify new areas of growth.

Joss Langford

Joss is Director of Arch Interface where he helps organizations to better manage design and innovation. Previously New Technologies R&D Director with Reckitt Benckiser, he has extensive insight on how companies make the most of their innovation activities.

Tim Jones

Tim is a Founder of The Growth Agenda network and Programme Director of the Future Agenda global open foresight project. Previously the Founder of Innovaro, he is a recognized expert in innovation, growth, and foresight, and advises a wide range of organizations on these issues worldwide.

Dave McCormick

Dave worked for Shell for over 30 years leading strategy development, developing business scenarios, identifying emerging growth opportunities, and supporting the organization in making pivotal strategic decisions. He is now an independent consultant and lecturer at Cass Business School.

Lisa McDowell

Lisa is a strategy consultant at The Foundation where she helps companies to see their world differently, from the outside in and so create organic growth. She was previously a planner with Barkers Group in the UK.

Satish Rao

Satish is a Principal at Clareo Partners in Chicago and helps clients address growth through new markets, products, customers, channels, and creating sustainable competitive advantage. He previously worked in strategy and telecommunications with IBM, Motorola, and Ericsson.

Hamsini Shivkumar

Hamsini is Founder of Leapfrog Strategy Consulting in Delhi and was formerly VP at JWT in India. With over 20 years of experience in consumer insight and branding, she is an expert in consumer-centric innovation, brand strategy, trends, and consumer culture.

Tobias Rooney

Tobias is with ?WhatIf! – The Innovation Company where he leads major growth strategy projects for clients. In the past he has been Strategy Director with Rhodia in France and Principal Consultant at both Cap Gemini and Innovaro with particular focus on life sciences and business model innovation.

Palie Smart

Palie is Senior Lecturer in Strategic Innovation Management at Cranfield School of Management and was previously Deputy Director, Innovation Leadership Centre. Her research focuses on topics including the culture of innovation, leadership for innovation, and innovation networks.

Neal Stone

Neal is Director of leapSTONE where he helps a number of organizations to make better use of design and design management. He was previously Head of Design at British Airways where, amongst other projects, he led the redesign of the award-winning new Club World cabin.

Introduction

Introduction

The Growth
Agenda

Nestlé
PepsiCo

Audi
Samsung

Reckitt
Benckiser
P&G

Starwood
Inditex

Amazon
Google

Narayana
Novo
Nordisk

Rolls-Royce
ARM

BASF
Shell

Tata
Bharti

LEGO
Apple

The Growth
Challenge

*Growth Champions **provides a distinct, informed perspective on how leading companies have been able to create, build and sustain growth to win the innovation battle. Drawing on a mixture of insights, research, interviews, anecdotes, and examples, it has been written to help business leaders to learn from the masters of innovation and understand the key lessons that really make a difference as they venture into the future.***

Why Growth?

Sustained growth is the ambition of most leaders. It has become not only the center of strategy but it is also a critical cultural focus for most organizations. If the sought-after goal of being a Growth Champion can be achieved then there are multiple positive impacts and implications – all high profile: think of companies like Apple and Google, PepsiCo and Nike. Most companies today place improved growth at the core of their businesses. Likewise, countries have growth at the heart of their economic strategies.

While the mergers and acquisition (M&A) route to growth has, at times, been favored by some organizations such as GSK, Pfizer, Boeing, and Alliance-Boots, most academic, consultancy, and government research over the years has highlighted that the organic growth option is seen to have a higher chance of success. If you consider mergers such as AOL–Time Warner, HP–Compaq, and Daimler–Chrysler, which have had to combine different cultures and streamline product portfolios, never mind integrate contrasting strategic objectives, it is clear that there are recurring icebergs to be navigated in any integration of different businesses from M&A. By contrast, growth driven by new market expansion and high-impact innovation has consistently achieved more sustainable success, and is thus becoming a core capability for many companies.

Adopting and adapting the proven techniques and approaches created in one sector and then transferring them to another has been the mainstay of many organizations' journeys to enhance their innovation capacity and so drive increased revenues and margins. As such, for the past 20 years or so, being a better innovator has increasingly been top of the chief executive officer's wish-list and who is best at this has been discussed repeatedly by the likes of *Business Week*, IBM, and industry bodies such as the Confederation of British Industry (CBI) in the UK. Delivering sustainable growth with greater impact than competitors and peers is therefore the Number 1 issue for many companies, and encouraging increased growth is a top priority for many national and regional governments.

Growth Champions

As a group working across the innovation and growth arena, we have spent the past 20 years or so collaborating with a number of the world's leading innovators, researching what approaches are having impact, participating in some ground-breaking growth programs, advising varied governments and companies on how and where to improve performance to drive sustained growth, as well as writing numerous books, papers, and articles on the subject. Now is the ideal time to share the essence of what we have learnt about the growth challenge.

Growth Champions is specifically focused on the core topics that many organizations are still struggling to master, and so has sought to answer many of the pivotal questions that chief executive officers (CEOs), chief innovation officers (CIOs) and their like are now consistently asking such as:

- Who are the real Growth Champions in key industries and why should we take note of them?
- With all the competition, how do Growth Champions in different sectors keep on growing?
- What do they do so well that helps them deliver continued revenue and margin growth?
- What strategic priorities are leading their approaches to organic growth and why?

- How and where are they placing more intelligent bets than their peers time after time?
- How do their organizations encourage and enable their people to deliver the goods?
- How do they keep their cultures fresh and their people focused on the big ideas?
- What are the Growth Champions doing in common and what are they doing differently?
- What is emerging onto the landscape right now that may change the rules of the game?

In a world where new competitors can emerge quicker than ever; where the 'developing world' organizations increasingly have more advantages than their 'developed world' peers; where information has become increasingly commoditized and understanding undervalued; where best practice moves quicker than people; and where keeping ahead of the rest of the pack has become ever more challenging, *Growth Champions* explores who is winning the battle for sustained innovation leadership, why, and how.

This book is focused on the linkage between two primary elements of the growth challenge – strategy and culture – and how they work together. While some may claim that it is process, new technology, and toolkits that make a difference, most experienced people in the field now see each of these as a commodity – something which is pretty well available to everyone, easy to imitate, providing no competitive advantage, and hence, at the end of the day, makes no difference. If everyone has a stage-gate process, uses social networks as part of their product development activities, and adopts 'BCG matrices' and McKinsey's horizon growth terminology to help them make decisions and prioritize activities, then how can any of them make a difference? Sure, if you don't have these in your portfolio then you are at a disadvantage to those that do, but even if you do have them, they are not in themselves enough to put clear water between you and your peers. We see that what really matters above everything else in order to be a leader in the growth arena is how organizations develop and exploit distinctive competences and specifically: how, why, and where to focus resources and capabilities; and how and why to create the right environment, bring together the best people, and stimulate the organization and networks to deliver growth.

However, before adding more on what this book is about, it is worthwhile taking a moment to first detail what it is not about – and why:

- This is not another book seeking to tell you everything you need to know about managing innovation – from how to develop an innovation strategy and what a good process looks like to how to organize your teams. There are hundreds of titles already focused on this and some of these are very good. If that is what you are looking for then we highly recommend that you get hold of a copy of the latest edition of *Managing Innovation* by Joe Tidd and John Bessant.
- This is also not another book explaining how to better understand your customers' needs so that you can deliver more focused products and services into the marketplace. If that is your issue then read something like *What Customers Want* by Anthony Ulwick.
- Neither is it a book on using creativity across the organization and having more and better ideas. There are literally thousands of books big and small on these topics, some clearly better than others: *Sticky Wisdom* by Dave Allan and colleagues and any of Edward de Bono's titles on lateral thinking are worth a look if this is what you are interested in.
- Nor is it a book focused on a single issue that is having impact on the way companies are thinking about innovation: If you want to know about open innovation read any of Henry Chesbrough's books and, if you are interested in the field of disruptive innovation, then take a look at those by Clayton Christensen.
- Equally this is not another book giving you just one company's view of innovation and how it has achieved success in a systemic manner. In this area we would recommend *The Art of Innovation* by Tom Kelley of IDEO or *Unleashing Innovation* by Nancy Tennant Snyder of Whirlpool.

Growth Champions is not seeking to meet any of these objectives. The books mentioned above do a very good job of their individual remits, we recommend them frequently, and the respective authors are probably some of the best placed to provide greater detail on their specific areas of interest.

Rather, this book is specifically focused on the strategic decisions and cultural dynamics of the companies that consistently win the innovation battle. Looking at the Growth Champions in 10 selected areas, it highlights the successes, the reasons for the success, and the learning that others seeking to emulate this success can therefore gain and build upon.

Navigating this Book

We have designed this book, the background research, and the accompanying website to bring together some of the most important developments in the innovation and growth spaces. We provide in-depth examples of those that are proven to be the exemplars at delivering growth – the companies we see from our analysis and experience as the Growth Champions. To best share the insights we have structured this book into three separate main sections each with a different focus and purpose:

Part I – The Growth Agenda: The Changing Dynamics of Innovation

Over the past few years there have been some interesting developments around how companies have changed their approach to delivering high-impact innovation and growth, therefore it is important that everyone interested in this subject has a good understanding of these developments. So this first section provides a detailed overview of those that we see as being most significant to companies today. From CXO level innovation leadership and strategic targets for growth to open innovation, broader collaboration and looking beyond the usual horizon for your growth platforms, we have provided concise explanations of what each of these have been focused on achieving, how they came about, which companies have been ahead of the curve in each area, and how they impact the growth agenda today. The intention here is to provide a good grounding for newcomers to the field as well as a refresher for more experienced practitioners. In addition we have specifically explored the implications of accelerating globalization on how and where different organizations have changed their game on the broader

Introduction

The Growth Agenda

Nestlé
PepsiCo

Audi
Samsung

Reckitt Benckiser
P&G

Starwood
Inditex

Amazon
Google

Narayana
Novo Nordisk

Rolls-Royce
ARM

BASF
Shell

Tata
Bharti

LEGO
Apple

The Growth Challenge

playing field. Supported by relevant examples this first section therefore provides you with a comprehensive understanding of the landscape within which companies operate as they seek to achieve sustained growth. More than just an introduction to the topic, it has been designed to share leading-edge views, provoke questions, and set up the subsequent exploration of the primary strategy and culture-focused issues that make a difference.

Part II – The Growth Champions

In the core central section of this book, we analyze 10 pairs of companies that are the proven Growth Champions across distinct sectors and highlight what they have been doing specifically in terms of culture and strategy which has made them the clear leaders. These companies and the sectors have not been chosen from a subjective CEO survey nor have they necessarily been promoting themselves as being the best of the best. We have selected these companies based on a decade of objective global Innovation Leaders' analysis, updated every year, of which companies are the most effective innovators. They are the ones that have consistently deployed their available resources and are able to access them in the most effective manner to deliver a constant stream of high-impact new products, services, and businesses that have resulted in increased revenues and profits. They are the ones that have tried new things, challenged the status quo, changed the game, pushed the boundaries, outpaced their rivals, and time and time again delivered the goods. Some of these organizations are well known in the business and consumer worlds, but some not. Few people would fail to recognize the names of the likes of Apple, Google, Nestlé, PepsiCo, and Samsung; but many outside of their immediate competitors may not be overly familiar with ARM, Inditex, Narayana Hrudayalaya, Reckitt Benckiser, and Starwood Hotels.

To provide a rich mix of insights in discussing what makes the 20 companies featured in this section special we have drawn on 10 years of analysis, our personal experience from working with many of these organizations and their peers, interviews with the individuals within these organizations responsible for delivering many of the successes, as well as discussions with their competitors, and debates with some of the world's leading analysts, consultants, and academics – a unique mix.

All of the associated insights are presented so that you can clearly understand the pivotal strategic decisions and cultural actions that have made the difference, delivered the goods, helped increase performance and share prices, and made these companies stand out from the crowd. In essence what has lifted them up from being one of many to be the growth leaders in each of their sectors, the most efficient and effective innovators, and hence the sustained Growth Champions of today.

We chose to specifically look at these organizations in pairs rather than in isolation so that you can gain an understanding of the alternative approaches that are delivering the impact.

- By discussing **Nestlé** and **PepsiCo** together we have shown the commonalities as well as the high-impact differences between these two organizations that have resulted in proactive change in the food sector. How they have both led the shift to healthier food but have chosen to achieve this by executing different strategies focused on alternative growth areas.
- The side-by-side comparison of **Audi** and **Samsung Electronics** demonstrates how, in two different sectors, these organizations have gained leadership through a combination of adopting a distinctive design strategy and building associated capability while also taking a different angle from peers on the use of technology to enhance performance.
- In the fast-moving consumer goods sector we have chosen to highlight **Reckitt Benckiser** and **Procter & Gamble**. Both have similar top-line growth targets, compete in many categories, and are increasingly battling in the same markets, but they have significantly different approaches to delivering the growth. Procter & Gamble is increasingly more interested in acting as a conduit for big ideas coming onto the market that will hopefully change the sector; while Reckitt Benckiser has become a highly tuned machine for delivering high growth from the rapid introduction of a host of incremental innovations.

- By looking at both **Starwood Hotels** and **Inditex** in the service sector, we profile two companies that have torn up the rulebook – through introducing more variety in the overall product mix built on common platforms; and by focusing more on rapid change of limited choice through building the world's leading logistics operation.

- With **Google** and **Amazon** we have two companies that are vying for leadership in the online world using their initially very different business models. As Amazon has used its technology focus to move from being a retailer of books and CDs to pretty much everything and then to developing web services, it has started to come head to head with Google by building multiple high-impact applications on the back of its core advertising revenue model. This is a sector in the midst of massive change and these two companies allow us to highlight some of the pivotal strategic changes taking place.

- **Novo Nordisk** and **Narayana Hrudayalaya** have outpaced their larger competitors in the healthcare sector by changing the way they work with the broader ecosystem. Both have pioneered different approaches to business model innovation – Novo Nordisk through building a world-leading interconnection of drug delivery and education and Narayana Hrudayalaya by completely reinventing surgery for scale. They have delivered the goods in this highly competitive arena but with different emphases.

- From the even more technology-dependent sectors we have two totally different approaches to growth to discuss. **Rolls-Royce** has been successful in changing the business model for engine supply by developing a service case business that now delivers greater contribution than its core high-tech product business across the whole market. While in the world of semiconductors **ARM** has become the essential hidden ingredient in every major smartphone as it is rapidly making the business of IP-based revenues very much its own.

- In an increasingly resource-constrained world, both **Shell** and **BASF** have continued to lead their respective energy and chemicals sectors through significantly changing their sources of material supply to be more future proof and lower carbon whilst simultaneously keeping an innovation edge over many of their competitors and so maintain constant growth across the board.

- From India, we have looked at two companies that have grown to become leaders in their domestic market and are now playing major roles internationally. In the manufacturing sector **Tata** has made significant shifts in both automobile and steel production to provide highly efficient global delivery of leading brands as well as low-cost products. And in the telecom arena **Bharti** has used a unique business model to allow the company to rapidly scale its activities at home and internationally.

- Finally we look at **Apple** and **LEGO** and see two companies that, despite increasing competition, continue to be at the forefront of how everyday activities are being continuously evolved with a little bit of magic. With its MacBook, iPod, iPhone, and iPad products setting the pace for usability and seamless technology integration, Apple has used disciplined internal control to become one of the most valuable public companies in the world; while LEGO, still a privately owned firm, has used fan-based collaboration to open up innovation in the toys sector and create a whole new dynamic for growth that is outpacing its larger competitors.

Collectively these examples provide a unique combination of insights on the companies that have been making all the right moves across multiple industries – and so enable us to discern both the common elements and the variations that make the difference.

Part III – The Growth Challenge: Lessons for the Future

The third section of *Growth Champions* builds on everything that has gone before to look at what the growth challenges are today and hence lessons for the future. Exploring the primary insights from the companies examined and what comes next for innovation and growth, this section looks at some of the accelerating issues that are starting to challenge organizations to think differently about how they achieve and sustain growth going forward. Using a range of examples we start to extrapolate from the lessons that have already been learned.

Introduction

The Growth Agenda

Nestlé PepsiCo

Audi Samsung

Reckitt Benckiser P&G

Starwood Inditex

Amazon Google

Narayana Novo Nordisk

Rolls-Royce ARM

BASF Shell

Tata Bharti

LEGO Apple

The Growth Challenge

Alongside bringing together common challenges that organizations around the world are now facing as they seek to enhance their growth performance, we have taken a view on what arenas in the innovation and growth landscape are likely to have high impact as they go mainstream over the next few years. Drawing on insights of what could take place, we have focused on the changes that are probable in terms of both scope and scale. This section includes a series of suggestions of where we might be heading and ends with a summary of the main issues for companies' growth strategies and organizational cultures going forward.

Resources and References

Finally, at the end of this book you will find a resource section that points you to a host of sources for additional information and insights. This book is inevitably a snapshot of today and things will change. So the profiles and changes will be regularly updated on the accompanying www.growthchampions.org website, which has been created to be a dynamic source of further insights as well as providing summaries of the key lessons from the examples that we have discussed in the body of this text. Seeking to act as a focus for informed ongoing discussion on what makes Growth Champions tick, which new approaches have impact going forward, and a means to highlight emerging issues, the www .growthchampions.org website provides you with an additional layer of information that, having read this book, we hope you will find a useful source of insight, debate, and learning. Researched and written by 20 innovation and growth experts from The Growth Agenda network, we hope that you find this a useful addition to the topic.

Tim Jones, Dave McCormick, Caroline Dewing – 2012

Part I

The Growth Agenda:
The Changing Dynamics of Innovation

Growth is a shared ambition for many companies and governments. For the vast majority creating more wealth by improving productivity and delivering innovation is a priority. It is a prerequisite for maintaining living standards in the developed world and building wider wealth creation and distribution in emerging economies.

Improving lives by building wealth is not a new idea. The industrial revolution in the 19th century heralded accelerated economic activity and production but as the post-colonial legacy steers nations from growth through regional aggrandizement, economic growth through the development of business has become a central focus for many. Economic growth comes with its own set of challenges, however. The cost to our environment is perhaps the most well recognized but as society becomes more global and we spend less time interacting with our local community, concerns around social issues are also beginning to emerge. Recently a sizable minority thinks that, in our resource-constrained world, we ought to look at the implications of unimpeded, consumption-driven growth and consider an alternative approach which will provide wealth without compromising on social and environmental well-being.

However it manifests itself, a growth engine that drives the economy, provides more choice for consumers, increases wealth, and so affords better health and hopefully improved happiness has been a virtuous circle that many have aspired to. Pivotal to this has been the success of some major organizations that are the economic heart of a country. The East India Trading Company and other state-granted monopolies paved the way in the 19th century and were the forerunners of General Electric, IBM, and Wal-Mart in the 20th. More recently, the likes of Google and Infosys have created scale and delivered more products and services, have employed more people, and so, through salaries, taxation, and occasional bouts of philanthropic activity, have been able to benefit society as a whole.

Today, after a couple of centuries of pretty much non-stop development, we are at a point where the balance of corporate power is changing. Asia in particular is experiencing huge growth and, as millions move out of poverty and into the world of increased consumption, both the drivers of and the appetite for 'more' are escalating rapidly. Simultaneously the European and American stalwarts are struggling to reboot their economies. To date most focus has been on consumption as a means to stimulate growth but the challenge is that, as more of us want more 'stuff,' it is becoming increasingly difficult to continue to deliver it without seriously plundering the finite natural resources. Serious questions are now being asked about what growth really is or indeed should be; what benefit it brings; whether higher growth in the East will follow the same trajectory as in the West or take an alternative, better path; whether GDP is a sustainable aspiration; how we can deliver prosperity within the planet's means; and whether it is possible to decouple economic growth and resource consumption.

Introduction

The Growth Agenda

Nestlé
PepsiCo

Audi
Samsung

Reckitt Benckiser
P&G

Starwood
Inditex

Amazon
Google

Narayana
Novo Nordisk

Rolls-Royce
ARM

BASF
Shell

Tata
Bharti

LEGO
Apple

The Growth Challenge

CHAPTER 1

Why Growth?
The Economist's Perspective

The growth of an economy has generally been seen as a good thing. Throughout history, nations have traded with each other and some have grown rich by exploiting their own natural resources and those of their neighbors or trading partners. The need to protect trade routes meant that from the Greeks and Romans right through to the British and the French empires, economies have grown hand in hand with military power. However, over the last half-century there has been a degree of rebalancing and a shift to create successful economic growth independent of 'empire.' Although the cases of oil and other mineral wealth may play against this, it is evident that when productivity improvements impact manufacturing and service-based economies at the same time as trading takes place, we experience economic growth.

Gross domestic product (GDP) is a widely adopted measure of national economic performance. Increases in GDP above and beyond what would be natural given population growth are believed to enable an increase in living standards for the population. Hence the interest in data such as GDP per capita both in real and relative terms. As wide-scale conflict between nations has been predominantly replaced by global trade, the post World War II decades have largely been focused on regions using growth to drive their economies forward, raise living standards, and increase influence. Over 30 years a growth rate of 2.5% of GDP per annum leads to a doubling of GDP. Growth of 8% per annum, as exhibited by many Asian economies in recent years, achieves this in a decade.

Pivotal technology breakthroughs have always enabled companies and countries to improve efficiency and so drive growth. The invention of the steam engine and processes for producing quality steel are often-quoted changes, but access to coal and oil and the 'invention' of electricity are also seen as inflection points.

So too we can consider that the creation of the train, the telephone, the car, the plane, the transistor, and the internet have all, over time, provided new platforms for growth.

The 18th-century economist Adam Smith is generally credited for shaping our views about how growth creates wealth, power, and stability. In *The Wealth of Nations*, published in 1776, Smith argued that 'productive capacity' was the engine of growth. Some 40 years later others such as David Ricardo with his theory of 'comparative advantage' saw that prowess in trade was the fundamental differentiator. In the mid-20th century Robert Solow and Trevor Swan contributed alternative theories – the neoclassical growth model – where the role of technological change is seen as significant as accumulation of capital and all countries eventually reach a steady state of growth. However, a decade earlier in 1942, Joseph Schumpeter made the connection between growth, innovation, and entrepreneurship upon which most companies and countries now base their respective economic policies. In his book, *Capitalism, Socialism, and Democracy*, Schumpeter saw an entrepreneur as someone who is able to convert a new idea into successful innovation. He popularized the idea of 'creative destruction' as creating new products, services, and business models across markets and so driving growth. It is this that is at the heart of successful long-term growth. The entrepreneur disturbs equilibrium and so causes economic development. Schumpeter argued that 'innovation is the critical dimension of change' and creates 'temporary monopolies that allow abnormal profits,' which are then competed away by rivals and imitators. These create new products and services that meet and drive demand and so improve profits and economic growth. Schumpeter also proposed that finance can have a positive impact on growth as a result of its effects on productivity and technological change. In recent years, many Asian economies have cited government-led investments as being a core catalyst for sustained economic growth. Back in the West, many see that Schumpeter's views stand firm and, for example, has had influence in such ambitions as the European Union's core development plan – the Lisbon Strategy.

Until recently it was generally assumed that growth is good for society. Indeed there is significant evidence to support this, for example the Cato Institute has undertaken research which shows that, up to a level of around $15,000 per capita, happiness increases with higher GDP. If – and sometimes this is a big 'if' – appropriately shared across a community, the benefits of growth have direct impact on alleviating poverty and enabling people to access the next rung on the economic ladder. On the other hand there are increasing and multiple arguments which suggest that growth fosters excessive consumerism, resource depletion, and unsustainable ways of living. As a result some consider that 'well-being' is a better ambition than mere growth while others call for alternative measures to be implemented, such as gross domestic happiness, as measured in Bhutan. Many of these arguments are clear, compelling, and visionary. However, today in the greater scheme of things, they are unfortunately largely marginal. In a decade or so mainstream attitudes may well have shifted but right now the majority is still focused on creating growth as a priority with other issues in second place. Decoupling growth from resource use, for example, is a great concept but one which many organizations have yet to get their collective heads around. For the moment it seems that most companies and countries are still abiding by Schumpeter's view of growth via innovation and change driving progress.

The Nature of Growth

Before exploring some examples of successful growth, it is useful to consider the nature of growth, how it occurs, and what some of the implications are. Taking the macro view, some see that economic growth and prosperity result from interaction at different levels ranging from the organization to the sector and then the national and international level. Growth within each of these can be supported or constrained by a number of factors such as the development of technology platforms, environmental fluctuations, political, economic or societal change, and regulatory changes that introduce new laws and standards at an industry or national level. Growth is driven by a complex amalgam of multiple issues – some of which are internal to a company or sector and can be more easily managed or stimulated, but there are also external influences which have to be accommodated as they unfold.

In order to try and gain some control of the changes that influence growth, the business of 'management' has evolved. New approaches, tools, and models have been created to help us be more effective in how we deploy available resources. These processes are often static 'command and control' methods that seek to impose order, hierarchies, and rules onto systems that are by their very nature complex, interconnected, evolutionary, and constantly shifting. One reason for this is that management theory has been largely dominated by thinking from the United States and based on large manufacturing businesses, where business models, underpinned by economic thinking, gained both relevance and resonance with business leaders. For example Alfred Chandler, Igor Ansoff, Peter Drucker, and Michael Porter arguably all used the U.S. manufacturer as a common reference point. Even 'Blue Ocean Strategy,' one of the most popular post-millennium models to have emerged from INSEAD, is grounded in product-based economics (see Kim and Mauborgne's book). Times have changed, however, and the problem is that in today's world this approach doesn't stack up. For a start, many of the high-growth businesses that have emerged in the past decade – think Google, Netflix, Facebook – don't play by the same rules as product manufacturers. In addition, the recent financial crisis demonstrates that, for many, the analytical models that were put in place to manage financial and economic systems simply don't work.

In truth growth cannot be rigorously controlled. As many now recognize there are levers that organizations, either corporate or governmental, can pull at different levels but, in an ever more interconnected world, most are nudges at best. Whichever metaphor you think of, from nurturing a growing plant to navigating an oil tanker, there are things we think we can do to improve efficiency and optimize the process but there also other factors – disease, hurricanes and the like, not to mention the caprices of human nature itself – that will inevitably occur from time to time and are outside our control. We will do our best to see them coming and have plans to deal with them, but we can't direct the what, where, or when.

However, we are where we are and know what we know. So, acknowledging the gaps, what can we learn from past economic thinking to help us see growth opportunities more clearly? For a start, we can see patterns that let us recognize and categorize what type of growth is taking place and we can understand some of the key characteristics. This can be done at both the national/regional and organizational company levels.

National/international economic growth

The economic view of growth is that increases in productivity lead to increased levels of economic prosperity. So, it follows that more competitive economies tend to be able to produce higher levels of income for their companies and citizens, not to mention higher returns on investment and hence increases in the national growth potential. The World Economic Forum's 'Global Competitiveness Report' provides an analysis of many of the drivers that enable national economies to achieve sustained growth and long-term prosperity. It divides countries into three different stages, which are consistent with general economic development theory:

- Stage 1 'factor' driven economies, where countries compete primarily on the use of unskilled labor and natural resources and companies compete on the basis of price as they buy and sell basic products or commodities.
- Stage 2 'efficiency' driven economies, where growth is based on the development of more efficient production processes and increased product quality.
- Stage 3 'innovation' driven economies, where companies compete by producing and delivering new and different products and services by using the most sophisticated processes.

So looking at the BRIC (Brazil, Russia, India, and China) countries, as of 2011, India is largely still in stage 1, while Brazil, China, and Russia are stage 2. Most of the developed world is in stage 3 for now, but, just as the performance of many European countries is starting to plateau, China's competiveness is way ahead of other developing economies and it is moving fast toward becoming a stage 3 economy. Although just one point of view, many see that this type of grouping is helpful in understanding what levers, regulatory or industry led, can be applied to different economies.

Company growth

Broadly speaking companies also grow across three dimensions:

- Dimension 1: 'existing market growth' – Once established a firm can expand by increasing existing market share through price and other sources of competitive advantage.
- Dimension 2: 'customer-driven market growth' – A business grows by helping to create new customers for existing offerings.
- Dimension 3: 'innovation-driven products and services growth' – This occurs when companies create new markets by offering innovative products, services, or business models.

Within each of these dimensions, different techniques to drive growth and improve efficiency have been used by organizations in order to win. It's what Michael Porter describes as competitive rivalry in the industry. High-growth companies excel across one or more of these dimensions. This means that they achieve disproportionate shares of growth.

Linking the national and company views together, it is clear that because high-growth firms contribute a disproportionate amount to employment levels and/or have higher productivity than their peers, they are also responsible for a significant proportion of economic growth. High-growth companies are attractive because they are more successful within a sector, but also help make a country more economically competitive on a global scale. Therefore they become the heroes – not just because they are the organizations people want to work for, but also because they are the companies that countries either want to nurture or to attract.

Established Growth Successes

Reviewing the varied archives of *The Economist*, the *Financial Times*, *Business Week*, and the *Wall Street Journal*, large companies have clearly been the main drivers of sustained growth over the last 50 years or so. The likes of Exxon,

General Motors, General Electric, IBM, Boeing, Procter & Gamble, United Technologies, AT&T, and Caterpillar in the United States; Tata and Reliance in India; and BP, Shell, Rolls-Royce, Ericsson, Bosch, Fiat, Novartis, and Volkswagen in Europe have all played a pivotal role. Big companies like these have grown in both scope and scale, increased incomes, employed more people, paid more dividends to shareholders, and taxes to governments. However, we argue that continued large company-led growth is no longer a certain bet. As new organizations are formed to tackle emerging challenges, the old models that supported large companies in the past are being replaced by new ones.

Taking a U.S.-centric view: of the top 100 companies in the *Fortune 500* in 1955, only 11 can be found in the same group 50 years later. Although oil companies still dominate, many leading firms from the 1950s were absorbed into larger entities or have died out to be replaced by banks, retailers, and a host of new technology companies: 10 years ago Amazon and Google were not even in the top 500. However, just looking at brand names can be deceptive and gives an inaccurate view of reality. A relatively recent UK study by the Department for Business Enterprise & Regulatory Reform on high-growth firms looked at a number of international factors that drive success. One interesting finding relates to the average age of the successful organization. Perhaps surprisingly many of the largest firms in the UK and the United States are over 100 years old and at least half of the firms in both countries can be tracked back to origins prior to 1900. So, presumably something has been going right?

Whilst some of the growth successes of today have been around for many years, many innovative companies, such as those highlighted by the likes of *Fast Company*, are relatively new: Groupon and Zynga are both in the *Fast Company* top 10 innovative companies for 2011 and neither existed five years ago. Alongside Google, other top 10 ranked companies such as Netflix and Epocrates can both trace their roots back to the late 1990s. There are evident growth successes from the past few decades that, all being well, will continue to prosper in the future. However, they are likely to be joined by newcomers ready to ride the next innovation wave. Just as Facebook, Twitter, and LinkedIn are driving high valuations today, so in the next decade we may see others of greater influence emerge from start-ups addressing new opportunities.

Such perspectives on successful growth companies also apply to nations. Countries such as Singapore, India, and China have all grown at twice the world average over the past 20 years. While many see China and India's growth being at the forefront of the rise of the BRIC economies, Singapore is seen as the leading example of government-influenced growth of an established economy. It is therefore the country that others seek to emulate: From Dubai and Qatar to Thailand and the Philippines, Singapore, with the pivotal roles of Temasek – its industrial investment vehicle – and the Economic Development Board – its catalyst for inward investment – is widely admired. Over the past 30 years or so, Temasek, 100% owned by the Singapore government, has placed some good bets: It has invested in markets and resources and supported companies – often financing strategic expansions – to such a consistent extent that it now has over $130 billion of assets for use by the nation. It is, by far, the most successful Sovereign Wealth Fund that links corporate growth and wealth creation to the assets of the nation, and hence the population.

CHAPTER 2

Alternative Strategic Approaches to Growth

The repertoire of success stories we can draw on to unpick the drivers of successful growth is extensive and we therefore need to be clear on the criteria we are using to select the best. However, before we do this, it's worth considering the relative merits of alternative strategic approaches to growth.

M&A-Driven Growth

For many years, growth via mergers and acquisitions (M&A) has been a much-vaunted strategic ambition for a number of companies. Rather than grow from within, the ability to buy market share or enter new markets via M&A has been a stalwart of the corporate toolkit. However, while the attraction of a quick fix is clear, the ability to deliver the benefits has been consistently inconsistent. KPMG, McKinsey, and Deloitte have all been quoted as saying that around 70% of mergers and acquisitions fail to achieve expectations and that more than half destroy value. Back in 1987, Michael Porter identified that between 50% and 60% of acquisitions were failures; in 1995 Mercer Management Consulting claimed that 60% of the firms in the *Business Week 500* that had made major acquisitions in the preceding decade were less profitable than industry averages; and in 2004, McKinsey found that only 23% of acquisitions have a positive impact on return on investment.

If it is true that the vast majority of mergers and acquisitions destroy value why do companies still take this course of action? Perhaps, while growth is the public rationale, the reality behind much M&A activity is that it has been driven by the desire to reduce the competitive pressures expressed in Porter's five forces model – power of buyers and suppliers, threat of new entrants and substitute products, and level of competitive rivalry. As we can see by the failures of AOL–Time Warner, HP–Compaq, Daimler-Benz–Chrysler, and Alcatel–Lucent, this does not always translate into creating value. Even, as with Daimler-Benz–Chrysler, when these are agreed mergers of equals rather than hostile takeovers, the lessons are clear: Generally M&A-driven growth in the West does not deliver the goods. Whether through cultural mismatch, leadership conflict or failed market synergies, a growing number of companies now see M&A as a poor option and one that many have made the decision to avoid. There are of course exceptions that make up the 30% of successes, but the odds are clearly tilted in favor of failure. It's not all bad news, however. There seems to be a role for smaller acquisitions as part of an organic strategy for sustained growth, and later we will highlight some emerging economy Growth Champions who are successfully using M&A.

Organic Growth Success

Time and time again over the past decades, academic research, consultancy studies, and empirical evidence have all pointed to the fact that organic growth as a core strategy for increasing value is more successful than large-scale M&A. The argument is that those companies that pursue internally driven innovation-led growth are the ones that outperform their peers: those that choose the organic option are now the more successful overall.

Way back in 1964, in an article for the *California Management Review* entitled 'Strategies for Growth' Peter Gutmann examined how over 50 US-based companies had achieved exceptionally rapid expansion in sales, total profits, and profits per share. He identified the reason for this success as the result of the careful selection of appropriate sector areas to be active in and participation in industries that were still in the early phases of industrial growth. In addition he noted that a combination of what he termed strong 'internal' and 'external' growth was key. Internal growth focused on delivering new products into new and existing markets while the external growth came from acquisitions. Although external growth was only found in less than half the companies he looked at, strong internal growth was prevalent in all successful organizations.

Introduction

The Growth Agenda

Nestlé
PepsiCo

Audi
Samsung

Reckitt
Benckiser
P&G

Starwood
Inditex

Amazon
Google

Narayana
Novo
Nordisk

Rolls-Royce
ARM

BASF
Shell

Tata
Bharti

LEGO
Apple

The Growth
Challenge

Over half a century later, with much interim work on innovation undertaken by the likes of Michael Porter, C. K. Prahalad, Gary Hamel, Clayton Christensen, Michael Tushman, John Bessant and Henry Chesbrough, similar success criteria for growth predominate. Here are just some of the key quotes:

Innovation is the central issue in economic prosperity (Porter, 1990)

Firms which are successful in innovation secure competitive advantage in rapidly changing world markets, and the economies which generate and support such firms prosper (Walsh, 1990)

It is only through the introduction of successful new products and processes that companies and nations can improve their competitive position (Porter, 1990)

Any company that cannot imagine the future won't be around to enjoy it (Prahalad and Hamel, 1990)

Innovation and new product development are crucial sources of competitive advantage (Tushman and Anderson, 1997)

Companies that don't innovate die (Chesbrough, 2003)

Countries everywhere are seeking their own sources of comparative advantage in the innovation landscape (Kao, 2007)

And again in a 2011 article for the *MIT Sloan Management Review*, Julian Birkinshaw and colleagues concluded that 'Innovation is the lifeblood of any large organization.' The academic view is clear: Innovation is critical, organic growth is pivotal, and without it companies fail and countries lose out to competitors.

The annual Innovation Leaders' research that informs some of this book also provides evidence that successful innovators deliver above-average growth. Throughout the last 10 years, this research has identified the companies in 25 different sectors that have been making the most of their innovation resources. By creating compelling new products, services, and businesses predominantly from within the organization, they have not only outpaced their competitors on a year-by-year basis, but their subsequent share price performance has also benefited. Every year, the subsequent two-year share performance of the innovation leaders' portfolio has bettered that of the Dow, NASDAQ, and FTSE 100.

The portfolio grew by over 60% in 2002 while the markets averaged less than 20%. Similar differences were true in 2003, 2004, 2005, and 2006. Even in the midst of the downturn, innovation leaders performed better than the markets. While indexes lost between 30% and 40% of their value in 2007, the innovation leaders' portfolio only dropped by 20%. In 2008 performance was around the same and in 2009 as global markets picked up and grew by between 40% and 70%, the average share price of the Innovation Leaders grew by 130%. Over the last decade, this provides clear evidence of the impact of innovation prowess on sustained growth in terms of revenues, margins, and value creation. Innovation-led growth works. The challenge, as everyone starts to realize and act on this, is in doing it better than the competition.

Five Approaches to Improve Performance (in the 1990s)

Over the past 30 years or so companies have sought to outpace their peers by adopting a host of new approaches to improve their strike rate on innovation and deliver growth. Some of these have come from academic analysis and others have simply migrated from one company to another as best practice. Here we highlight five different approaches that achieved wide attention towards the end of the 1990s.

Core competences

Perhaps the most significant strategic view to stand the test of time was centered on core competence thinking. In *Competing for the Future*, C. K. Prahalad and Gary Hamel built on others' views of the drivers of sustained success and high-lighted that an ability to develop and maintain core capabilities and core competences is behind the sustained growth of many major companies. According to Prahalad and Hamel, core competences represent the 'competitive strength' of an enterprise, defined and agreed upon by the company's general management. Building on this gives an immediate competitive advantage as others need to assemble similar abilities prior to entering the competitive race. From General

Electric to NEC to Canon, they argued that focus on the competences of the organization was the mainstay of successful strategic growth.

While General Electric has built new core competences over time in such areas as materials technologies now used in jet engines and wind turbines, Canon's focus on maintaining its strength in four key areas of precision mechanics, fine optics, microelectronics, and electronic imaging has been at the heart of its sustained success in the office products and imaging markets. These and other examples from the 1990s are often quoted to support the notion of core competence thinking and its continued relevance.

Multifunctional teams

On the organizational side, a major focus during the 1990s was on making teams work more effectively. As large companies had become more structured around divisions and business units and consequently developed into silos, so the use of cross-disciplinary multifunctional teams became a means of bridging the gaps between different areas of capability. An issue for many was the divide between marketing and R&D functions, which often talked different business languages, had different perspectives on common issues, and fundamentally looked at innovation through different lenses. Whether by creating temporary 'lightweight' teams or going the whole hog and setting up 'skunk works' with autonomous teams operating independently of the mother-ship, changing the culture of large companies towards greater collaboration between groups became a major challenge. Honda was highlighted early on as a leader in team-based approaches but soon pretty much every major company from HP and IBM to Sony, BP, and even some of the banks were adopting team-based approaches for innovation and growth programs.

Stage-gate processes

Aligned with this strategic and organizational shift was a change in development processes. In order to accelerate the creation and launch of new products and services, and to help different groups of resource to cooperate, most companies started to adopt a phased development process. 'Ideation' was separated from concept development, testing, and launch. Decision gates introduced between each stage allowed the cross-functional review of progress and a wider portfolio perspective of growth opportunities to be brought together. Built on the popularity of the thinking of people like Robert Cooper of McGill University, stage-gate processes and later IT-enabled versions became the prevailing theme. Whether adopting a four-, five-, six-, or even a seven-stage approach, pretty much every major organization had a program to improve its development processes.

Customer insight

Another area of change towards the end of the 20th century was greater interest in what customers think in order to identify and better articulate their needs – be they 'met' or 'unmet' needs. Rather than just using focus groups for pre-launch product validation and fine-tuning, the idea of involving customers earlier on in the development process became popular so that customer insight could inform and stimulate important growth decisions about what to launch and where. The notion of the 'voice of the customer' came into parlance as organizations adopted new quantitative and qualitative techniques such as conjoint analysis and ethnographic research to respectively analyze preferences and observe products and services in use and then develop more 'user-centered' solutions. Organizations from Philips and Procter & Gamble through to Intel, Hasbro, and Boeing all established consumer insight programs to better inform innovation and growth activities. Many of these have ensured that the respective organizations were able to produce products that were a better fit for the market need than in the past.

Technology licensing

Given the important role that new platforms can play in enabling growth, there has also been a long-term interest in being able to access the best technology. While many firms have invested in their internal R&D to create new technologies that will support these platforms, others have chosen to license technologies from others. As organizations saw value in creating intellectual property, not just in a defensive capacity to stop others copying their ideas but also in a value-creating

Introduction

The Growth Agenda

Nestlé PepsiCo

Audi Samsung

Reckitt Benckiser P&G

Starwood Inditex

Amazon Google

Narayana Novo Nordisk

Rolls-Royce ARM

BASF Shell

Tata Bharti

LEGO Apple

The Growth Challenge

manner, many started to get excited about their IP portfolios. Led by companies such as Dow and Texas Instruments, the likes of Philips, IBM, and Ericsson have all been active in deriving substantial revenues through the licensing of their technology and associated intellectual property to others. Starting with its patents around CDs in the 1980s, Philips grew a successful revenue stream from licensing its proprietary technologies across the consumer electronics sector. IBM used its extensive patent portfolio as leverage for some major global deals and, perhaps most notably, Ericsson created the Bluetooth patent pool which enabled this protocol to become an industry standard. As a means to increase revenue from internal assets, licensing of intellectual property quickly spread from technology to other product and business model areas.

Hygiene Factors

These five approaches – core competence thinking, multifunctional teams, stage-gate processes, customer insight, and technology licensing – were the battle-grounds for a lot of growth platform successes for a good few years. At the start of the 1990s everyone was keen to develop these capabilities within the organization. By the end of the decade pretty much every major company had effectively achieved this and so, in essence, they all became 'hygiene factors' – things that had to be done in order to meet the same standards as everyone else but actually didn't make them different. To further improve innovation and growth performance, companies had to look for new sources of potential differentiation in their ability to grow.

Recent Approaches for Improved Performance

In the last decade, few would argue that the biggest driver of change in terms of how companies innovate, access new markets, interact with new audiences, create new channels, and so deliver growth has been the internet. The scale and scope of how increased access to better information can deliver step-changes in efficiency has been breathtaking. From the advent of online marketplaces like eBay; the birth of aggregators such as Expedia and Groupon; and the reinvention

of media consumption via YouTube, iTunes, Rhapsody, Spotify, Netflix, and www
.CNN.com; to shifts in efficiency achieved by internet-only banks and real-time
logistics tracking for UPS and FedEx; and the invention of completely new spaces
from the likes of Amazon, Facebook, Twitter, and Foursquare, the impact of the
internet on society, consumers, and companies alike is irrefutable.

Alongside taking advantage of new opportunities provided by a more connected
and more interconnected data-sharing world, there have been a number of other
specific developments over the past few years that have also changed how organizations think about their options and opportunities for growth.

Open innovation

Perhaps the most widely recognized development has been concept of open
innovation. Although trading intellectual property and technology transfer have
been well-established activities in some sectors for decades, Henry Chesbrough's
labeling of sourcing ideas from outside the firm and the external exploitation
of concepts as 'open innovation' caught the corporate imagination big time.
Particularly with the proactive embracing of this concept by the likes of Procter
& Gamble, it has become the mantra for organizations operating across multiple sectors and markets. The potential from getting new ideas from outside as
well as inside the firm has been so compelling that Chesbrough recently suggested: 'around 70% of major companies have now set up open innovation
programs: Although only around 10% of these have actually seen tangible
results so far.'

A well-promoted 2000 *Harvard Business Review* article by Huston and Sakkab
on Procter & Gamble's Connect + Develop open innovation program laid down
the aspiration that many others have sought to emulate. The CEO of Procter &
Gamble at the time declared that the company would derive 50% of its revenues
from ideas sourced from outside the organization. Although internal R&D would
continue to drive innovation within established categories, new products from
outside the boundaries of the organization would provide significant additional
growth. The external sourcing of ideas has taken hold and, in the first few years
of Connect + Develop, R&D productivity at Procter & Gamble increased by nearly

60%. As individuals and small companies have proved eager to share their ideas with larger organizations, global organizations have been lining up to establish open innovation programs, most of which have been focused on providing a conduit for new ideas into the firm: France Télécom, Unilever, Vodafone, Henkel, AkzoNobel, Kraft, Boeing, the BBC, and Google are just some examples.

Smart M&A

Although large-scale M&A has not been a great success, there are a number of companies that have successfully delivered sustained growth by using M&A as part of their core innovation growth strategy. The list is populated with companies that are actually more focused on small acquisitions than large ones. They do this as a key component of their innovation and growth strategies but not at the expense of internal innovation. Top of the list of 'smart M&A' experts is Cisco – a company whose innovation through acquisition strategy has become a best practice example. Cisco was the first to have grown through buying and successfully integrating other companies and their technologies into its portfolio and has been followed by the likes of Google and Medtronic, which have also become leaders in the early acquisition of emerging technological capabilities. Rather than wait until small university start-ups have grown to scale, they have become expert in spotting potential winners early and bringing them into the larger corporate tent. Google has also been one of the leaders in spotting new technology platforms, buying them as soon as they show promise and before valuations rocket and then integrating them into the wider Google ecosystem. Yes, the company has made some major acquisitions such as YouTube, but the vast majority of its M&A activity has been focused on buying small companies with great technology or business models to scale.

Over the past five years, Minnesota-based Medtronic has acquired around six organizations a year giving it access to new capabilities in areas from heart valves and minimally invasive catheters to cardiovascular disease treatments. These relatively small acquisitions, made early and at a point where costs are relatively low, give Medtronic the ability to significantly enhance its future technology and growth portfolios in a highly efficient manner.

Customer engagement

Back in the world of consumer interaction, Eric von Hippel, Professor of Technological Innovation in the MIT Sloan School of Management, wrote a seminal book in 2005 entitled *Democratizing Innovation* in which he focused on the benefits of allowing 'users of products and services – both firms and individual consumers – to increasingly be able to innovate for themselves.' Whereas the initial 'user-centered design' and 'voice of the customer' approaches had led to techniques for bringing insights around attitudes and needs of customers into the organizational consciousness, von Hippel brought attention to allowing customers to become active parts of the innovation process and hence the growth activities within a firm. Companies as varied as BMW, Unilever, and Staples have all been making shifts in how they enable customers to become part of product, technology, and service development.

However, by far the most significant change, and one covered in more detail later, was that made by LEGO where, using platforms such as www.legofactory .com, the company enabled its millions of customers to design their own products online and then buy the ones they liked best. LEGO became a conduit for its customers' ideas and in doing so brought the notion of fan-based innovation into the commercial mainstream.

In a more recent example, in 2011, ahead of an official release, rock band the Kaiser Chiefs put 20 new tracks onto a website where fans could select 10 tracks for a digital album, design a cover, pay for and download the album for their own use, and then use the web to market and sell the album that they had designed. Subsequent customers were able to select an already created album with the original creator being reimbursed for each copy downloaded so any fan only needed to sell a few copies in order to make a profit.

Strategic collaboration

Alongside the open innovation movement there has also been a shift in how organizations collaborate around new growth platforms. The term 'strategic partnerships' has been a widely and poorly used description of what, in many instances, are simple contractual outsourcing arrangements where one company (such as Accenture, IBM, or Infosys) delivers capabilities better, cheaper, or quicker than the likes of BT, Colgate-Palmolive, or General Motors can do internally. Although effective as a means of improving operational efficiency this is not innovation. What has had greater impact on companies' growth strategies and associated revenue and margin enhancement over recent years has been deeper and wider collaboration across the board. Companies have recognized that while they have core competences in some areas that allow them to be effective in delivering specific assets into the marketplace, there are often areas where they are not so strong and where others can complement internal capabilities.

An increasing number of strategic collaborations have been evident particularly when organizations are entering new geographic markets, expanding into new categories, or embracing new technology platforms. Taking just one sector, that of mobile connectivity as an example, we can see strategic collaboration on markets occurring between Vodafone and Verizon and around new categories between Google and device manufacturers such as Samsung and HTC. In these cases, companies are working together to deliver experiences and functionality that are richer, better, and deeper than they can achieve in isolation. In addition, with a clear shift to sourcing new molecules from biotech firms as part of their own take on open innovation, a number of pharmaceutical companies have formed deep strategic collaboration partnerships with new organizations. While some, such as the relationship between Genzyme and Roche, have followed a bilateral approach, Novartis, with over 400 research collaborations now in place, has been one of the companies to have made the most of strategic partnerships with biotech firms, start-ups, and universities. Strategic collaboration has moved from being a label for subcontracting low-value activities to one focused on true partnerships for growth.

Using foresight

As short-term consumer and customer insight has become a commodity capability the battleground has shifted to the area of foresight – having a clearer view on emerging opportunities that are over the usual horizon. Given the increasingly cross-sector nature of growth opportunities and the speed of change enabled by the global adoption of new technologies, companies are keen to search harder. In the past few years, companies ranging from Cisco and Procter & Gamble to Vodafone and Microsoft have all started to scan the emerging horizons to identify potential opportunities. Many companies now use foresight to look for early signals of what might be happening to markets. What sets the successful companies apart is their ability to use this foresight to drive decision making. To do this, good foresight needs to not only be insightful but it must also be effectively communicated to the relevant decision makers at the right time.

Although there have been organizations such as Shell, whose scenarios activity has been running for many decades, over the past few years, others have also established formal foresight programs. IBM first used its Global Technology Outlook to keep a handle on what developments were underway around its core business activities. It then added the Global Innovation Outlook (GIO) program to undertake a more wide-ranging regular view. Using a very similar approach to Shell's Technology Futures program, the GIO brought together around 100 experts from many different companies into workshops to discuss emerging issues, challenges, and opportunities. Picking three topics a year (e.g. healthcare, transport, and water) helped IBM to keep better track of developments outside its core business and so inform it on new growth opportunities. When attractive areas are identified, they are passed into the Emerging Business Opportunity (EBO) program for development. This systematic approach to turning opportunities into multibillion dollar activities has proven its worth as demonstrated by the Advanced Water Management business launched in 2008, which has clear linkage back to the original GIO programs.

With initiatives such as the 2010 FutureAgenda open foresight platform now having impact, more companies are adopting foresight as a core part of new growth strategies; balancing emerging long-term opportunity activities with shorter term capability development and innovation programs. Moreover, with business model innovation high on many agendas, the ability to see opportunities early and leapfrog established players with new approaches to big problems is increasingly attractive.

Adoption and Commoditization

Open innovation, smart M&A, customer engagement, strategic collaboration, and foresight are clearly where the action is right now and are the areas where organizations believe they can gain competitive advantage over their peers. However, in sectors such as fast-moving consumer goods (FMCG), consumer electronics, and telecommunications, some would say that these approaches are, like the initiatives of the 1990s, fast becoming hygiene factors themselves and will soon evolve into necessary business commodities. We are not there quite yet but these five approaches may soon become the status quo for all.

So, what next? New arenas are emerging that may provide the basis for future growth but before we look at these we should first consider the factors that are changing the nature of growth – the current drivers of change.

CHAPTER 3

Drivers of Change

Small Companies Acting Bigger/Big Companies Getting Smaller

In the past 'scale' mattered and large companies were able to exert wider influence, deploy more resources, and so reap greater rewards than small firms. For many countries having a few strong national champions was enough to more or less guarantee ongoing economic success. Influential multinationals such as IBM, Unilever, General Electric, and Ford were seen to be growth drivers and so encouraging such companies to set up facilities in different locations has been core to many national innovation or foreign direct investment (FDI) strategies. There used to be clear blue water between what could be achieved by these large multinationals and by smaller organizations. Today that gap is rapidly closing.

In Western economies small- and medium-sized enterprises (SMEs) have played a crucial role in job creation in the early part of the 21st century, and maintaining this momentum is central to many national growth plans today. In the United States, for example, small businesses (with fewer than 500 employees) now account for around half the nation's GDP and more than half its total employment. In addition small businesses account for around a third of all exports. This is double what was achieved a couple of decades ago.

As more accessible technologies (e.g., cloud computing) are enabling small companies to act like big ones, the productivity gap between large and small firms has narrowed. Small companies can now have global reach, serve customers in many countries, and use a plethora of internet-enabled platforms to provide support anywhere in the world. Similarly the wage gap has shrunk and SMEs have become significant magnets for the best knowledge across the global talent pool. Indeed, in both North America and Europe, in recent years SMEs have outperformed their larger counterparts in job creation and become stronger sources of innovation. Whereas in the past SMEs' lack of resources was a barrier to growth, today their flexibility and speed of response has made them better innovators. As technology has enabled global reach without scale, we have seen the emergence of multinational SMEs that are integrated into international value chains.

Simultaneously, many large companies are becoming smaller. With offshoring and outsourcing still growing in impact, many back-office roles such as HR, procurement, and logistics have shifted outside the organization. We can also see more strategic roles like R&D moving externally, with increasing use of flexible contract or freelance talent. Many large companies today directly employ around 50% of the people they did a few years ago. Microsoft's HQ in Seattle has around 120,000 people working on site but only half are employees – the rest are contractors or consultants. Companies are still growing and increasing revenues, but with less people 'within the tent.' So the gap between large and small is again blurring. What used to be the difference – small companies were flexible but big companies had the resources to implement change – is no longer the case. As such, the choice about how companies grow and who they work with is less constrained by size and reach and more by ambition.

A key element in this is the role of networks and multilateral partnerships. Today, with the right connections, it is relatively easy to put together a bespoke team of individuals, and so more and more companies are choosing to go the network route. As long as there is coherent choreography, sharing activities to deliver innovation across a network has become easier. In the world of apps and open source, most of the attention has focused on software development, but organizations from ARM to Zipcar are also using networks as part of their future development activity.

The other major organizational catalyst for change around growth has been the rise of new business creation or corporate entrepreneurship – that is, how large companies successfully build brand new businesses. Traditionally many organizations focused on core competence thinking have only felt comfortable delivering new growth platforms within their comfort zone. However, given that many emerging growth opportunities are found at the intersection of different companies' capabilities – and not at the core – organizations are keen to experiment and grow at the edge. Medtronic has had success in allowing an organization to engage outside the periphery of current activities in order to invest in new opportunities, but this is not the only route. The ambidextrous organization is increasingly looking at how best to grow and maintain the core and also simultaneously create major opportunities that can drive growth. Through working with a venture capital mentality for investment, collaborative partnerships for execution, and, most significantly, a more open-space approach to opportunity identification and development, firms from General Electric and IBM to Shell and Procter & Gamble are embracing corporate entrepreneurship to make the connections between the talent and capability and then deliver the best opportunities.

Emerging Economy Growth

Alongside the size of the organization being a significant success factor, prevailing views around location have also been challenged in the past few years. Global growth is now largely being driven by the emerging economies. There has been a shift from the West being the market for 'Made in China' to fast-growing Asian economies serving their own needs – 'Made in China for China.' Since Jim O'Neill at Goldman Sachs termed the abbreviation in 2001, growth in the 'BRIC' economies of Brazil, Russia, India, and China has been a priority for the financial markets and associated investment activities. While each is growing in their own way, exploiting different assets and capabilities, it is clear that, with total BRIC GDP fast catching that of the G7, the contribution to world growth is shifting quickly – and actually far quicker than many expected. Six years ago Goldman Sachs forecast that China's economy would pass that of the United States in real terms somewhere around 2040. In 2011 they revised this down to 2018: In five years, the estimate of Chinese relative economic growth was effectively doubled. The increasingly dominant role of the Asian rather than the US consumer for global companies is causing many to rewrite their growth strategies.

Across fast-growing economies companies such as Embraer, CEMEX, and PETRONAS are delivering sustained growth, not just locally but also on a global stage. From being a me-too manufacturer of domestic aircraft in the 1980s Brazil's Embraer has used design and strategic focus to become the leader in regional jet production globally and the fourth-largest civilian aerospace company in the world. In the world of construction, Mexico-based CEMEX has been growing on all fronts and alongside market expansion has been delivering a number of product innovations, addressing the sustainability agenda using recycled materials such as glass. And with a strong domestic base to build on, the Malaysian PETRONAS organization is now exporting its skills to other national oil companies as they seek to become more effective in oil and gas exploration and production.

While these achievements are well earned and well deserved, much media attention, however, is on companies that are growing from within the two largest emerging economies of India and China. With GDP growth rates of nearly 10% and wider wealth generation and distribution, another one billion middle-class consumers will enter the local markets over the next decade.

With India and China the primary growth engines in the world today, we can see firms in both countries that, as well as meeting domestic demands, are also making major inroads in the export markets and deriving growth beyond their national boundaries. Success in their huge home markets has enabled these companies to develop the economies of scale, specific capabilities, and financial strength that allow them to compete and win at the regional and global level.

India

In India, companies driving growth are in many different sectors of the economy. The IT sector has been international from the start. However, while it began with the likes of IBM and Accenture reducing costs by offshoring in order to serve their US and European customers, this is no longer the case. Today companies like Wipro, Infosys, and Tata Consulting (TCS) have all shifted from cost reduction to value creation. Infosys, India's best-known IT company, has revenues over $6 billion, employs over 130,000 people, and, with major campuses in Bangalore, Chennai, and Pune, has become a leader in design as well as software development for many of the world's major organizations. With 2010/11 revenues up 18%, Wipro is a major force in collaborative innovation technologies, while TCS, the company that pioneered IT services in India, now has over 100,000 employees.

In the automotive sector Tata Motors, India's largest car and truck company, is exporting a good proportion of its products, and, through its ownership of Jaguar Land Rover, has international brands that support global growth. However, while Jaguar and Land Rover are the high-profile brands, Tata-branded products that have traditionally addressed the home market are now also generating significant export income. The domestic market leader, Maruti Suzuki, is also looking to external markets in Asia for new customers. In addition Mahindra & Mahindra has been innovating its way up the domestic market with rural transport, SUVs, and urban utility vehicles now being exported to many countries. With its recent acquisition of Korea's SsangYong, Mahindra's reach now extends to over 90 countries giving it a footprint across Latin America, South East Asia, and Eastern Europe with ambitions to go fully global over the next few years. With revenues growing at 27% the company is now valued at $10 billion. Together, all three are becoming a major force in the global automotive sector and are seen by some as future challengers to the Toyota/General Motors/Volkswagen trio that currently lead worldwide markets.

In the healthcare sector, three organizations that have grown on the back of domestic need are now having multinational impact through medical tourism. Hyderabad-based Apollo Hospitals is one of the world's biggest telemedicine hubs and Aravind Eye Care has reinvented cataract surgery performing over three million operations a year, 70% of which are either free or at minimal charge: at only $50 for full-cost surgery, many thousands from other countries are therefore flying to India for high-quality eye treatment. And then we have Narayana Hrudayalaya based in Bangalore that has taken a similar philosophy with cardiac surgery. As detailed later, over 600 heart operations a week are now performed at Narayana facilities, where, supported by process and business model innovations, surgeons provide world-class cardiac operations at less than 10% of the cost in the West. Across all three companies, the ability to re-engineer healthcare to meet the needs of the millions of people at what Franklin Roosevelt first termed 'the bottom of the pyramid' and then use the efficiencies to scale-up the business is providing new growth opportunities.

The big challenge, however, remains; that is, while success has enabled India to have more millionaires than any other country, the wealth is yet to migrate down. Millions of people in India remain in abject poverty and the gap between rich and poor in many cities is increasing. Going forward many commentators see that the onus is for private India to better support public India and help to share the benefits of its high-impact growth success more widely. Innovation at the bottom of the pyramid in India is increasingly seen by companies such as Narayana Hrudayalaya as the way to not only address the needs of the many, but also as a means of replacing expensive approaches with simpler, equally effective, and lower cost models.

China

In China, most attention is usually focused on the banks and oil companies that dominate the listed company indexes. Organizations such as the Industrial and Commercial Bank of China (worth $239 bilion in mid-2011), China Construction Bank ($225 billion), and PetroChina ($324 billion) feature in many listings of the top 10 companies globally by market value and their influence compared to firms such as ExxonMobil and HSBC cannot be underestimated. However, alongside these headline-grabbers, there are a host of other organizations to note.

In *Fast Company*'s 2010 analysis of the 10 most innovative companies in China, four particularly stand out:

1. Huawei Technologies is one of the world's leading telecom equipment suppliers competing with Ericsson and Alcatel to provide 4G connectivity both in the primary Asian growth markets as well as in Europe and the United States. From its origins as a lower cost copycat, Huawei has invested heavily in R&D and is now one of the world's leading patent-filers as it seeks to be at the forefront of mobile technology.
2. BYD (Build Your Dreams) is widely acknowledged to be a leader in new battery technologies that will enable the electric car to become mass market. With major investment from Warren Buffett under its belt, 'its lithium-ion ferrous phosphate battery makes the Shenzen-based company a front runner,' and with its all-electric E6 now on the market, BYD is both providing the core technology to others and building its own automotive brand presence.

3. Suntech Power is fast becoming a leader in the solar energy market. Given that this is the most significant and long-term growth area for sustainable energy globally, Suntech's photovoltaic cells, which are 50% more efficient than the industry average, have been attracting much attention. With exports now being supplemented by international production facilities in the United States, Suntech is seen as one of the leading clean-tech companies for the future.

4. Baidu, China's leading search company, dominates the space domestically with more than 75% of the market. Even if Google manages to remain active, in China Baidu is in the lead. Although competitors such as Sohu have been developing improved accuracy and easier ways to search, with its significant market share and partnerships with Microsoft, Baidu is well positioned to benefit from the fast growth of internet connectivity in China, especially via mobile.

Emerging Market Country-to-Country Expansion

Returning to the role of M&A, as well as internally driven organic growth, several emerging market companies have also been making strong acquisitions of both brands and capabilities by buying some or all of established operations in other companies. In 2010 the Economist Intelligence Unit made special note of the purchase of a stake in the African business of Portugal's Banco Espírito Santo by two Brazilian institutions – Banco do Brasil and Bradesco. According to the banks, only around 15% of Africans currently have a bank account against 45% in Latin America. Having dominated their domestic markets and created effective new services that reach the 'unbanked,' these institutions see great potential in such emerging market country-to-country expansion. Indian telecommunications company, Bharti Airtel, has recently added significant presence in Africa through its acquisition of Zain and is now distinctively exploiting its home-market experience with customers who generate low revenues. In several sectors, emerging market companies are also expanding steadily into developed markets. With Lenovo and Tata seen as the pioneers, many are lining up to look at global not just local and regional opportunities.

Western Companies' Success in Emerging Markets

While the growth successes of companies from emerging economies is clearly significant, the addition of an extra one billion middle-class consumers over the next decade in the BRIC economies alone is a great attraction for many established Western companies from retailers such as Wal-Mart and Tesco, to luxury goods producers like Prada and Louis Vuitton. And with more middle-class consumers predicted in 2020 than the United States and European Union combined, the biggest focus for many is on Asia and particularly China.

As well as those above, others such as Procter & Gamble, Philips, Nestlé, and Visa are all making Asian growth core to their future plans. For some this means selling more of the same global products such as Pampers, Nespresso, and credit cards in new markets. However, for others this is more about designing new products for the Asian consumer. Whether this is noodle snacks from Nestlé or cleaning products for Chinese apartments from Procter & Gamble, goods that are specifically designed for the new markets are delivering growth. Alongside the domestic products that are 'Made in China for China' the attraction of China as an export destination rather than a source is accelerating and finding successful routes to growth in Asia is the priority for many a global organization.

However, not all attempts by Western companies to gain footholds in emerging markets have been successful. Really understanding different cultures and consumers is notoriously difficult and many companies are finding it hard to adjust their practices to different business and market environments. A few have made good progress. The most successful strategy to date has been to achieve growth by entering into local partnerships with companies which have distinctive and complementary capabilities that have developed out of specialization.

Whereas Wal-Mart and Carrefour have largely failed to get significant traction, after a bit of trial and error, UK-based Tesco has powered ahead with the majority of its growth now coming from non-domestic markets. In the past the general approach was for a team of expats to manage local operations but this has changed. In South Korea Tesco established a joint venture with Samsung – Home plus – which is now the second-largest retailer in the country with over 350 stores and 23,000 employees of whom only four are British. With revenues of over £5 billion and 13 million members of its loyalty card scheme (25% of the country's population), Home plus's success has been credited to that fact that it is a Korean company, run by Koreans for Koreans, which benefits from Tesco's retailing capabilities.

Elsewhere Western companies are gaining successful footholds through acquisitions. But these are not simply to buy market share. Rather they are capability growth driven enterprises that create new platforms. Take for example Reckitt Benckiser's 2011 purchase of India's Paras Pharmaceuticals, a privately owned company that has brought to the Reckitt Benckiser portfolio a number of leading over-the-counter health and personal care brands. This creates a material healthcare business in India – one of the largest future markets in the world – while adding strongly established brands to the mix. 2010 Accenture research highlighted that 'access to higher-growth emerging markets has been an important driver of multinational performance in the downturn.' Partnerships that bring local input to the mix rather than simple expansion of the Western model are seen as the way forward for many companies.

Fragmenting Markets

Yet another driving force is the changing shape of markets – as we become more connected we are arguably becoming more fragmented and distributed. Like-minded consumers may not be geographically bounded – city dwellers in China may have more in common with those in Paris and New York than with their countrymen in rural areas. We need to be careful when looking at growth opportunities at the country level. Whilst the growth potential in countries like India and China is very high there are significant variances within those countries. Rather than having one growth strategy for the whole of China, which has 150 cities with populations over one million, there may be greater benefit in segmenting the country into sub-regions where scale opportunities still exist and there are sufficient similarities within the region to make growth prospects attractive.

As the global diaspora grows larger, it is also increasing in its influence, repatriating capital and ideas to the motherlands but also creating substantial markets for products and services that meet the cultural needs of the dispersed and offer entry routes into new markets.

It is estimated that over 40 million Chinese people live outside of China and in 2010, according to World Bank estimates, they remitted some $51 billion back home. With significant expansion of the Muslim population in some parts of Europe, growth opportunities are opening up for companies that can satisfy these differing cultural needs. From halal foods to Islamic finance products we can see an emerging shift in the European product mix. As technology allows for greater tailoring of offerings and enables more detailed profiling of what consumers are searching for so more considered segmentation of markets may be needed in order to tap into the best growth opportunities.

The Impact of the Financial Crisis

If the emerging economies have some very strong cards to play going forward, how has the financial crisis impacted how the developed world approaches growth? The opportunity for innovation in a downturn is well documented and during the financial crisis many of the arguments have been rekindled. A report by Charles Leadbeater and James Meadway from NESTA in the UK in 2008 was one of many that called for investment in innovation at a time of crisis. Citing the creation of the Federal Reserve System in response to the 1907 San Francisco earthquake, the development of the internet in response to the threat of a nuclear attack, and IBM's shift to services in response to a crisis in its mainframe computing market, this report argued for the need to invest in innovation and growth in a downturn. In order to avoid the sort of decline in world trade that happened during the Great Depression, investment in change at a time of crisis is a well-honed argument.

Over the past couple of years we have seen multiple stimulus programs designed to kick-start economies and incentivize growth via innovation. The Green Stimulus Program in the United States, the German car scrappage scheme, and even China's infrastructure investment program are all examples of cooperation between governments and industry to drive increased growth. Just as a similar combination in post-war Japan helped to create an economy that averaged growth rates of 8% during the 1950s and 10% during the 1960s, so these programs were designed to stimulate growth. However, while the German car scrappage scheme helped the automotive sector in this European powerhouse to remain strong, many of the other programs are yet to pay dividends.

It is natural for any organization facing hard times to tighten its belt and cut back on costs. A top candidate here is R&D investment as it often has little short-term payback. While the logic of investment for the future makes sense, for many business leaders cutbacks in a downturn affect innovation and operational activities equally. What was different for some countries over the past few years was the inability of public-sector innovation to pick up the slack and maintain the national growth engine. In places such as the UK, as well as the usual examples of Portugal, Ireland, Greece, and Spain, the austerity measures introduced to cut back on spending and reduce the deficits have meant decreased investment in public-sector growth at the same time as relying more on the private sector at a time of economic hardship. Taken together this has clearly caused lasting problems for some economies.

In 2007, before the financial crisis, average growth across the world's economies was 5.2%. In 2009 this dropped to 0.6% but there were differences between the so-called advanced and emerging economies. In the West, average GDP growth dropped to −3.2% while in the fast-growing Asian economies it only dropped to 2.4%. Two years later, the West was just reaching 2% GDP growth per annum before dropping back again, while the developing world average was back up at over 6%. If you talk to many industrialists in India and China about the global recession, they ask 'what recession?' – it was merely a minor bump in the road!

What has changed over the past few years has been the ways in which companies and some countries have sought to collaborate around innovation-driven growth. Whether at G20 level or more regionally there has been increased focus on the power of networks to enable faster and more effective growth than many nations have experienced in the past. Closer links between cities and the global centers of growth, rather than between regions within countries, are seen as the general way forward. With organizations such as the C40 (the mayors of the 40 largest megacities) having increased influence on global change, many see that it is the direct connections between Mumbai, New York, Shanghai, and London rather than economic relationships between London and Birmingham or New York and Philadelphia that will have greatest impact.

For some, the downturn has also caused a fundamental questioning of assumptions about how we do things and how wealth is created. While a good number of sectors, such as health, transport, and communications, carry on as usual because the macro global changes around population growth and technology adoption are seen to be the main driver of future growth, for companies that have their main focus on the Western markets and are hit by declining demand there is clearly a longer hangover period. However, taking the global view, others argue that the overall impact of the financial crisis was that it has forced many to clean out the cupboard, stop doing the incremental activities maintained out of habit, and instead focus on the bigger opportunities on the horizon.

Whilst the long-term impact of the recession on the growth prospects of different countries in the developed world is unknown, it is clear that there are still significant opportunities, especially for those who can support the development of markets and institutions fit for the 21st century and for those who provide products and services that meet the needs of its consumers.

CHAPTER 4

New Approaches to Growth

Introduction

The Growth
Agenda

Nestlé
PepsiCo

Audi
Samsung

Reckitt
Benckiser
P&G

Starwood
Inditex

Amazon
Google

Narayana
Novo
Nordisk

Rolls-Royce
ARM

BASF
Shell

Tata
Bharti

LEGO
Apple

The Growth
Challenge

Whereas core competence thinking majored on organizations concentrating on what they were good at, the idea of a *distinctive competence* is focused on doing something that organizations are uniquely capable of and so offers greater competitive advantage. This is an area that has been attracting much discussion in both academic and business communities and is key to how many organizations are now looking at their overall strategies for growth.

Back in the late 1950s when Philip Sleznick first coined the term, the concept of distinctive competence came from the belief that there are certain market-facing strengths in some organizations (such as a strong brand) that enable them to succeed. In the 1970s Kenneth Andrews and Howard Stevenson built on this view, suggesting that distinctive competence is a set of activities, such as technology development, which an organization could perform particularly well in comparison to its peers. This generated wide-ranging debate because what one person may see as distinctive another may well view as a commodity. The challenge, and the opportunity, is for a company to not only be clear about what its distinctive competences are and why they matter, but also in developing them so that they are a unique source of differentiation.

Resource-Based View

In recent years, academic focus on distinctive competences has moved on to what has been termed the 'resource-based view' of how companies succeed.

This shift has become a prominent perspective moving away from a sole focus on the external issues (as depicted in Porter's five forces paradigm), and more towards an equal consideration of internal capability development for sustainable, competitive advantage. The resource-based view essentially explores the link between the internal features of a firm and its performance, and, as Barney first detailed in 1991, at its heart sees organizations as bundles of resources, which are simultaneously 'valuable, rare, inimitable and non-substitutional.' So, as explained in an influential 1995 *Harvard Business Review* article, 'Competing on Resources,' by David Collins and Cynthia Montgomery: 'no two companies are alike because no two companies have had the same set of experiences, acquired the same assets and skills, or built the same organizational cultures.' Valuable resources are what make the difference and these can be physical assets, intangible resources such as brands and intellectual property, or an organizational capability that is 'embedded in a company's routines, processes and culture.' Competitive advantage can therefore be gained from the ownership of a valuable resource that enables a company to perform activities better or more effectively than competitors.

Dynamic Capabilities

While the ideal is that distinctive competences remain unchanged over time, many recognize that this is increasingly unrealistic, as a faster world demands change in order to stay in the lead. A recent elaboration of the resource-based view therefore looks at what has been termed 'dynamic capabilities' and examines more deeply the underpinning organizational routines that can be adapted and are associated with future resource creation. This focuses more on the capacity of an organization to renew resource 'bundles' or as Teece and colleagues put it: 'to integrate, build and reconfigure internal and external competences to address changing environments.' Whilst the functionality of dynamic capabilities is generic, their value lies in the resource configurations they create, and not in the capabilities themselves.

One organization that has successfully evolved its distinctive competences and developed dynamic capabilities is IBM. In 1993 the services unit of IBM provided 27% of revenues – a percentage which more than doubled by 2001. Ten years later, the share of IBM revenues associated with software and services had risen to over 70% and much of this is attributed to the dynamic capabilities that the organization has developed. Looking in particular at the role of management in building and adapting competences to address rapidly changing environments, a *California Management Review* article by Harreld *et al.* stated that 'with dynamic capabilities sustained competitive advantage comes from the firm's ability to lever-age and reconfigure its existing competences and assets in a way that is valuable to the customer but difficult for competitors to imitate.' Through the creation of new approaches including deep dives, strategic leadership forums, and emerging business opportunities programs, IBM has been able to build a unique set of evolving capabilities that are embedded into the internal resource and thus provide what it sees as its distinctive competences that enable it to continue to grow in a continually competitive landscape. With 2010 revenues of $99.9 billion and profits of $14.8 billion, up 10% on 2009, its share price has now eclipsed the peaks of the dot.com boom in 2000/2001. Although a company that has been around for 100 years, IBM sees that developing these unique competences can keep it at the fore and help it to continue to evolve its fields of activity and opera-tion and successfully compete with the fast-growth entrants creating new markets.

Distinctive competences are unique combinations of skills, assets, and capa-bilities that set companies apart in a market or a sector and so enable them to lead in sustained value creation and growth. Whether the underlying capabilities are fixed or dynamic, these are what academics and business leaders are increas-ingly seeing as pivotal for future growth.

So, at a time of rising global competition, faster change, and more rapid devel-opment of capabilities, the focus for many CEOs is to build or reinforce their organizations' distinctive competences. As accessible new approaches are quickly adopted by the mainstream, the challenge of protecting competences and prevent-ing them from becoming a mere commodity is matched by the need to refresh, rebuild, and even create anew those that will be distinctive in the future. As we will see later, those companies, like Apple, Amazon, LEGO, Rolls-Royce and Shell, that achieve this become and remain the winners in their fields.

Sustainable Growth

The downturn in the West and the resultant search for new sources of growth are having a potentially game-changing effect on the sustainability agenda. Coming at a time when the world population increases by another 750 million people in the next decade, many of the countries that will be impacted by this change are taking a new approach. More companies are starting to challenge their views of unfettered growth and some are even exploring the potential to decouple growth from increased resource consumption.

As cost reduction and resource security have aligned and become greater challenges for companies, many are seeing the growth potential for 'responsible business.' Across companies as varied as Google, PepsiCo, and Wal-Mart, sustainability has moved from the corporate social responsibility office to being embedded in business strategies and plans for the future. Simultaneously the language has changed from discussions about saving the planet to practical solutions for the responsible and efficient use of increasingly constrained resources and how the 'green economy' can be a primary driver of growth.

It is not just in the boardroom that this is happening – institutions and country leaders are also putting growth and sustainability on the agenda. For example, at the 2010 World Economic Forum (WEF) 'Summer Davos in Asia,' China focused on 'Driving Growth through Sustainability.' In his opening remarks the Premier of the People's Republic of China, Wen Jiabao, pledged that China, will 'continue to conserve resources, protect the environment and raise the efficiency of resources.' Although some may shrug this off as mere greenwash, there was widespread recognition that now is the time to 'embed sustainability in companies, mindsets and cultures. Organizations are trying different ways of accomplishing this goal and it is not clear if there is one "right" way.' But it is evident that many believe that sustainability can be a source of competitive advantage and a driver of growth. For example André Schneider, managing director and chief operating officer World Economic Forum: 'Driving growth through sustainability is fundamental for global, national and business competitiveness in the 21st century.'

In parallel, the OECD has developed an Innovation Strategy to promote innovation for the 21st century. This is underpinned by the belief that 'innovation can help accelerate the recovery and put countries back on a path to sustainable – and greener – growth . . . innovation is essential if countries and firms are to recover from the economic downturn. It is a powerful engine for development and for addressing social and global challenges. And it holds the key, both in advanced and emerging economies, to employment generation and enhanced productivity growth through knowledge creation and its subsequent application and diffusion.'

A growing number of organizations around the world now see that in our increasingly resource-constrained world, sustainable growth is no longer a 'nice to have' option but the only way we can all really go forward. The debate is about the degree and timing of the necessary change in approach, motivation, and reward for growth. One significant view that has been gaining traction is that we must rebalance our economies so that we are using less than the planet's resources can sustain. The one-planet view of growth, which is endorsed by a number of organizations including the World Wide Fund For Nature (WWF) and the World Business Council for Sustainable Development (WBCSD), is focused on bringing us down from the current level where we use 1.6 times the resources the world can naturally replenish every year.

A big challenge in the past has been to find a common currency and language between the world of economic and shareholder value and that of social capital. When the net present value of things in the future is calculated, discounting techniques can make future benefits appear less valuable in the money of today and so potentially less relevant to decision making. The measurement of societal well-being and the understanding of relationships between economic prosperity and happiness are still in the early stages of development and adoption although there are increasing signs of these issues becoming mainstreamed. In July 2011, the UN General Assembly passed a resolution that invites countries 'to pursue the elaboration of additional measures that better capture the importance of the pursuit of happiness and well-being in development with a view to guiding their public policies.'

The resolution notes that the GDP indicator 'was not designed to and does not adequately reflect the happiness and well-being of people in a country,' and 'unsustainable patterns of production and consumption can impede sustainable development.' So perhaps the financial crisis does have a silver lining – as French President Nicolas Sarkozy is quoted in *The Telegraph* back in September 2009, 'the crisis doesn't only make us free to imagine other models, another future, another world. It obliges us to do so.'

Other recent attempts to reframe the growth debate in terms of economics and sustainability, whilst adding to our understanding of the challenges and potential solutions, have tended to remain on the margins. It might be enlightening to see how many leaders are familiar with the recommendations of publications such as the 2009 Sustainable Development Commission report 'Prosperity without Growth? A Transition to a Sustainable Economy.' In both this report and the subsequent book, Tim Jackson argued strongly that capitalism and growth can indeed be decoupled from such issues as energy consumption. In concert with the one-planet view, he sees 'a vision of prosperity as the ability to flourish as human beings – within the ecological limits of the planet.' But he also goes further suggesting that voluntary simplicity and frugality are the way to go and that 'people engaged in attempts to live more frugally seem happier than those driven by materialism.' He proposes that a 'Cinderella economy' geared to improved flourishing and increased resource productivity is needed but recognizes that this 'is problematic in conventional terms because its potential for productivity is almost negligible.'

Although most would agree that we need an end to relentless growth, this may be a step too far too soon. Right now growth in many developing countries is being driven at one level by the need to provide the basics of sanitation, electricity, and fresh water to all and this is largely being achieved by adopting traditional views of economic growth. However, the impetus for change is clearly there in some quarters and momentum for a new approach is steadily building. In the financial world there has been a marked rise in areas such as socially responsible investing, ethical funds, and ethical banking, whilst consumers are increasingly responding to such things as fair trade, carbon and calorie labeling, and showing increasing loyalty to companies such as Unilever and Marks & Spencer who they see as being leaders in the sustainability field. In the companies highlighted as Growth Champions we can see financial growth success but at the same time a number are also showing how the sustainability agenda is fast becoming embedded in many core business strategies and processes.

In the short term, shareholder value is created when the perception of future profits is enhanced. However, sustainable shareholder value growth is produced when the needs of all stakeholders (including employees, customers, suppliers, local communities, governments, and shareholders) are addressed. Innovation can clearly create new economic value by developing new products or introducing new ways of doing things. In addition it can create utility or emotional value and also help to bring about change in societal value systems and choices.

More of us agree that growth is about much more than providing a boost to sales, margins, and the bottom line. It is about creating value for all stakeholders; economic value for the shareholders; social value for employees, their families and friends, local communities, and social networks; as well as value for ecosystems and the environment. This applies equally in developing markets where growth is steadily rising as in many developed regions where the priority is to kick-start new growth. While economic growth is vitally important it is critical to deliver this in a way that does not elevate pure profit above societal or environmental value. The organizations profiled in the core section of this book are, to varied levels, achieving their growth ambitions within this perspective.

Introduction

The Growth Agenda

Nestlé
PepsiCo

Audi
Samsung

Reckitt Benckiser
P&G

Starwood
Inditex

Amazon
Google

Narayana
Novo Nordisk

Rolls-Royce
ARM

BASF
Shell

Tata
Bharti

LEGO
Apple

The Growth Challenge

Part II

The Growth Champions

The companies we have profiled are those that, over the years, have chosen to do the right things and do them well. They have not just followed the mainstream and kept up with their peers. They are the companies that have pushed the boundaries; the ones that have challenged convention – the ones that have reinvented themselves and how they run their operations. In a world where access to knowledge has created an increasingly level playing field, they have been brave enough to try new things, learn from the associated experiences, and adopt successful practices into their activities.

With over a decade of analysis of innovation and growth performance to draw on, we have chosen to profile the companies that have consistently made the most of their innovation resources. These are not necessarily the ones that spend most on innovation or those that make the most noise about their innovation activities. They are a distinct group that, over time, has delivered the greatest impact in relation to the resources that they have deployed.

Using the past 10 years of *Innovation Leaders*' analysis, we have identified 20 organizations that have consistently delivered sustained growth ahead of their peers. Combining detailed analysis of their performance from public data with internal insights we have highlighted the companies that have been able to deal with the big challenges, have broken new ground, and have delivered consistent sustained growth through accommodating these challenges and reinventing the status quo.

In this section, we profile 10 pairs of companies that have been growth successes over the last decade. Each pair of companies has achieved impact in the areas discussed, but they have done it in their own way, using their unique capabilities to create greatest value. We do not lead each discussion on the distinctive competences that have been built, but instead concentrate on the impact that has been achieved as we believe this provides a more coherent way to understand the achievements. In each case study we have, however, brought to the surface the specific distinctive competences that are making a difference for the respective organizations. We selected the following companies to discuss further around the associated issues:

- Changing food and drink for the better – Nestlé and PepsiCo
- Design as the growth driver – Audi and Samsung Electronics

- Making the most of insight – Reckitt Benckiser and Procter & Gamble
- Delivering a unique customer experience – Starwood Hotels and Inditex
- Expertly using data to get ever closer to customers – Amazon and Google
- Reinventing healthcare – Narayana Hrudayalaya and Novo Nordisk
- Technology partnerships for growth – Rolls-Royce and ARM
- Growth in a resource-constrained world – BASF and Shell
- Leapfrogging from India – Tata and Bharti
- Bringing magic to the everyday – LEGO and Apple

The mapping below is used throughout to not only visualize but also link the distinctive competences and impact so that the specific approaches are clearly evident.

Introduction

The Growth
Agenda

Nestlé
PepsiCo

Audi
Samsung

Reckitt
Benckiser
P&G

Starwood
Inditex

Amazon
Google

Narayana
Novo
Nordisk

Rolls-Royce
ARM

BASF
Shell

Tata
Bharti

LEGO
Apple

The Growth
Challenge

Nestlé	KEY DATA
Total revenue (2010)	CHF 109.7 billion
Average revenue growth p.a. (2005–2010)	4.5%
Net profit (2010)	CHF 35.4 billion
Average net profit growth p.a. (2005–2010)	47%
Revenue per employee (2010)	CHF 390,500
R&D investment (2010)	CHF 1.9 billion
Average share price growth p.a. (2005–2010)	12%
Number of CHF 1 billion brands (2010)	20

PepsiCo	KEY DATA
Total revenue (2010)	$57.8 billion
Average revenue growth p.a. (2005–2010)	12.5%
Net profit (2010)	$6.3 billion
Average net profit growth p.a. (2005–2010)	8.0%
Revenue per employee (2010)	$576,000
R&D investment (2010)	$488 million
Average share price growth p.a. (2005–2010)	5.2%
Number $ billion brands (2010)	19

CHAPTER 5

Nestlé and PepsiCo
Changing food and drink for the better

Competition across the food and drink sector is intense. Traditional players are being confronted by new challenges around health and sustainability whilst regional players are increasing their reach and influence, particularly in emerging markets. Asia and Latin America provide the greatest attraction for both existing and new product growth, but other markets need to revise and rejuvenate their product portfolios to produce healthier but just as palatable food. Today companies such as Nestlé, General Mills, PepsiCo, Coca-Cola, Kraft, and Kellogg's have the largest market share and are battling to access new customers and provide better products for their existing ones.

Satisfying growing demand in emerging markets has become a stated priority for many of the large food and drink manufacturers. Approximately one billion new middle-class consumers will come into the market over the next decade and often one of the first things they do with their newfound wealth is to change their diet. For some this is about improving nutritional quality, increasing their protein intake, and helping their families to become healthier. For others, the attraction of cheap fast foods, convenience snacks and sodas, and more sugar-based products is an equal pull. Nutrition, health, and wellness are the buzzwords for most companies as they seek to make healthier products without compromising on taste. Equally, improving the quality of low-cost foods, especially in emerging markets, is a priority for many.

With an increasing number of people consuming more food, many see a fundamental supply problem on the horizon. As we climb up the protein ladder, we tend to eat more and especially more meat. Add in bio-fuels demanding extra wheat and sugar and the competition for land is a major concern. Companies such as Monsanto and Cargill have been making major investments in the science of food to improve yields of key crops such as wheat and soya. Using GM seeds that can make wheat drought-resistant or improving the life of soya beans have been key areas of focus. Jim Kirkwood, vice-president of R&D at General Mills, sees that, given the challenge going forward, major 'technical breakthroughs are required for a second agricultural green revolution that will enable us to feed the world.' We simply need more sustainable supplies of food.

Alongside the demand for more food, the other big issue for food and drink companies is the impact that their products have on obesity and hence diabetes.

Organizations such as the Center for Disease Control and Prevention (CDC) in the United States have been highlighting this issue for many years and now many of the world's governments are finally starting to regulate against high-fat and high-salt foods. Historically, the food and drink sector was focused primarily on taste and convenience. While these are still important factors in consumers' choice, many companies, perhaps because of regulatory pressure, are concentrating on improving the nutritional and sustainability characteristics of their products.

Over the past decade there are two of the larger companies in the food and drink sector that have proactively started to tackle the health challenge. Neither has chosen to exit major categories, but rather have made what they see as significant moves to change the nature of their product portfolio. This has been achieved both by introducing new products and by making existing products healthier. Nestlé, the world's largest food company, and PepsiCo, the biggest food and drink firm in the United States, have both grown substantially. Nestlé is now a $200 billion company and PepsiCo has shifted to become more focused on foods than drinks.

Nestlé

Nestlé is the world's largest food company by market value: Over 1.25 billion of its products are consumed every day. Headquartered in Switzerland and operating in over 80 countries, it employs nearly 300,000 people and sells a huge range of products. With over 6000 brands including Nespresso, Perrier, Kit-Kat, Häagen-Dazs, Cheerios, Buitoni, and Felix, chances are that pretty much every Western household is a customer. Twenty brands each have sales of over CHF 1 billion a year. Tracing its history back to 1867, Nestlé now also owns around a quarter of L'Oréal, the world's largest cosmetics company, and is part of major joint ventures including Cereal Partners with General Mills, Beverage Partners with Coca-Cola, and Dairy Partners with Fronterra.

Foremost amongst all of the major food and drink companies, Nestlé aims to be 'the world's leading nutrition, health and wellness company and the industry reference for financial performance.' Judging by the past few years, it has been doing a good job of this. It has clearly positioned itself as the company that marries nutrition and taste across the range, has topped $100 billion in sales, and has increased profits by over 400% in the past five years.

Nutrition, Health, and Wellness

The health focus for Nestlé has been a long-standing platform, and one that, over the past decade, has become more prominent. Through education, improved ingredients, and the launch of new products, the company is seeking to shift consumers away from obesity-fuelling foods and beverages towards healthier products. Sanjay Sehgal, head of Nestlé's Corporate Wellness Unit, sees that its global R&D infrastructure and closeness to markets have positioned the company at the center of a contemporary drive for increased nutrition: 'From 2003 onwards, Nestlé was the first company in the food industry to put comprehensive policies in place for the systematic reduction of specific nutrients that are considered to be detrimental to health when consumed in excess, and also to offer consumers more essential nutrients or nutritious ingredients.'

The company's '60/40+ program' aims to systematically improve its leading products. Firstly, it aims for 60% of consumers to prefer its version over the nearest competitor in a blind taste test. Complementing the taste advantage with nutrition, it then requires that it offers additional nutritional benefits as outlined by leading health authorities. Among many improvements, Nestlé has managed to significantly reduce salt content across a range of its mainstream products.

Pharma Foods

A major recent focus for Nestlé is its medical foods division with the creation of both Nestlé Health Science and the Nestlé Institute of Health Sciences. These are bridging the gap between foods and pharmaceuticals, and developing the innovative area of personalized health science nutrition to prevent and treat health conditions such as diabetes, obesity, cardiovascular issues and Alzheimer's disease. Nestlé CEO, Paul Bulcke, sees that 'this is an opportunity in the making . . . It is linked to the equation of food and health. Food is the best medicine and we are looking for personalized science based platforms.'

With chewing gums for people who have chronic kidney inflammation and a number of products that counterbalance the negative effects of chemotherapy, Nestlé believes that its new foods can play therapy-supporting and preventative roles across many chronic illnesses. Chairman, Peter Brabeck, sees that compared to pharmaceutical companies like Abbott that are also active in this area, Nestlé's food expertise will be pivotal – 'Nestlé has the major advantage because we know how to texturize the product. If you can't swallow, we can give a product a texture that allows you to swallow.' Nestlé firmly believes that it has the capabilities to not only lead technologically in what have become termed 'pharma foods' but also profit the most in the market.

Emerging Market Growth

Over 35% of Nestlé's sales are currently from emerging economies and it is expecting to add an extra billion customers or so and another 10% of sales by 2020. With this in mind Nestlé uses local manufacturers, with 47% of factories now in emerging markets; it builds long-term relationships with suppliers and farmers and encourages and supports home-grown, local talent to work at the regional HQ.

The company's range of what it terms 'Popularly Positioned Products' accounted for 10% of annual sales in 2009 and grew to 26%, substantially faster than Nestlé's other products. These are high-quality, nutritionally enhanced, and affordable products aimed at emerging (mostly cash-based) markets and lower income consumers in developing and developed (mostly East European) markets – combined a market of some three billion people. In the emerging markets, Nestlé touches the customer in multiple ways, through local markets, mobile street vendors, and door-to-door distributors as well as more established shops and supermarkets. The same product category can be offered in cheap and expensive versions in the same markets, so appealing to a wider consumer demographic.

Sustainable Sourcing

In the late 1970s and early 1980s, Nestlé was in the headlines for promoting infant formula in favor of breast milk to mothers around the world and especially in developing companies. This was the biggest controversy to hit the company,

Introduction

The Growth Agenda

Nestlé PepsiCo

Audi Samsung

Reckitt Benckiser P&G

Starwood Inditex

Amazon Google

Narayana Novo Nordisk

Rolls-Royce ARM

BASF Shell

Tata Bharti

LEGO Apple

The Growth Challenge

and one that still has residual impact in some regions. More recently, Greenpeace has highlighted the problems associated with deforestation to make way for palm oils for Nestlé products. In response the company has made significant changes in its practices over the last few years. Not only does it now clearly advocate that 'breast is best' but it has also rethought its supply chain. In carrying out the research for this book we found that, in parallel with the nutrition, health, and wellness priority, what most people highlight about Nestlé today is the major shift it has made in how and where it sources its key ingredients.

Starting in 1995 with environmental reporting, in 2001 Nestlé then began reporting on issues related to rural development and particularly farmers, employees, and economic development in Africa and Latin America. Since 2007, under the 'Creating Shared Value' banner, Nestlé has made a big push toward creating value not just for its shareholders, but also for 'the societies in which it operates.' The focus is on creating shared value across three linked areas of risk and opportunity: water, nutrition, and rural development. While other companies have similar initiatives, the focus on rural development has attracted greatest attention. Nestlé sees that 'the objective of rural development is to reduce poverty and hunger, and improve the quality of life in non-urban areas.'

This objective has delivered tangible change as we can see from the 144 rurally located Nestlé factories in emerging markets. By 2010, 70% had a company-built water treatment facility, 58% a formal apprenticeship program, and a third provided literacy and numeracy programs. CHF 500 million is being invested in the Nescafé coffee plan aiming for '90,000 tonnes of production to be grown according to Rainforest Alliance principles by 2020' – and the company is sourcing twice this amount directly from farmers. The Cocoa plan aims to ensure '10m plants being provided to farmers within ten years.' For Nestlé value is created through more secure supply of better quality raw materials, lower procurement costs, and consumer preference for its products. It sees that for society the value is in the 'advice and technical assistance provided; increased yields; higher quality crops; increased rural income and reduced poverty and wider employment and economic development.' By 2015, Nestlé aims to source all its palm oils from sustainable sources.

Although initially derided by some non-government organizations as greenwashing, in recent years the Creating Shared Value program has been gaining a great deal of praise. Having built up momentum internally, Nestlé is now seen as a leading example in this field. John Elkington of Volans sees 'the creating shared value concept as a significant step forward.' Already the subject of a *Harvard Business Review* article by Michael Porter and Mark Kramer, the program is also creating an alternative view of how to manage a multinational business in tune with the societies in which it operates:

Embedded in the Nestlé example is a far broader insight, which is the advantage of buying from capable local suppliers. Outsourcing to other locations and countries creates transaction costs and inefficiencies that can offset lower wage and input costs. Capable local suppliers help firms avoid these costs and can reduce cycle time, increase flexibility, foster faster learning, and enable innovation. Buying local includes not only local companies but also local units of national or international companies. When firms buy locally, their suppliers can get stronger, increase their profits, hire more people, and pay better wages – all of which will benefit other businesses in the community.

Growth via Innovation

Paul Bulcke sees that Nestlé is 'looking for growth in the whole world: Growth should come from developed and developing markets.' The company achieved organic growth in revenues of 11.5% in 2010 and is targeting similar figures for the next five years. He sees that foremost 'we need food products that people like but ones where we can also build in nutrition.'

For Nestlé, 'innovation and renovation is the process through which we keep our brands consumer relevant and competitor differentiated.' The world of food and drink is characterized by lots of small changes on an ongoing basis. Flavor and packaging tweaks are the standard approach for regular refresh of many brands, but with the nutrition, health and wellness focus, ingredient change is also a priority. 'Each of our product categories, from Chocolate to Baby Food, has a specific strategy to ensure that it can be the nutrition leader in its space.'

Equally, there are now nearly 5000 Popularly Positioned Products available around the world through a variety of distribution models. Many of these include nutritional ingredients. For example, around 90 billion Maggi bouillon cubes are sold annually. These are iodine-enriched and fortified with micronutrients to address deficiencies in certain markets.

The other major trajectory of change in the sector has been 'premiumization' where 'affordable luxury' is the name of the game. Whether through its Häagen-Dazs ice cream or its Nespresso coffee products, Nestlé has developed a premium strategy for each of its categories. With Nespresso, success has come from a combination of patience, experimentation, and willingness to challenge assumptions. Although now a CHF 3.2 billion leader in the super-premium coffee category, it has taken 10 years to build it to this point. Initially conceived within the Nescafé-dominated product group, the willingness to launch a product that competed with the existing portfolio was, at the time, a bold move which required extensive collaboration with the coffee machine manufacturers and establishing a new direct-to-consumer distribution channel supported by dedicated retail stores. However, with over 10 million members of the Nespresso Club and many more additional regular consumers, this product has become not only a star in the Nestlé portfolio but also a reference point for many in the innovation arena.

For Nestlé innovation runs across the whole company and is fundamentally about 'finding the sweet spot between what is technically possible, commercially viable and what consumers and society actually need.'

Global R&D

In all, Nestlé spends 1.6% of revenue on R&D – more than any other food company. Alongside its brands, people, and geographical reach, it considers its R&D as a core competitive strength: 'It is science-based, consumer-centric and focused on differentiation from our competitors. It goes beyond food to cover new products, packaging, technology and manufacturing, quality and safety.' With 17 R&D centers around the world employing 1300 people in 275 application groups, Nestlé considers that it has an 'unparalleled global R&D infrastructure' in the sector. In line with other companies such as IBM, Novartis, and Philips, the decentralized network approach in Nestlé allows it to match global platform development with local need.

Nutrition is a complex subject demanding significant scientific expertise and close proximity to local tastes, needs, and capabilities. Placing scientific centers in diverse locations, Nestlé has developed a significant, localized R&D competence that it can tailor and exploit globally through its application teams. The proximity to the consumer of R&D, manufacturing, and distribution, helps the company deliver global platform products with high local relevance. Through its close collaboration with local farmers, manufacturers, and distribution mechanisms, Nestlé demonstrates a unique and vertically integrated view on developing ethical, nutrition-rich products that competitors find difficult to match.

Nestlé's USP?

While the global/local R&D is highlighted by many as the organization's distinctive competence, others in the company like to add the breadth of Nestlé's operations:

Nestlé's Food and Beverages business has the scale to touch consumers all over the world; the intimacy to provide the food and beverages they want; the diversity to do so at a great many eating occasions and to provide balance; the ubiquity to provide it whenever and wherever consumers want it; the presence to be there throughout consumers' lives; and the know-how to advance nutritional science and to bring nutrition, health and wellness arguments to all food and beverage categories. These are the pillars on which we make our claim of leadership in Nutrition, Health and Wellness: unmatched scale, intimacy, diversity, ubiquity.

In an industry where the focus is shifting towards an appreciation for the nutritional, health, and wellness benefits of eating and drinking, Nestlé's physical presence in emerging and developed markets has served it well. It has moved from being a largely product-based, technology-driven company to a science-based one.

Global scale, built in its early years, has organically created an international foundation of localized scientific competence that is difficult to replicate. This 'up-skilling' of the enterprise has moved in step with the growing sophistication in consumer choices, creating a brand that is increasingly trusted in a health-conscious society.

Challenges

With billions to feed and thousands of companies, the food industry is intensely local. Maintaining global leadership in such a diverse sector requires focus not just on local trends but also on the big issues that can disrupt the business model. Food commodity prices, for example, rose between 40% and 60% between 2009 and 2010 and are set to continue on that trajectory. Nestlé chairman Peter Brabeck sees that 'the world has made some politically wrong decisions like subsidizing and fostering bio-fuels, which increase the demand for an already limited supply of food in an unsustainable manner.' Moving forward his view is that 'there has to be a ban on using food for fuel. A move in that direction would have an immediate effect on bringing down the stress on the food supply.'

Given that Nestlé envisages that the world will need to double food production by 2050, the basics of raw material supply and pricing are critical. While the company's 'shared value' approach is a step in the right direction to mitigate this, some feel that it may not be enough if there is greater food security activity by key producers.

PepsiCo

PepsiCo is the world's third-largest food and drink company. No longer just Pepsi, it includes other major food and drink brands including Tropicana, Quaker, Lay's/Walkers, and Gatorade. In all, very much like Nestlé, it has around 20 $1 billion brands that are sold in over 200 countries worldwide. What makes PepsiCo so well regarded in the sector is that not only has it made the old Coke vs. Pepsi debate irrelevant by outmaneuvering its rival, but over the past decade it has substantially changed its product portfolio. Ahead of most of its peers, PepsiCo saw the obesity epidemic on the horizon and recognized the need to change. Most significantly, rather than exiting the category, as it had previously done with fast-food restaurants such as Pizza Hut, Taco Bell, and KFC, it chose to change its product portfolio and move towards a healthier product mix. This has been a gradual process but one that over the past five years has had significant impact. It has involved a new focus for the company – 'performance with purpose' – and has also incorporated a splitting of its portfolio into three categories – 'fun for you,' 'better for you,' and 'good for you.'

'Fun for you' products are part of PepsiCo's core food and beverage businesses, such as Pepsi, 7-Up, and Lay's potato chips; 'Better for you' products are foods and beverages that have levels of total fat, saturated fat, sodium, and/or added sugar that are in line with global dietary intake recommendations. 'Good for you' products are foods and beverages that deliver positive nutrition through the inclusion of whole grains, fruits, vegetables, low-fat dairy, nuts and seeds, or significant amounts of important nutrients, while moderating total fat, saturated fat, sodium, and/or added sugar.

Led since 2006 by Indra Nooyi, CEO and chairman, and formerly CFO, this change has involved acquisitions such as Tropicana in 1998 and Quaker in 2001, and more recently the whole-scale renovation of core company brands to make them healthier. She explains the last few years of change thus:

Big companies can be a force for good in society and help address big problems. Too often companies have forgotten that we owe society a duty of care. So the PepsiCo operating philosophy is about 'performance with purpose' – how can we as a company deliver great performance while also doing right by society? It is not 'performance and purpose' or 'performance or purpose' – it is 'performance with purpose.' Purpose has three planks: 'human sustainability,' 'environmental sustainability,' and 'talent sustainability.'

So what is the logic? If we don't transform our portfolio, we can't deliver the numbers. If we are not environmentally prudent, NGOs and governments will shut us down. And if we don't have the best people who can bring their whole selves to work, we won't have the right talent base to feed performance going forward. So it is a virtuous circle that results in performance with purpose. When I leave, I want people to look back and say that PepsiCo was a good company – good commercially and good ethically.

Outmaneuvering the Competition

Coca-Cola used to always be better than Pepsi. Throughout the 1970s and 1980s whatever Pepsi tried it could not move from number 2 to number 1 in the drinks market. However, as PepsiCo changed its portfolio to become a lower fat food and drink company, it made progress. While Coca-Cola focused primarily on renovating the drinks market, PepsiCo expanded into orange juice, oats and snacks, and in 2005, after a century of being number 2, PepsiCo surpassed Coca-Cola in market value. Although in the last few years Coca-Cola has gained significant international market share in carbonated drinks in emerging markets, many see that it is vulnerable to the emerging changes around sodas. Fat taxes and regulation by governments against obesity may hit Coca-Cola hard. While Diet Coke is now Coke's number 1 product, many analysts see that it is Pepsi that has the more sustainable and future-proof portfolio. PepsiCo is now two-thirds a food business and one-third a drinks producer. The company has also committed to remove its drinks with high-sugar content from primary and secondary schools worldwide by 2012 and, since 2006, has adopted voluntary guidelines to replace 'full calorie' products with 'lower calorie' alternatives. Moreover, as Indra likes to highlight 'with $12bn of "good for you" products we are one of the top two health and wellness companies in the world.' The aim is to have $30 billion 'good for you' product sales by 2020. Although some like to criticize PepsiCo for staying in the snack-foods and carbonated drinks sector, the view of the company's CEO is clear:

Any product consumed in excess is bad for you. Our products are not bad for you. We provide people with a balanced portfolio of fun for you, better for you and good for you products. The consumer worldwide has to eat differently so they can remain healthy. We therefore have to bring goodness to people but in ways that are authentic, affordable and available. We can take products like oats and make them taste great.

In achieving this ambition, by 2020 PepsiCo sees that its 'business will be based on delivering fruit, vegetables, wholegrain, and fiber.'

Growth Ambition

With 'performance with purpose' at the heart of the company strategy, delivering sustainable growth is very much at the fore. While aiming to achieve shareholder returns in the top quartile of its sector, global growth is a priority and the target is to grow international revenues at two times real GDP growth rates in each country. In the top 20 developed markets, the aim is to 'grow market share in savory snacks and drinks through a combination of building and extending the snack portfolio through healthier product varieties and new flavors in line with local tastes.'

One card the company likes to play with retailers is that of the combined snack and drink purchase which it calls the 'Power of One':

Studies show that, 85 percent of the time, when a person eats a snack, he or she also reaches for a beverage. No company on earth is better positioned to fulfill both sides of that equation: As an integrated operating company across snacks and beverages, we now can provide incredible benefits to our retail partners and consumers. For example, we can respond to retailer needs with increased speed and agility; we can incubate new products in our distribution systems for a longer time; we can offer integrated in-store displays tuned to occasions and day parts; we can leverage our in-store merchandising better and we can truly bring the power of PepsiCo to all our retail partners.

Changing the Portfolio

In the last few years, much effort has clearly been applied in reducing saturated fat, salt, and sugar. Compared to a 2006 baseline, for key global food brands, in key countries, Pepsi aims to reduce the average amount of: saturated fat per serving by 15% by 2020; sodium per serving by 25% by 2015; and of added sugar per serving by 25% by 2020.

In addition PepsiCo is busy increasing the range of foods and beverages that offer solutions for managing calories, like portion sizes. In 2010 Naked Juice introduced two 100% juice smoothies that have 35% fewer calories than regular Naked Juice Smoothies; while Tropicana added new flavors – such as Pomegranate Blueberry, Pineapple Mango, and Farmstand Apple – to its Trop50 line, which offers 50% less sugar and fewer calories with no artificial sweeteners: 'On the foods side, we utilized our expertise in baking and air-popping technologies to manage calories. In Mexico, a baking technique is used to produce a version of Sabritas potato chips that has 20 percent fewer calories.'

Shifting the Center of Gravity

CEO ambition and targets are one thing, but how has change actually been delivered? Simon Michaelides, formerly marketing and innovation director at PepsiCo UK, has some views.

In the quest to shift an organization, the language used internally becomes all-important and defines the way employees see the company. Encouraging the right kind of vocabulary can change a company dramatically. The company set a goal to move the consumption of 80% of its products from 'Fun for you' towards 'Better/Good for you' and this needed a shift in attitudes. 'Internally this became known as the 'Real Foods' initiative. I would overhear people say to each other; 'so, what are you working on? . . . I'm on Real Foods.' We knew then that a step change was taking place in the company, almost through the conversations people were having. PepsiCo has a strong internal culture of innovation and the business is comprised largely of impulse businesses where the key is constant news and noise.

A brief look at the company's acquisition portfolio supports this. The acquisition of Naked Juice – a business similar to Innocent Drinks in the UK – is a typical example of this huge global organization buying up entrepreneurial, *beach-bum* businesses and turning them into huge successes. 'We used to say to ourselves, right, what are the two or three really exciting things we are going to do with our snacks next year and we'd look for fun to eat products that would make for exciting news and exciting noise internally.'

Twenty years ago, the market was all a battle of attrition that became known as the 'Cola Wars.' PepsiCo was David to Coke's Goliath and had sought ways of diversifying beyond the core product. Simon attributes PepsiCo's growth ambition and recent success to four distinct competences.

The first is the nature of growth. PepsiCo has absorbed entrepreneurial businesses across many related food and drink sectors. Naked Juice, Gatorade, Quaker, Frito Lay, and Tropicana were all born out of the dreams of entrepreneurs. This focus on acquiring entrepreneurial businesses defines and refines the internal culture of PepsiCo and contributes to the company's innovative culture.

The second aspect to PepsiCo's innovative growth is a focus on principles. The businesses that it acquires all have some raison d'être: Anthony T. Rossi founded Tropicana in 1947 with the goal of bringing Floridians the kind of orange juice found in Rossi's home country of Italy. 'PepsiCo is an incredibly principled organization. All the businesses it acquires mean something; they've started out with and maintained a clear purpose.'

Third, the customer is at the heart of everything PepsiCo does. In the midst of a zeitgeist focused on health and well-being, it's perhaps all too easy to dismiss a business founded on sugary drinks and snacks. PepsiCo directly appeals to the customers' desire for fun and liberation from mediocrity. PepsiCo has always been about fun and there seems no reason why fun and health cannot live together.

The fourth pillar of growth is perhaps less surprising: a relentless focus and obsession on the competition. PepsiCo has become highly reactionary to Coca-Cola, in its marketing, product, and brand innovation. Where Coca-Cola has primarily focused on developing its core product, PepsiCo has diversified. This diversification has meant that PepsiCo has been able to move much faster than its old rival. When you're focused on carefully steering the development of a single brand, dramatic change can bring dramatic disappointment and Coca-Cola's foray into new derivatives of the core drink product have become the focus of many a business school case study.

PepsiCo's focus on rapid innovation and new business acquisition has produced some challenges for the business. 'PepsiCo has all the know-how in the world to create products, but its operating model requires massive scale to reap the returns.' True innovations need time to mature in the market. The PepsiCo model has always been to throw huge marketing resources in a short time at new products and then wait to see if they take off. 'We'd launch something new, spend massively on TV ads for month and the news and noise would suddenly be everywhere. But then we'd switch everything off.'

PepsiCo's success shows that this often works, with highly successful brands like Quaker and Red Sky – though other products such as PJ Smoothies and Potato and Cheese Heads have fared less well. New products often need a more sustained marketing effort to bring consumers with the product on a joint journey. Simon continues, 'The company would often cite Innocent Drinks, elevating it upon a pedestal as something that went crazy very quickly. We would forget that it took 10 years to build Innocent into a £140m business.'

Future Growth

In a similar move to Nestlé, PepsiCo has recently moved to regional centers of excellence (CoE), each focused on a product category. For example, there is a fruit and vegetable CoE in Geneva. In the medium term, such a CoE focuses on questions such as 'Where's the juice business heading?' and longer term ones such as 'How can we create vegetable-based snacks?'. The CoE's connections with the regional marketing teams should provide a more sustainable system of innovation for the future.

The company's clear targets, not just around financial growth but how it is going to achieve this in terms of product and portfolio change, are clear to all. As with Nestlé there will be challenges around food supply at a global as well as local level. However, with an increasing focus on the sustainability not just of its products but of the sources of the ingredients used and their supply – right back to the field and seed, PepsiCo believes it is addressing the right issues. The days of Coke vs. Pepsi are well over and as the company looks to the future, it too has aspirations to be the world's largest food company, and like Nestlé, to have health and nutrition as a core part of this.

Key Insights – Nestlé and PepsiCo

Both Nestlé and PepsiCo have clearly nailed their colors to the dual masts of nutrition and sustainability. While they are not alone in their sector in this, their achievement in doing so while maintaining steady growth is notable. Some such as Danone and General Mills are following similar approaches but do not yet have the same business impact, while others such as Coca-Cola are seen to be more focused on revenue growth than doing the right thing.

Three other elements also seem to link the Nestlé and PepsiCo successes:

- *Clarity of purpose* – Both of these companies clearly now have health, nutrition, and environmental sustainability well cemented in their core approach to business. However, both have also gone further than many of their peers in areas that have helped to shift the organizations. While completely different in ambition, Nestlé's 'shared value' and PepsiCo's internal focus on development plans for people are major, culture-changing initiatives that tie the businesses into the long term. As well as driving growth organically, PepsiCo also internalizes innovation through acquiring entrepreneurial businesses with a sense of purpose, while Nestlé externalizes it through developing and up-skilling local communities in developing worlds.
- *Global/Local* – Nestlé's global network of R&D centers is evidently addressing the combination of global research priorities while at the same time accommodating and seeding regional developments. The tie-in with local production and supply chains is already making a difference and bearing fruit. In PepsiCo, again global brands and developments are taking place but there is also a local focus. Whether in Turkey, Mexico, or the UK, local brands are developed and sometimes acquired to shift the product mix and provide platforms that can then spread.
- *Ahead of the curve* – While it is easy in retrospect to see obesity, food supply, and local production as three major issues impacting the food and drink sector, both of these companies recognized them over a decade ago. They had the foresight to see the challenges and the willingness to be proactive about

addressing them. Rather than just reacting to market sentiment, in their own ways, each has been bold with their ambitions and sought to change their portfolios and improve their supply chains so that a new model is evident and now plainly part of the system. Global businesses this big and complex, can't simply be reactive – they have to form long-term positions and move hundreds of thousands of employees in different cultures and billions of customers with them, so their continued leadership reveals a focus on the longer term.

In addressing these issues, what is also notable is that both companies are taking their consumers with them. They are not preaching but are rather shifting the nutritional balance and eco impact of their products while still providing fun, taste, and convenience. The organizations rise above their individual brands; while their long histories define themselves in the minds of consumers in terms of one or two brands only, they actually have very diverse portfolios and so are able to shift consumer tastes without losing customers.

Nestlé

Growth Impact

The world's leading nutrition, health,
and wellness company

Distinctive Competence

Creating shared value

Underlying Capabilities

| Nutritional product improvement | Global/local R&D organization | Scale, diversity, and ubiquity of operations |

PepsiCo

Growth Impact

Steady revenue and profit growth while
shifting the center of gravity of the
corporate product mix

Distinctive Competence

Performance with purpose across human,
environmental, and talent sustainability

Underlying Capabilities

| Managing proactive portfolio change | Embedded customer centricity | Shared future direction and ambition |

Audi AG	KEY DATA
Total revenue (2010)	€35.4 billion
Average revenue growth p.a. (2005–2010)	6.9%
Net income (2010)	€2.6 billion
Average net income growth p.a. (2005–2010)	28.4%
Revenue per employee (2010)	€598,000
R&D investment (2010)	€2.5 billion
R&D intensity (2010)	7.0%
Average share price growth p.a. (2005–2010)	25.1%

Samsung Electronics	KEY DATA
Total revenue (2010)	KRW 154 trillion
Average revenue growth p.a. (2005–2010)	KRW 19 trillion
Net income (2010)	11.4%
Average net income growth p.a. (2005–2010)	14.1%
Revenue per employee (2010)	KRW 740 million
R&D investment (2010)	KRW 9.1 trillion
R&D intensity (2010)	5.9%
Average share price growth p.a. (2005–2010)	15.1%

CHAPTER 6

Audi and Samsung Electronics

Design as the growth driver

Globalization and the fast diffusion of new technology and ideas have short-ened the lifecycles of numerous products. New versions are released in ever-decreasing timescales and the so-called 'fast followers' are quick to launch imitations. Many products can be copied and ready for sale within weeks of the original launch. Across many different sectors, differentiation is not about just price and positioning – it is about the product itself. This presents a challenge as many manufacturers now have access to and use the same technology plat-forms as their competitors. Therefore the role of design as the driver of visible innovation has come very much to the fore.

On one level this is nothing new. For companies that want to generate higher margins and grow revenues, better design has been a long-standing focus. Indeed, throughout the second half of the 20th century, leading manufacturers embraced design as a source of differentiation. Some companies built in-house teams to not only develop new product concepts but also define what became known as the language of the brand and how to apply it across multiple product lines. Braun, Herman Miller, Sony, and Philips are perhaps some of the most long-standing examples of this. More recently, high-growth companies such as Dyson, LG, Virgin Atlantic, and Apple have all taken a similar approach. Sometimes there is very much a collective design ethos and style as you find in Philips and Dyson, and sometimes a lead designer within the organization has played a formative role in creating the corporate blueprint – think of Dieter Rams at Braun, Jonathan Ive at Apple, or David Lewis with Bang & Olufsen.

After many success stories, design is now an essential ingredient for any product that has ambitions to succeed. For the companies who want to take the lead in their sector more often than not pioneering design is placed at the heart of their innovation and growth strategies. Unsurprisingly, competition for the best engi-neering and product design talent is intense and, as companies seek to maximize their design capacity, applying it in the most effective way has become a major challenge. When a company gets it right and connects great design, class-leading technology, and a compelling brand, the growth rewards can be significant.

In this chapter we look at two firms, Audi and Samsung Electronics, who have not only developed design excellence within their organizations, but as a means to move their brands up-market, have also used this as a core driver of growth.

Audi

VW and Audi

In 2010 more vehicles were produced globally than ever before. Despite the hangover effects from the Western recession that hit the market hard, there was a 26% rise in sales, and total production was nearly 78 million. In terms of country of manufacture, China was producing around 18 million cars a year – twice as many vehicles as Japan; while the United States and Germany maintained number 3 and number 4 positions – a good distance ahead of the likes of South Korea, Brazil, and India.

Since Toyota eclipsed General Motors as the world's number 1 car producer, attention has focused on the growing rivalry between Toyota and VW – two companies with global operations, strong stakes in China, and multiple brands in their respective stables. Toyota, with its 11.4% share of the market, now includes the Lexus and Daihatsu brands, while Volkswagen Group's 9.4% share of the market comes from a wider range, including SEAT, Skoda, Audi, Bentley, Bugatti, Lamborghini, and, since 2009, Porsche.

In 2010 Audi provided nearly 40% of the VW Group's profits from just over one million cars – less than 15% of total group production. With rising sales and average growth in net profit over the last five years of 35% per annum, a doubling of share price, and numerous accolades, Audi is very much the star of the VW Group's growth story.

The Audi Growth Ambition

Today, under the leadership of Ferdinand Piëch, the Volkswagen Group is aiming to become the largest, most profitable business in its market and is widely expected to overtake Toyota as the global #1 manufacturer by 2018. Audi's global production has grown from 354,000 in 1993 to 1.09 million in 2010: sales have just overtaken Mercedes and are forecast to surpass BMW by 2014. Audi's aim is to become the number one premium brand in its sector by using its expertise, passion, and agility to 'create the best brand experience through innovative and emotional products' that all bring to life its core brand values of being 'sophisti-cated, progressive and sporty.'

Achieving this ambition demands not only great products and the nurturing of a leading automotive brand but also continued leverage of the VW organization and its capabilities. Audi brings significant profits and status to the VW Group, but VW's technology and platform sharing are in turn major assets for Audi.

The Role of Design

Key to Audi's strategy to become the number 1 brand is its focus on leading-edge design both in terms of technical engineered design and aesthetic product design. And this is not a new approach.

'Audi design is distinctive – it is the harmony of form and function,' says Royal College of Art trained Stefan Sielaff, head of design at Audi AG. 'Above all, it is the proportions, the sculptures of our automobiles which portray the interplay of technology and design. This philosophy has a remarkable past – it is the key facet in Audi's history.' Audi is now recognized across the industry as the design benchmark – not only for external form but also for interiors where, from a quality and craftsmanship point of view, the company is up with the very best of the high-end brands like Aston Martin and Bentley.

Technology Landmarks

Audi's use of technology to lead brand development can be traced to 1971, when the company, with a growing range of respected models, chose to start using the 'Vorsprung durch Technik' slogan to share the intent behind them. Translating as 'progress through technology,' this line has been used in advertising campaigns across the world and remains central to the brand's ethos and communications.

This approach was cemented in 1974 when Dr. Ferdinand Piëch, grandson of Ferdinand Porsche, became Audi's head of technical development. He not only rose to run the brand, and subsequently the entire Volkswagen Group, but cru-cially for Audi, he oversaw the development of a number of award-winning tech-nological innovations including the five-cylinder engine, the introduction of four-wheel drive, and aluminum bodyshells, and the adoption of aerodynamic design.

In concert with the VW Group, in recent years Audi has continued to take a lead on technical developments: voice control, TDI diesel engines, the direct shift gearbox, drive select, and the multimedia interface are just some of high-profile technologies introduced in the past decade.

Aesthetic Icons

When it comes to the aesthetics of car design, over the years the Audi design teams have created a number of iconic products. The fundamental philosophy of its design-led approach enables Audi to make different choices from its competitors. If Mercedes is driven by comfort and BMW by improving performance to create the ultimate driving experience, Audi starts with design and is good at it. Over five years, Audi has won the world's 'best performance car' award no fewer than three times: in 2007 with the RS4; in 2008 for the R8 sports car; and again in 2010, with the V10 version of the R8. In recent years, Audi has won more design awards than any other brand with two models seen as being game-changers in the sector. These are the A2 and the TT.

The A2

The A2, Audi's smallest car when launched in 1999, was way ahead of its time, providing a combination of small and premium. Here executive comfort met the super-mini; it looked like nothing else on the market with a narrow, tall one-box shape. Part of the reason for its height was the 'sandwich' construction of its floor that had an upper and a lower portion. This created a cavity in the center of the car that housed the fuel tank and the engine's electronics, freeing up space for passengers to sit in greater comfort. It was constructed primarily from aluminum making it lighter but also more expensive than its competitors. However, its average consumption of 79 mpg – gained from its highly efficient tapered profile that gave it a drag coefficient of only 0.25 – has not yet been bettered by a production car. 'The A2 epitomizes Audi design of the late nineties,' says Stefan Sielaff: 'It was purist and plain, and practically dogmatic in design. It was not an emotional vehicle – sensible more than anything. But it embodied that timelessness which designers always aspire to. Even today, the A2 strikes a bold pose. It is one of the cars which have been most significant for Audi.'

The TT

Launched in 1998 and designed by Art Center College of Design Pasadena alumni J. Mays and Freeman Thomas, who also created the 'new' VW Beetle, Audi's two-door TT compact sports car quickly gained iconic status. Unique and distinctive, it challenged the notion of what a coupe should be. It was a mixture of sporty, with very hard design (for example, sharp edges), and luxury (hand-stitched leather seats), underpinned by technical competency. Some of the features were extremely difficult to manufacture, but rather than softening the design and saving money, Audi invested in new processes, for example laser-braising to attach the rear of the roof to the body in a sharp crease – a detail that only design-obsessives would be aware of, but which added up to a car that looked different and somehow elegant. Stefan sees that 'the TT was a kind of untypical situation because, if you do a normal portfolio strategy, this car would not have fit because at that time it was not a typical Audi. It was kind of a separate product. I still have to admire the braveness of the Board at that time to decide to do this. Dr. Piëch was very much involved himself at that time because he saw the proposal for it at that time and he said "go for it, do it".' Not only did the TT gain a host of admirers at launch, but the second version in 2007 also won many design awards including World Car of the Year.

Throughout the last decade, Audi has adopted a number of common design features across its range that have created a new design language for the company – and one that many others are now busy trying to emulate. This started off with the adoption of the full depth front grille that defined the head-on image of the cars and was followed by LED running lights; the lights for each model are clustered in a different shape, adding to their distinctiveness and clearly signaling the presence of an Audi on the road ahead.

Audi Design Focus

If awards are the measure of success and a reflection of prowess in the automotive sector then, across the board, Audi is plainly making the running. Although it shares many platforms with VW and uses common technology in its engines and drive trains, some see that the Audi design team 'lives and breathes different air,' and the numerous award-winning and commercially successful products have ensured that design remains at the very heart of the Audi organization.

VW Group Platforms

In terms of the advantages of being part of VW, foremost for Audi has been the ability to gain access to new technology far earlier than would be possible in smaller companies with lower development budgets. This comes from platform sharing where the engines, floorplans, and other components are shared across different models. So for example around 15 different models including the VW Golf, Beetle, and Audi TT are all built on the same vehicle platform. Audi also gains from sharing the VW Group's back office systems, distribution network, dealerships, financing support, and media buying. Although each brand maintains a separate profit and loss, sharing and collaboration deliver margin enhancement across the group.

Design Team

As with other car firms, the role of the core design teams in Audi is embedded in the dual delivery of new concept cars to demonstrate the latest thinking and regular new model launches to bring some of that thinking to life. Although nowhere near as hierarchical as in the past, today most automotive groups have separate design teams for each brand and a chief designer leads each team. While the decision of which concepts to put into production is clearly made by the board of directors of the company, as with Jonathan Ive at Apple, Stefan Sielaff and his colleague, Wolfgang Egger, head of design for Audi, are the key influencers on this and overall product portfolio direction.

Overseen by Stefan, each project has a design lead with separate individuals responsible for exterior and interior. The exterior lead looks after the whole treatment of the front and the rear light and the wheels, while the interior lead looks after cabin architecture, seating and driver interaction, and the human–machine interface. In addition there is expertise in color and trim and a design strategy group that looks into the long-term development of the design language and the relationship with the brand.

Stefan's view on Audi today is that 'Audi design is still a very, very clean design language . . . in which there is a strong combination of dynamic lines and proportion.' Given that most other car marques now reference Audi as the benchmark in car design, his repertoire of peers for inspiration is rather small. 'Outside the VW Group, I have to say Aston Martin. They are doing very emotional products with good design quality. Land Rover is also a brand I like. I like the authenticity and clean design language.' Originally winning an Audi scholarship to go to the Royal College of Art in 1988, outsiders point to the fact that Stefan has been part of the Audi design team for 20 years as one of the reasons that the brand coherence is so strong across so many models. Like Jonathan Ive, Dieter Rams, and David Lewis, he is very much the power behind his company's design language.

Business Performance

The combination of leveraging the VW Group capabilities and leading-edge design has enabled Audi to become one of the most profitable in the sector. Across the Audi range, a core element of the design strategy has been to maintain overall brand consistency year on year, to prevent rapid aging and help support high residual second-hand values – both issues that support premium pricing: Audis have a strong sense of timeless style and the cars don't age as badly as some brands; for example Hondas depreciate in value by 15% year on year, whereas Audis only depreciate by 2.5–4.5%.

Audi has sustained margins by adopting a 'pull/retail' model, avoiding a rush towards too great a volume growth and dependence on the model sectors that rely on fleets. A danger in the car industry is growth of excessive capacity or production of the wrong product mix, both of which lead to forced discounted sales, driving down prices to attain volume, reducing margins, and taking out funds to invest in new models. Audi (and the VW Group) have funded investment into new models by creating a virtuous cycle – concentrating on 'pulling' the retail market. The high-quality design and investment in image and technology creates desirability, demand, and robust premium prices, increasing the margins to reinvest in more high-quality design. Higher residual values than most other brands also reduce costs for their buyers, despite the higher initial price of the car. By protecting product quality, maintaining brand desirability, not becoming too trend-led, and managing model aging, the real cost of ownership for customers stays low while the price of the car is high.

Future Growth

Audi's future growth strategy is aiming for 1.5 million cars to be delivered to customers in 2015, with much of the growth expected to come from the United States, China, and India enabled by an expansion of the Audi portfolio to 42 cars. Between 2010 and 2012 the company is investing €5.5 billion to sustain its technology and design lead. For the expanding development team of 8000 engineers and 200 designers, 'in the future, the strength will lie in the interaction and innovation of design, technology and production. A beautiful wrapping won't be enough. Customers want a holistic product that answers all the environmental questions.' Given that Audi has recently acquired a 90.1% stake in the Italian automotive design house Italdesign Giugiaro, it will be interesting to see how the future designs emerge.

Moving ahead to 2020 where the company's vision of being the world's number one premium brand is firmly set, the continued desire to 'delight customers worldwide' through innovative and emotional products and Audi brand experience looks like a good bet. While other firms are striving to catch up with Audi, given its current lead, the resolute determination to steadily shift upmarket, the commitment it has to continuing to lead automotive design, and its growing and loyal customer base, for now many in the sector see that Audi is firmly in the driving seat.

Samsung Electronics

Samsung Electronics is the world's largest consumer electronics company. Producing everything from phones, TVs, cameras, and laptops to microwaves and freezers, it is a top three brand in pretty much every category in which it is active. 2010 sales were in excess of $135 billion with net profits of over $14 billion. Samsung Electronics is now twice the size of Sony, the company which 20 years ago was the undisputed leader in the sector. While Sony's revenues grew by 22% total in the last decade, Samsung Electronics' revenue rose by over 400% and, over the past five years, the company has maintained growth at an average of 16% every year. In the TV market, Samsung Electronics has been market leader by a good margin over Sony and local rival LG since 2006 and is way ahead in LCD panels; in the camera market it is number 2 to Sony and despite intense competition; in the cellphone market, Samsung Electronics has just over 20% of the global market and is rapidly closing in on Nokia. Most significantly, in the DRAM and NAND flash memory arenas where it competes with Intel and Toshiba, Samsung has over 40% of the market share. This is hugely important because it highlights how, even when not used in Samsung-branded products, its technologies are often found in those of its competitors: Samsung Electronics wins both ways.

The company is part of the larger $200 billion revenue Samsung Group that accounts for a fifth of Korea's exports. Samsung has become the flagship of the South Korean economy and the source of much of the innovation that is taking place across the consumer electronics sector. Given that it was a low-cost 'me-too' manufacturer of imitations of Sharp's microwaves in the 1970s this is a huge achievement. Whereas people used to look at Philips, Sony, and Toshiba for the latest developments, today it is Apple and Samsung Electronics. Indeed, as Apple has moved across some of the consumer electronics market with its high margin products; it has become the only real challenger to Samsung's dominance. Pivotal to Samsung Electronics' success over the past decade or so has been the way it has embraced design as the source of competition. Growing from 2 to 900, the Samsung Electronics design team now consistently takes most awards at the prestigious annual design events as the company's products are time and time again seen as leading the category in performance, quality, and value.

The Early Years

Born out of the larger Samsung *chaebol* that was in the food-processing and textiles sectors, Samsung Electronics started off in 1969 manufacturing low-cost black and white TVs, fridges, microwaves, and washing machines.

Although by the early 1990s Samsung Electronics had grown to be a significant manufacturer with its products sold around the world, at heart this firm was still producing low-end products and, in its part of the market, was facing increasing competition. To grow it needed to continue to win in its core area but also move up-market and compete at a higher level.

Two Design Revolutions

According to company lore, in 1993 Kun-Hee Lee, chairman of Samsung Electronics, visited an electronics store in Los Angeles and was struck by the fact that its products were viewed as a cheap commodity. Although good value at the low end of the market, they were not seen to be in the same class as products from competitors such as Sony that stood out on the shop floor and were given premium positioning. The lack of a coherent design identity was highlighted as a major weakness for Samsung Electronics, in comparison to Sony and Philips where design was seen as a core corporate asset.

Samsung Electronics recognized that, if it was to grow, design quality should play a leading role in its organization alongside technology leadership. The chairman made things clear: 'Management is still clinging to the concept of quantity at the expense of quality. We will become a third-rate company. We must change no matter what.' He then famously said: 'change everything except your wife and kids.'

To become more innovative, Samsung Electronics needed a cultural transformation and a key part of this was in creating a facility for nurturing and developing talent. 'In 1995, the company set up the Innovative Design Lab of Samsung (IDS), an in-house school where promising designers could study under experts from the Art Center College of Design in Pasadena, California, one of the top US design schools. Samsung designers were dispatched to Egypt and India, Paris and Frankfurt, New York and Washington to tour museums, visit icons of modern architecture, and explore ruins.'

According to Gordon Bruce who, along with James Miho, helped Samsung Electronics set up the IDS previously 'there was no design involved. It was all about keeping the price down and outselling the other guy.'

In typical style, Samsung Electronics declared 1996 as its first design revolution year. Chairman Lee shared his view that, 'An enterprise's most vital assets lie in its design and other creative capabilities. I believe that the ultimate winners in the twenty-first century will be determined by these skills.' Although Samsung Electronics was a technology- and process-obsessed company this laid the seeds for how it would become more competitive by placing design center-stage.

Whilst initial progress was slow, by 2005 Samsung had established additional Global Design Centers in San Francisco, London, Los Angeles, China, and Milan.

These design centers became Samsung Electronics' windows on global markets. As Geesung Choi, chief design officer for Samsung Electronics from 2005, explained, 'We use design centers overseas to learn about lifestyle trends, then when we are deciding on a product, we collect those inputs. We also let the overseas design labs design their own concepts from their own understanding of the tastes of their market.' Indeed, each center brings a different cultural insight to Samsung Electronics design: 'The English are strong in engineering, the Japanese in fine finishes, the Italians in shapes, and the Americans in pragmatism.'

However, despite the awards an ex-member of the UK design team recalls: 'Design was initially seen as something applied to a product' after the technology had been developed and 'only gradually did the company recognize that design had to be involved from pretty much day one.' Joint-concepts projects between different groups such as 'the future of home appliances' were used by the design team to start the ball rolling and help to, for example, redefine how marketing communication narratives developed.

By 2005 Samsung Electronics had made significant progress, winning 65 design prizes and surpassing Sony in Interbrand's rankings to become the world's largest consumer electronics brand. However, in April 2005, at the opening of Samsung Electronics' sixth global design center in Milan, chairman Lee urged the organization to go further: 'Samsung's products must meet global premium standards. In order to do that, we must strengthen competitiveness in soft areas, such as design and brand, and leap over emotional walls in addition to functional and technical ones.'

The speech and further actions inspired what became known as the Second Design Revolution. The next challenge for the company was set and improving design research was a key step.

'The difference between marketing research and design research,' explained Young-Jun Kim, vice president of Samsung Electronics' Design Research Lab, 'is that marketing research is focused on the current situation – market share, and so forth. Design research is focused on user behavior and user experience.' Samsung Electronics' designers visited people in their homes to see how they actually used products and the company ramped up its associated ethnographic activity. 'With this kind of research we can persuade the marketing team what will work. To understand users, the Design Research Lab also carries out trend research on home interiors, furniture, fashion, and so on – trying to apply those trends to product development.'

An early success was the 2007 launch of the Bordeaux TV. The design team was aiming at creating a unique piece of glossy, thin, and sculptured furniture that people would want to buy just to have in their home. The product that emerged became the first TV model to sell more than 1 million units in its first year on the market.

With well-designed, award-winning new products emerging almost monthly, consumers reacted well. In 2007 Samsung Electronics overtook Motorola to become the world's second-largest cellphone maker and spent more on R&D than IBM; and in 2009 it eclipsed both HP and Siemens to become the world's largest technology company.

Emergence of Apple as a Competitor

Having pushed aside Philips and Sony in some core categories and becoming increasingly focused on Nokia in cellphones, Apple's growth outside the computer market became an increasing concern for Samsung Electronics. Back in 2004, 'Apple was not seen as competition as it was not mass market.' But as Apple's products became global bestsellers the situation changed. According to members of the design team, 'the problem is that Apple does not behave like Samsung's traditional peers. It is not technology led but rather focuses on the whole package and sometimes the technology is not the best it could be. Even though Samsung created the MP3 player way ahead of Apple, the iPod's simplicity and design took the world by storm. It used off-the shelf technologies and won on design and the business model. This was a new paradigm for Samsung Electronics to accommodate.' Today with its Galaxy Tab collection, Samsung are going head to head with Apple in Apple's backyard.

Samsung Electronics' Current Growth Capability

Samsung Electronics' vision still focuses on its technology and process prowess:

Samsung is dedicated to developing innovative technologies and efficient processes that create new markets, enrich people's lives and continue to make Samsung a digital leader.

While design has become important, and clearly far more so than in the past, we should not kid ourselves that Samsung Electronics is first and foremost a technology company. Today over 50,000 people work in R&D at Samsung Electronics across 42 facilities around the world, collaborating on developing what the company sees as strategic technologies for the future that will set new standards. These are split into three groups: the Samsung Advanced Institute of Technology (SAIT) identifies growth engines for the future and oversees the securing and management of technology; the R&D centers of each business focus on technology that is expected to deliver the most promising long-term results; and division-based product development teams are responsible for commercializing products scheduled to hit the market within one or two years. Each year Samsung Electronics invests around 9% of revenues in R&D.

Samsung Electronics' component business is the leading producer of many of the best technologies; whether it is memory, integrated circuits, storage, or LCD panels Samsung Electronics makes great products. And it doesn't just make them for use in Samsung products – most of its competitors' products also source their components from Samsung Electronics. Whether you buy a Samsung or another brand, chances are you are still buying Samsung Electronics' technology.

Delivering the latest technology at a competitive price is thus still the core purpose of Samsung Electronics, but is not the only one. While the company makes good money selling its components to others, it makes far more when they are in its own branded products and hence the importance of making these the most compelling and attractive for the customer is key. Alongside this formidable technology powerhouse, Samsung Design now has over 900 designers in its design centers. As in Audi, the ratio of engineers to designers is around 50 to 1. In total, Samsung Electronics now has seven design centers, with six regional design centers in London, Los Angeles, Milan, New Delhi, Shanghai, and Tokyo. Research activities cover industrial design, graphic design, interaction design, human factors, lifestyle research, creative business planning, visual brand strategy, materials exploration, color theory, and computer-aided design.

Most significantly therefore in this increasingly competitive sector, Samsung Electronics wins best when it delivers the total package – really good solid technology and very good design. Recent successes include the Galaxy S smartphone that sold over 10 million units in its first six months and became the #1 Android device.

Future Ambition and Challenges

While the continued development of new technologies that allow products to be faster, smaller, quieter, and cheaper is a mainstay of Samsung Electronics' future growth, facing as it does more mainstream competition from Apple, the role of design is clearly again being dialed up. Design strategy is an important tool in Samsung Electronics to effect organizational change. Having now had two 'design revolutions' a third phase is in the mix. Old silos between design and marketing have been addressed with more focused speed of action very much at the fore. Whereas in the past 'impatience as a virtue' became an issue resulting in some things being rushed to stay ahead of the competition, in a world where hits like the iPad or the Galaxy phone are essential, some see that Samsung may start to take a more 'Apple-like' view of innovation and growth. Quantity of products and hence breadth of choice has always been part of the Samsung Electronics' approach to winning in the marketplace and with its well-honed capabilities is something that Samsung Electronics excels at. Releasing fewer but higher impact products will be another step for the company and one that it may try in a few categories – but not all.

Samsung Electronics is still very much a vertically integrated hardware company: it makes the product and pretty much every component that goes in it. As such it is increasingly relying on partners for the software. Its relationships with Google and Microsoft for mobile operating systems have so far proved successful and are spreading across other categories. Given Apple's unique advantage of being in hardware and software, Samsung Electronics may need to shift its capability mix. It is highly unlikely to try and compete with Google and Microsoft, so how will it cope if, as is expected, both of these use recent and proposed acquisitions to accelerate their moves into the hardware arena?

Samsung Electronics has also so far succeeded by being the challenger. Back in 1993 Sony was well ahead and therefore Samsung Electronics upped its game across the board to win, and by 2005 had eclipsed Sony. Having overcome Motorola in the mobile market in 2007, Nokia is very much in the company's sights and several telecom analysts see that Samsung Electronics may take number 1 position in that market pretty soon. Clearly Apple owns the high margin high ground in the categories in which it plays but it is the likes of Sony and Nokia with broad product ranges that have been Samsung Electronics' traditional peers for competition.

Samsung Electronics has 'moved from zero to hero in the consumer electronics space' and that itself is a great achievement. But it is clearly not without strong competition. As it gains overall global leadership in more categories like mobile, the big challenge is to really differentiate itself. If Samsung Electronics does become the number 1 design brand in the world, as some anticipate, former employees question whether it has the mindset to lead rather than challenge. If

Samsung Electronics is breaking new ground across multiple fronts at once, this may need a different approach. The company is currently 'relentless and driven by process' so how will that need to change?

In the TV sector Samsung Electronics has taken market leadership so now the designers can no longer benchmark anyone else. This is a whole new world that requires a whole set of new activities and perspectives. This has happened in the last two years. Samsung Electronics now has its own identity but it knows it needs to change its processes and behaviors to exploit being a market leader. It is going to be tough to make that break and make the move.

Lastly, faced with rising competition, not just from its long-standing Sony and LG adversaries but also from competitively priced Chinese and Taiwanese manufacturers like Lenovo, HTC, and Acer, many see that Samsung Electronics' future growth prospects are less assured than some commentators believe. As such the big challenge therefore will be to continue pushing the technological boundaries, competing on quality with its Asian peers, and using its now recognized design competences to produce the products that the vast majority of the world's consumers clearly want to buy.

Key Insights – Audi and Samsung Electronics

Design often sits in isolation producing things of beauty that make little money. The hard part is to integrate design with technology and business in order to find the sweet spot where design, technology, and business combine to deliver great products that people love and that take into account human behavior, needs, and preferences.

Design thinking brings a designer's mentality into the business and shifts things from arm's-length market research to research based on direct observation of potential users. By placing design thinking center-stage, the organization may end up being redesigned and this can increase the risk of reduced attention on process efficiency, cost control, and profitability.

There are a number of common features between the two companies. Both Audi and Samsung Electronics have successfully combined strong leadership, continued to focus on business performance and technology with a design mentality that has enabled them to maintain the benefits of being part of a larger group whilst being distinctively different.

The focus on products that connect with consumer needs is clear in the different ambitions of the two companies:

- Audi: 'create the best brand experience through innovative and emotional products'
- Samsung Electronics: 'dedicated to developing innovative technologies and efficient processes that create new markets, enrich people's lives and continue to make Samsung a digital leader'

Audi and Samsung Electronics have made a major success of product design, but this has not been done in isolation from great technology. In both companies it has been the increasingly close and symbiotic relationship between the engineering and the aesthetic design that has made the brands stand out more from the crowd.

They are both resolutely determined to continue to move upmarket and see global leading-edge design as a key part of this. Technology access is plainly a vital ingredient – for Audi internally and via the VW group and for Samsung Electronics through its multiple divisions.

As a result profitability for both companies has been growing steadily as they have got the balance right between brand, technology, and design. As Samsung Electronics now takes on Apple and Audi seeks to put distance between itself and BMW/Mercedes, the question is how long can this be maintained? For now, both companies believe that they are good bets for strong future growth.

Audi

Growth Impact

The profit center of a number 2 global automotive group

Distinctive Competence

Creating a unified premium brand experience built on a common platform

Underlying Capabilities

| Iconic consistent product design | Shared technology platform development | Deep engineering design expertise |

Samsung Electronics

Growth Impact

The world's most vertically integrated consumer hardware company

Distinctive Competence

Value-focused development of challenger products across multiple categories

Underlying Capabilities

| Essential ingredient technology platform development | Highly efficient internal processes | Prioritization of leading-edge design |

Reckitt Benckiser	KEY DATA
Total sales (2010)	£8.4 billion
Average sales growth p.a. (2005–2010)	14.1%
Net income (2010)	£1.6 billion
Average net income growth p.a. (2005–2010)	18.8%
Revenue per employee (2010)	£311,000
R&D investment (2010)	£125 million
R&D intensity (2010)	1.5%
Average share price growth p.a. (2005–2010)	15.3%

Procter & Gamble	KEY DATA
Total sales (2010)	$78.9 billion
Average sales growth p.a. (2005–2010)	7.6%
Net income (2010)	$12.7 billion
Average net income growth p.a. (2005–2010)	13.3%
Revenue per employee (2010)	$622,000
R&D investment (2010)	$1.95 billion
R&D intensity (2010)	2.5%
Average share price growth p.a. (2005–2010)	3.7%

CHAPTER 7

Reckitt Benckiser and Procter & Gamble

Making the most of insight

The world of 'fast-moving consumer goods' (or FMCG) in Europe or consumer packaged goods (CPG) in North America has long been characterized by soap powders, cosmetics, and shampoos. But if you look at the largest FMCG companies today you can see that the range of products has become far broader than that. Although Colgate Palmolive is largely all about toothpaste, soaps, and deodorants, Unilever stretches from tea and ice cream to bleach and shower gel. Henkel's portfolio encompasses hairspray and glue. Procter & Gamble covers everything from shavers and hairdryers to batteries and perfumes and Reckitt Benckiser stretches from mosquito repellant to air fresheners and dishwasher tablets. Between them, these five companies control the majority of the non-food consumables market and dominate global advertising. Although sharing the same customers, they each have their own unique products. Other than the Procter & Gamble merger with Gillette, there has been limited major consolidation in the sector but there have been quite a number of tactical acquisitions of brands and small companies. In terms of growth overall, the businesses with a better balance of emerging and developed markets are just beginning to translate this into better results.

It's difficult to stand out in the FMCG sector. The five top companies today all have a global footprint and compete aggressively in all markets but they are being squeezed on a number of levels. Consumers are increasingly less loyal to specific brands and 'white label' supermarket products are gaining shelf space and market share. While some may claim that their product in a certain category is better than their peers, often performance differences are marginal. That said, consumers worldwide are making monthly if not weekly buying decisions based on a belief that product A is better than product B and that it will therefore do the job more effectively. It is little surprise therefore that, alongside core product and technology development, one of the largest costs for FMCG companies is their media investment. In an increasingly crowded market it is critical for a brand to broadcast the 'reasons to believe' in it. FMCGs are driven more and more by a near obsession with consumer insight, not just to help them to identify unmet needs but also to ensure that their products resonate best with target customers and will be selected from the shelf.

Over the past decade, two of these five companies have nudged ahead of the pack. Based on a 10-year view of share prices as a reflection of value creation, it is clear that Reckitt Benckiser and Procter & Gamble have been the ones that have made greatest headway in growing their brands, engaging more customers, and consistently delivering better performance than their peers. Reckitt Benckiser and Proctor & Gamble have followed different approaches with different levels of success, but both are clearly doing the right thing as they lead growth in this most competitive of product areas.

Reckitt Benckiser

Reckitt Benckiser is the fastest growing of the major FMCG companies. Although the original Benckiser business was started in Germany in 1832 and Reckitt in the UK in 1840, Reckitt Benckiser very much sees itself as beginning from the merger of these two companies in 1999. That is very much day 1.

Reckitt Benckiser has used organic growth powered by fast incremental innovation to move into leadership positions in the vast majority of categories in which it operates. In 1999 Reckitt Benckiser had around 20,000 employees, produced net revenues of just over £3 billion, and had an operating profit of £357 million. Ten years later, with only an extra 5000 employees, revenues had more than doubled to nearly £8 billion and profits had risen by more than five times to nearly £2 billion. How this is achieved is very clear: as Bart Becht, former CEO, said in 2010:

We have a very simple approach to the business: focus on powerbrands in fast-growing categories, innovate and invest behind them – and do so in every market.

In 2009, these powerbrands accounted for over 60% of net revenues and over 80% of the company's growth.

For Reckitt Benckiser growth of the business and success for all employees comes from one thing – innovation. It is the number 1 focus of the company by far: 'Our primary focus is on growing the business organically. That does not mean we do not like to do acquisitions, but we are only doing them if they make sense for us because they fit strategically.'

Innovation at the Core

More than anything, the main topic of conversation at Reckitt Benckiser is organic growth via innovation – and ideally high-impact innovation via new product development (NPD). The purpose of this is clearly articulated by Bart Becht, 'We believe innovation does two things: it drives category growth and it drives our market share within those categories.'

It is new product development that holds the innovation hot seat and this view permeates throughout the business: 'NPD' is king. Career histories of senior executives are illustrated by the products they have launched, and specific examples of successful launches are used to motivate and illustrate success. Everyone, from lab assistant to marketer, aspires to be involved in a product launch. And every time Reckitt Benckiser talks to the outside world – be that investors, the media, retailers, or customers – innovation and new product launches are the lingua franca.

Big Company Acting Small and Young

Although now a global organization of nearly 30,000 people, and so considered to be a major multinational, Reckitt Benckiser at heart still behaves like a small company. Its global HQ is a compact, low-profile facility where everyone shares the same car park, entrance, cafe, and lifts so people can easily interact with each other. The structure is very flat and therefore information flow and ideas can quickly spread and evolve. Small groups work together but interact with others naturally and frequently. As Becht shared, 'I believe high-calibre, smaller teams always outperform larger organizations, because if you double the organization you don't get double the productivity; you lose a substantial amount of productivity because now you have to organize all these interrelationships between people.' Despite its growing size, Reckitt Benckiser retains a firm command and control structure, with the CEO very much at the helm. It is highly focused on a common objective and this is clearly reflected in the structure: nearly everyone works for a category, even R&D, and the categories report to the CEO.

This clarity of purpose combined with simple structures enables Reckitt Benckiser to respond quickly to challenges, align resources, and exploit growth opportunities. And it also influences the way in which the company works more with outside organizations rather than trying to do everything itself. As recently appointed successor to Becht, Rakesh Kapoor puts it, 'the more a company depends only on its internal capabilities, the slower it will be in bringing ideas to action. That's why Reckitt Benckiser works with outside organizations to a significant degree, to complement its own good internal capability.'

Three Things That Set Reckitt Benckiser Apart

So, as well as being innovation obsessed and behaving like a smaller company, what are the key capability areas where Reckitt Benckiser outperforms the sector? Current and former employees all cite the same three – speed, focus, and culture.

Speed

As indicated above, the way the organization is structured makes the flow of ideas fast and efficient without the need to go up and down functional silos to share perspectives and recommendations. On top of this, there is another facet of the organization that enables things to happen quickly.

Processes in Reckitt Benckiser are slimmed down as much as possible in order to focus on what is important. NPD has only two decision stages: deploy R&D resource and then launch. These decisions are based on two questions – whether the idea will deliver a product that is better than anything else already on the market and whether the target consumer will see the benefit and so ideally pay more. While some companies could take months to answer this, Reckitt Benckiser do so in a matter of days. It prizes an attitude of conflict over consensus. Decisions do not need 100% alignment in the room and ultimately 'payer decides and decider pays.' Or as Becht puts it, 'Get 80% alignment and 100% agreement to implement. And move quickly.' This pared-down approach is a major asset when capitalizing on immediately relevant insights.

Reckitt Benckiser sees that being 80% right is fine for a national launch and if a product goes well then it can be scaled and refined. All NPD projects have a lead country and a roll-out plan: A central team coordinates the launch supported by a lead-country marketer to create local buy-in and improve market relevance. So, as an example, for Cillit Bang, an original product was launched in Hungary and, when it was seen to be a success after the first two weeks, it was scaled globally and launched in over 20 markets within a matter of months. Simultaneously 50% of the costs were taken out of the product and its packaging through what is known internally as the 'squeeze' process.

Focus

The next core ingredient in the Reckitt Benckiser growth engine is clarity of focus. This is not just on the big picture of how the company is to succeed, but it is also translated right down to individual goals in order to improve performance. Reckitt Benckiser has a strong focus on institutional shareholders as the key audience for messages around growth and innovation setting, and reporting on specific financial targets such as net revenue growth. And there is also clear alignment between the targets promised to the analysts and those set internally.

There is a very strong flow of annual objectives from the top of the business to manager level. These objectives are heavily quantified and cover three main areas: in-market performance; new launches; and tested ideas for launch in the coming two years. These metrics translate directly to financial rewards – so 'a manager who blows the targets out of the water can earn a bonus of up to 144%.' Although they attract much media attention, especially with Bart Becht's record-breaking £92 million payment in 2009, bonuses are used to drive the adherence to clear objectives set from the top.

For the powerbrands innovation is about margin improvement. New benefits are continuously introduced that enable higher prices to be charged. Most notably this can be seen in the flagship Finish brand that dominates the dishwashing category. Over the years this has moved from being a basic tablet to having multiple additional features, and each stage of the evolution has been incremental – gradually advancing the user experience and shifting the price. From '3 in 1' to the addition of a 'powerball' and then 'dissolving wrappers' each step forward is associated with a price increase that largely goes unnoticed by the consumer. This focused approach continuously builds the existing brands and maximizes the return from existing markets.

Culture

Reckitt Benckiser's culture is the number one driver of success – no question. It is our only sustainable advantage. Everything else can be copied, but it's close to impossible to copy culture.

While the bonus system is an important element, it is not the sole driver of the Reckitt Benckiser culture. Individuals are highly empowered to make decisions and to do everything in their power to achieve their objectives. The general instinct of management is to work at arm's length and judge on outcomes while progress is good.

The Reckitt Benckiser organization is also highly culturally diverse with pro-portionally far more nationalities in the mix than found in comparable firms. This is actively encouraged. As Rakesh puts it; 'If you want to have a diverse workforce to promote the DNA of innovation, you need to be in a place where people can be attracted.' Evidently this can lead to challenges, but not insur-mountable ones: 'We are one team with one language. English isn't most people's native language, and often our English isn't pretty. But the way we see it, it doesn't matter as long as you give a view. If you don't express your opinion, you don't have an opinion, and that's a fatal weakness for people who want to do well at Reckitt Benckiser.'

Another cultural advantage in the world of collaborative and open innovation is that, unlike many firms, Reckitt Benckiser has never had a 'not invented here' problem. 'We'll look at ideas from anywhere. Some come from our competitors; we see if they are doing something new and see if we can do it better.' Consequently, in comparison with other companies, Reckitt Benckiser has always been a low spender on internal R&D, preferring to access others' technologies rather than invest heavily in expensive internal experimental activities. Growth is all about new products but not necessarily developing the associated new technologies – in

Becht's eyes, 'Innovation is generated by new ideas, not by messing around in the lab.'

Being a growing, successful business with real responsibilities, new opportunities, and financial rewards linked to its success, there is very low staff churn: only 12% of the top 400 managers left the company in 2010. As a signal of the staying power in a pretty intense environment, many see that this reinforces that, for those that want to keep pace, the company culture is absolutely fine.

The Role of Insight

Although speed, focus, and the culture are very much the three things most visibly different about Reckitt Benckiser, the way the company makes use of insights is also interesting. This is not so much in the information that the company gets, much of which is similar to its peers, but more in how it uses it. 'There are many similarities between us and the rest, such as our consumer insight and research. But once we find the right idea or project that we believe will make a difference to consumers, the entire organization gets behind it with an intensity, a drive, a passion and an energy that is rare and unseen elsewhere.'

Within Reckitt Benckiser, an insight is defined as the line at the top of a written concept that defines the position and relevance of a new product in a consumer's life and the importance of consumer market tests in particular is elevated above all other sources of insight and concept validation. Unlike Procter & Gamble, it is not about an exploration of deep and motivating consumer truths – products and product concepts are very much the insight discovery vehicles. There are interesting consequences of this approach:

On the positive side, you know that the insights are tradable now and there is little to invest in consumer education. On the negative side, you don't what is coming and it is difficult to have a view on future capability requirements.

The confidence the company has in its ability to execute fast and with focus means that brand ownership for insights with a maximum 12-month horizon is the norm. There is a distinctive in-market media model where new product launches are backed harder the faster they grow and then media is cut early as growth fades. A former marketing executive reinforces the fact that 'insight drives not only innovation but also advertising: Reckitt Benckiser has had some great growth from new messages for the same product. It can be very quick to market, no new product, no new shelf requirements etc., just some packaging.' And spending on getting the new messages heard is an integral part of growth: in Becht's words, 'Our corporate strategy is very much focused on driving our powerbrands behind high levels of [media] support and continuous innovation.'

Media investment as a percentage of net sales is typically well over 10% and is one of the top 10 key performance indicators by which Reckitt Benckiser tracks and reports its success. 'We were the third biggest TV advertiser in the UK last year. When you consider the size of the company that is quite astonishing. And if the government cuts [advertising] spending we might become the second after Procter & Gamble.'

Reckitt Benckiser has an insight–test instead of an insight–explore approach. The requirement to have good consumer test scores on concepts ties the business to insights that are relevant to consumers now but not necessarily in the future. While successful for the short-term focus, some have concerns about the medium to longer term view and Reckitt Benckiser's current inability to assess future capabilities needs.

Building through Acquisition and Expansion

The focus on brands shapes the acquisition activity. Although primarily driven by organic growth, the company has bought a series of companies in order to build the brand portfolio and expand the geographical footprint. Notable examples are the acquisition of Boots Healthcare International in 2005, adding Neurofen, Strepsils, and Clearasil to the portfolio, and the purchase of Paras Pharmaceuticals, which added new health and personal care products as well as significantly improved presence in India.

Integrations following these acquisitions have been fast and the market channels very tightly managed. Typically Reckitt Benckiser will complete an integration of people, brands, and facilities with six months and see clear financial benefit to the top and bottom line in 12 months.

Going Forward

Looking ahead, CEO Rakesh Kapoor and other business leaders all speak the same language in terms of their aspirations for the future – expecting the business 'to at least double in size over the next decade.'

The company recognizes that it will need to deal with future challenges. These range from moving into the digital marketing arena later than its peers – but probably faster; maximizing geographic expansion potential; and achieving growth in China where, unlike India, the company currently has no major business. However, above all, as it seeks to continue growing, most see that the core of Reckitt Benckiser's approach will continue to be focused on the capabilities already in place.

Procter & Gamble

Incoming CEO A. G. Lafley knew he had some pretty major changes to identify and implement when he took over from Durk Jager in June 2000. They were dark days. Procter & Gamble had just issued profit warnings after its stock had nearly halved in value and had been the worst performing component of the Dow industrial average in the first quarter. After years of continued growth, the world's largest FMCG company had hit a major barrier and a different approach was clearly required.

Over the next nine years Lafley rebooted the company, changed the way it thinks about innovation, and fundamentally changed its approach to customers. He did a pretty good job. By the time he left in 2010 Procter & Gamble had 18 $5 billion brands and another 20 or so billion dollar brands. 'In 2000 only 15% of innovation efforts met profit and revenue targets. Today the figure is 50%.'

As Lafley reflects, back in 2000, 'stretch, innovation and speed were the orders of the day. Stretch for higher goals. Innovate in all we do. Go fast. Take more risk. All these are good things in and of themselves. In hindsight though, we were trying to change too much too fast. Too many new products, business and organization initiatives were being pushed into the market before they were ready.'

He saw that foremost, 'Innovation must be the central driving force for any business that wants to grow in both the short and long terms,' and that 'winning requires finding a new way to sustain organic revenue and profit growth and consistently improve margins.' While these views are not unique, the approaches that Procter & Gamble have taken in achieving its goals over the past decade are certainly noteworthy.

Connect + Develop

Although there were 7500 people in R&D, several senior managers in Procter & Gamble felt that there was untapped potential for extra innovation outside the company. With internal innovation failing to hit its targets, the company decided to seek ideas from the external ecosystem of 'around 1.5 m worldwide whose knowledge they needed to tap into.' Having run several years of experiments in the area, Larry Huston, vice president R&D Innovation and Knowledge, was asked to lead a new approach which became known as Connect + Develop. With a CEO-endorsed goal of 'getting half of our innovation from the outside' the initiative was heavily promoted in a number of imaginative ways. In addition to the usual *Harvard Business Review* articles, a vehicle for reconnecting with former employees – www.yourencore.com – was launched. There were also multiple bilateral co-development programs with selected companies and universities and a team of 70 technology scouts.

By 2010 Connect + Develop had helped bring more than 250 new products into the marketplace. Larry describes Procter & Gamble's strategy behind this success as 'matching what's needed with what's possible and doing fact-finding in between – Procter & Gamble's 'Connect + Develop' program represents a cultural shift from in-house advances toward external collaboration of all kinds.'

Connect + Develop has meant that innovation has become the lifeblood of the company. As the CEO puts it, 'We know from our history that while promotion may win quarters, innovation wins decades.' From a cultural perspective, Mike Addison, section head of R&D for Procter & Gamble in Europe, adds; 'innovation is discussed all the time in Procter & Gamble and success celebrated and communicated. Every individual is assessed on their contribution to growing the business and their contribution to growing the organisation. For R&D, innovation is woven all the way through this. People build their own stories on where they have been involved in great innovation. This is being refreshed all the time – being shared on the Internet, publications and intranet.'

Integrated Design

Inspired by how others were putting design more centrally in the business, Lafley was keen to make a better job of this at Procter & Gamble. He chose to 'integrate design with the innovation process and use it as a mechanism to improve collaboration' and appointed Claudia Kotchka as vice president Design Innovation & Strategy to lead this. Over five years the company hired over 150 designers and worked closely with IDEO, a design, innovation and consulting firm, as a preferred strategic design partner.

The drive to integrate design was emblematic of a shift of focus from the product and the sales channel to the consumer as customer. As Claudia put it at the Institute of Design Strategy Conference in 2008, 'science starts with analysis and looks for the right answer. Designers start with the user and don't believe there is one right answer.'

Organizing for Growth

Procter & Gamble is clear about the role of incremental and disruptive innovation – the company understands the difference and focuses on the two in different ways. Not only does it segment incremental innovation into three types – sustaining, commercial, and transformational – but Procter & Gamble also sees that disruptive innovation has to have a separate focus and hence a different team.

In common with Reckitt Benckiser, Procter & Gamble uses acquisitions to help deliver its growth ambitions: 'When we acquire, we acquire to build the core.' Examples being the purchase of Wella and Clairol to expand its beauty business, and, as the company grew to be a top player in personal care, the acquisition of Gillette for $57 billion in 2005. These days Procter & Gamble drives its high levels of growth through three key groups.

1. The Future Works organization whose objective is to seek out innovation opportunities that create new consumption. It is not constrained by existing category paradigms and is free to search for new opportunities in totally new spaces.

2. The New Business Development organization focuses on creating both disruptive and incremental innovation for a specific category – usually based on ideas developed within the business.

3. External Business Development works with all categories to help identify and close deals with external parties. It accelerates the flow of ideas from outside the company.

Although this is not unique to Procter & Gamble, the company sees that the way they work together and interact not only with each other but also with the varied categories is what creates a distinctive competence that competitors have yet to either imitate or better.

Deep Understanding of the Consumer

Early on, Lafley saw that 'our goal at Procter & Gamble is to delight our consumers at two moments of truth' and so 'Procter & Gamble's definition of innovation focuses not just on the benefits a product provides, but also on the total consumer experience from purchase (the first moment of truth) to usage (the second moment of truth).' And this meant that the primary focus was on the consumer not the category. Seeing the consumer as the boss, the mantra became all about 'earning the loyalty of our bosses.'

Over the past decade Procter & Gamble has been at the forefront of creating and adopting new research approaches from in-store shopping and in-home usage immersion through to more investigative ethnographic and semiotic analysis of consumers, culture, and society. The company has developed a series of proprietary consumer research methods that 'not only enable deeper understanding, but also broader understanding across 40 product categories in more than 80 countries.' In contrast to Reckitt Benckiser, as well as gaining short-term views, these also look out further than most in the FMCG sector and include what are termed 'Lighthouse projects,' which set the ambition for category development 5–10 years out. Taken as a whole, no other company in the world has this level of insight capability.

Mike Addison's view is that at Procter & Gamble 'we really believe we are best at understanding the consumer, we have a variety of touch points with the consumer throughout the development and marketing processes – that results in superior products and world class marketing and we really believe we are the best marketers in the world . . . The thing we are better on now is using insight to create a holistic analysis of what we are going to do. As a company we recognise that insight is not always only based on observation but also on deep understanding of the consumer. I can't imagine that there is a mechanism that could engage with consumers better than what Procter & Gamble is already employing.'

Washing powder and disposable diapers provide two examples of how this approach works:

- *Tide Naturals:* 'Ethnographic research in India highlighted that the majority of consumers wash their clothes by hand and that they therefore chose products that were relatively gentle on the skin but not very good at cleaning clothes. Tide Naturals was launched in 2009. It cleans well but without irritation and was priced 30% below regular Tide. It is now the market leader and accessible to 70% of Indians.'
- *Pampers:* 'We were too internally focused. So we shifted Pampers' focus from the diaper to the baby and the mother and so discovered insights we would not have found previously. In India we discovered that babies who sleep through the night develop better and this gave mothers a reason to want to use disposable diapers so that their babies did not have disturbed sleep. The problem shifted from the diaper to babies' sleep. The advertising campaign reinforced the insight – "babies in disposable diapers sleep 30% faster and 30 minutes longer"'.

Another perspective widely shared within Procter & Gamble is that because the company has access to so much insight, it really wants to make best use of it. As such 'getting everything 100% right before launch' is an often-cited ambition that is seen as both good and bad: good in that it makes sure that project teams pay attention to detail, mine the insight, and ensure that the products really hit the mark; and bad in that, compared to competitors such as Reckitt Benckiser, the company may well 'delay' launch of a product by six months to get it to 100%. And the view of most is that making sure that products they launch are as good as they possibly can be is a higher priority than speed.

Longevity

For Procter & Gamble employees two things are important – the history of the company and that long-term careers are the norm. Being 174 years old is really important to the company and its employees – not just because of the products and brands it can trace all the way back to the Ivory soap bar in the 1880s, but also how the company has led the industry. From the creation of a corporate R&D lab in the 1890s, a market research department in the 1920s, and brand management in the 1930s to being at the forefront of introducing the eight-hour day, five-day workweek and minority hiring, employees have a great sense of pride in their company.

Accompanying this is a company that still very much provides a job for life. Although in recent years a higher ratio of mid-career external recruits have entered the organization, Procter & Gamble has traditionally promoted from within. Mike Addison concurs: 'Most of our employees join the company when they are really young and leave when they are really old. The whole leadership in the company has spent a lifetime in the company. Even people who are not in leadership posts have spent many years in the company and we all have been brought up in a company that is totally focused on innovation, focused on doing the right thing, focused on our consumer. That gives us a capacity, in my view, to execute hopefully with greater excellence than our competition, more often.'

New Leadership

By the time that Lafley retired in 2010, Procter & Gamble was in far better shape. 'We identified the key issue and developed a strategy that prioritized top line growth and are now earning profit in the right way.' Reviewing his performance,

Forbes magazine summarized his impact thus: 'Diligently and methodically, he spread the word that Procter & Gamble had to focus on big brands, big markets, and big customers. He said that Procter & Gamble, to win with powerful discounters, must slash costs and reinvest savings in marketing and product design. Focusing on those things, Lafley became the best organic-growth guy in the consumer-products industry.'

The changes that had been introduced were well embedded in the organization and Bob McDonald, the COO, had overseen much of this. It was therefore of little surprise that he became the new company CEO. Several analysts commented that, 'Procter & Gamble's current situation makes it a good time for a COO to take charge.' On his appointment Bob McDonald saw that 'this is a period of what we would describe as continuity with change,' and today in interviews he reinforces the view of the importance of the Procter & Gamble purpose, on the significance of consumer-focused innovation, and the need to grow the company's business in emerging markets:

It all starts with our purpose – touching and improving lives: I joined Procter & Gamble because I wanted to be with people who are motivated by a higher purpose. This is the idea of improving lives.

We are a company where innovation is our lifeblood. We have to innovate and bring innovations to market to touch and improve lives. It all comes down to having the consumer insight. When I travel I visit people in their homes. I watch people using our products and go shopping with our consumers.

If you are the one who has the consumer insight, you can better segment the category and create better loyalty and more indispensability and as a result have a higher market share. We want to delight but not dilute for the bottom of the pyramid. As an example, in the Philippines people do their laundry by hand. Water is very limited. They judge the quality of their soap by the amount of suds – but it takes up to five rinses to get rid of this. We developed a product that only requires one rinse and that is about designing for the purpose.

Future Growth

In 2010, as an evolution on its past decade's success, Procter & Gamble updated its growth strategy to connect it explicitly to the company's purpose:

We focus on three specific choices:

- *To grow Procter & Gamble's core brands and categories with an unrelenting focus on innovation;*
- *To build our business with un-served and underserved consumers; and*
- *To continue to grow and develop faster-growing, higher-margin businesses with global leadership potential.*

These strategic choices are unified by one simple, overarching growth strategy: to touch and improve the lives of more consumers in more parts of the world more completely.

The challenges ahead are varied and numerous. In addition to the usual competitor threat, they include a growing presence of private label brands; the power of Wal-Mart, which distributes over 15% of Procter & Gamble's total production; the need to embrace digital marketing 'to be where the customer wants to shop'; accommodating rising environmental constraints and higher raw material prices; and sustaining growth in Asia. Bob McDonald believes the company is ready to deal with whatever is thrown its way. 'We talk a lot about having an 'AND' not an 'OR' culture at Procter & Gamble. We believe you can find another way: an 'AND' way without tradeoffs.' Like Bart Becht at Reckitt Benckiser, he sees that above all the company culture is the real distinctive competence both for now and for the future.

Key Insights – Reckitt Benckiser and Procter & Gamble

Both Reckitt Benckiser and Procter & Gamble are successful Growth Champions. Although they are in the same sector, how this is achieved is different. Reckitt

Benckiser's focus on speed and incremental innovation means that its fast decision-making culture has become finely tuned to driving innovation that, year on year, hits the mark and impresses the market. Procter & Gamble may not be as fast, but what it does is to focus specifically on disruptive innovation and inherently therefore the longer term.

While both make core use of consumer insight, here too there are major differences. Reckitt Benckiser is focused on an insight–test instead of an insight–explore approach. Consumer insight for Reckitt Benckiser is about proving the concept or giving short-term evidence of an unmet need. In Procter & Gamble this is important, but having deeper understanding of the consumer has greater significance.

Reckitt Benckiser behaves like a global business that was born in 1999 despite its much earlier roots. Procter & Gamble celebrates its longer term heritage. Reckitt Benckiser is nearly 10 times smaller and thinks of itself as more than 10 times younger. Despite these differences, it is clear that there are also some common traits. The clarity of strategic focus, the high growth ambitions, the role of the CEO, and the need to leverage the organization's capabilities are present in both businesses.

Both companies have had inspirational leaders for much of the last decade and now have new CEOs, promoted from within, in place. As they both aim to significantly increase revenues and profits over the next decade, umpteen more comparisons of the two companies will be made. In the short term, many see that Reckitt Benckiser's highly efficient growth will continue to be faster than that of Procter & Gamble but others also see that despite its size, the fact that Procter & Gamble can continue to achieve such strong organic growth is testament to its prowess in innovating at scale. Some question whether Reckitt Benckiser's lack of long-term focus will eventually become its Achilles' heel and allow Procter & Gamble to consolidate its position, but then, given the past decade, perhaps 'late and fast' is just fine for an organization like Reckitt Benckiser.

Reckitt Benckiser

Growth Impact

Sector-leading creation of shareholder value
from organic growth and powerbrand development

Distinctive Competence

Delivering insight-driven fast incremental
margin-enhancing product innovation

Underlying Capabilities

Acting and delivering faster than the competition	Focused top-down targets with no ambiguity	Bonus-driven culture with high empowerment

Procter & Gamble

Growth Impact

Remaining the world's largest FMCG
company under increasing global competition

Distinctive Competence

Making big brands bigger through
consumer-focused global and local innovation

Underlying Capabilities

Deep understanding of the consumer	Mastership of open innovation	Purposeful and motivated leadership

Starwood Hotels	KEY DATA
Total sales (2010)	$5.1 billion
Sales growth (2009–2010)	9%
REVPAR growth (2009–2010)	10.1%
Average share price growth p.a. (2005–2010)	16.5%
Number of hotels (2010)	1041
% Hotels owned or leased (2010)	6%
% Hotels managed (2010)	45%
% Hotels franchised (2010)	49%

Inditex	KEY DATA
Total sales (2010)	€12,5 billion
Average sales growth p.a. (2005–2010)	14.6%
Net profit (2010)	€1.7 billion
Average net profit growth p.a. (2005–2010)	18.7%
Average share price growth p.a. (2005–2010)	20.0%
Number of stores (2010)	5044
Number of countries served (2010)	77
Average sales per store (2010)	€2.5 million

CHAPTER 8

Starwood Hotels and Inditex

Delivering a unique customer experience

A cross the service sector, a consistent concern is how to provide an excellent customer experience while still making money. In addition to the traditional problems around customer loyalty, supply chain management, and staff retention, globalization has meant that access to common service standards has increased and there is growing awareness of what is available. Customer expectations are high and it stands to reason that the consistent provision of affordable and memorable experiences really is the Holy Grail for service providers.

At the luxury end of the market, where customers pay premium prices for premium services, the margins are pretty healthy. From corporate jets to designer fashion and boutique hotels, brands such as NetJets, Prada, One and Only and their peers provide luxurious experiences for the few who have the money to enjoy them. These brands focus on building a high media profile, whether through advertising or celebrity endorsement, to articulate the dream of a lifestyle few have but many want. Millions are spent communicating with people who will most likely never be able to afford what's on offer: think of watch manufacturers such as Rolex or Omega. It's all about reinforcing exclusivity.

The big challenge is lower down the service sector in the land of RyanAir, SouthWest Airlines, Aldi, and Lidl. Being able to deliver a memorable service and an enhanced customer experience to the many is really difficult; ensuring that this is simultaneously differentiated, profitable, and scalable even more so. For those that have managed it there are considerable rewards around growth, brand value, customer loyalty, and profit.

This chapter explores two companies that have achieved this in different ways. One delivers a differentiated set of experiences through a largely franchise operation; the other through direct involvement throughout the supply chain. They are known more by their customer-facing brands than their corporate names – Starwood Hotels and Inditex. While they have different approaches, both organizations have commonalities that have positioned them ahead of their industry peers. Inspirational leadership has been successfully passed from the founders to the next generation; each has a strong corporate culture which establishes the brand and attracts and retains the best staff; and both have nurtured high levels of customer loyalty. They are head and shoulders above their competitors in the service sector in delivering mass customer experiences that are highly efficient and very profitable.

Starwood Hotels

Sheraton, Westin, Four Points, the St Regis, W Hotels, Le Méridien, The Luxury Collection and, more recently, Aloft and Element are all brands that you may have come across or even experienced. Each is focused on different markets and consumer segments and is highly efficient in how it operates. They are all part of Starwood Hotels, a US-based company worth over $10 billion.

A relatively new player in the hospitality sector, Starwood Hotels was founded in 1999 by Barry Sternlicht, a youthful Harvard MBA and real estate entrepreneur running a Connecticut-based firm called Starwood Capital. In 18 months between 1995 and 1997 he went on 'a shopping spree, purchasing two of America's largest and best-known hotel groups, Westin Hotels and ITT Sheraton. Starwood Hotels was created as a standalone hotel-operating company in 1999.

With properties in nearly 100 countries, Starwood Hotels can justifiably claim to be the most 'global hotel company,' citing the unstoppable flows of globalization, capital flow, and wealth creation as cornerstones of its future growth strategy. More than 80% of Starwood Hotels' 85,000-room pipeline will be built in international markets, with Asia Pacific representing its largest source of future growth with 50,000 new rooms coming on stream. Starwood Hotels is now the world's second-largest hotel group by market capitalization and the eighth largest by guestrooms with approximately 300,000 rooms in 1000 hotels around the world. In the face of strong long-standing businesses like Hilton, Hyatt, and Marriott and exciting new local or regional brands such as The Standard, the Mondrian, and Amanpuri, Starwood Hotels is making an impact.

Hotels are measured by their 'revenue per available room' – room revenue divided by the number of nights available. Competition is intense particularly in the high volume arena where global brands such as Hilton, Marriott, and Crowne Plaza compete with more regional operators like Shangri-La and Jumeirah. In a crowded market where everyone is fundamentally playing the same game, Starwood Hotels has been able to match, if not better, the experience provided by the newcomers at a global scale and do this while being more efficient than the incumbents.

According to current CEO Frits van Paasschen, 'Innovation is core to who we are and gives us our competitive edge.' This certainly seems to be the case and this ethos, alongside a focus on the creation and development of a portfolio of strong brands, has enabled the company to transform a stuffy, conservative industry with low margins into one of relative growth and innovation.

Starwood Hotels' Prowess

Through a combination of high-impact innovation to attract customers and financial efficiency in running the business, over the past five or so years, Starwood Hotels has been able to both double the number of hotels and maintain comparable average room revenues. While this does not stand out as momentous growth when compared to that achieved by some of the other companies profiled in this book, it is significant in relation to the hotel sector where many competitors have seen net decreases in average room revenues over the same period.

Three Strategic Pillars

Like many organizations, Starwood Hotels has a small number of areas that it sees as critical to its future success. Otherwise known as the strategic pillars, these are 'great brands,' 'financial flexibility,' and 'global scale' – each of which gives a strong insight into both how the company thinks and what has made a tangible difference to its performance in the hotels business.

1: Building Great Brands

Brand identity has been a primary focus for Starwood Hotels. Starting with Westin and Sheraton, Starwood Hotels' ambition has always been to build world-class hotel brands. Indeed van Paasschen sees Starwood Hotels' mission as: 'to be a global operator of lifestyle hospitality brands.' According to Scott Williams, chief creative officer from 1997–2007, Sternlicht's initial intent was to revive a portfolio of tired brands (i.e. Sheraton, Westin) and then create new desirable alternatives, giving more choice and opportunity to customers. This strategy seems to have been pretty effective so far.

With every launch Starwood Hotels aims to reinvent each hotel category by going beyond the usual expectation. Barry Sternlicht set the standard when he created the W Hotel chain in 1999. Dreamed up around the kitchen table with his wife, Sternlicht's concept offered a modern, hip experience for the contemporary traveler, successfully marrying the attractions of an individualized boutique hotel with the benefits of being part of a rewarding global loyalty program.

As van Paasschen says, 'We are the only global hotel company with a brand like W. The reason is that this is not easy to do: creating a cool, design-driven environment is only half the story. Creating an economic model that delivers for owners and ourselves, and continuing to replenish that, takes some intellectual capital.' It's certainly a fine balance and many others have tried to imitate it, but a decade after the launch with 40 properties across the United States and in locations such as Seoul, Santiago, and St. Petersburg, the W remains the only global boutique hotel brand.

Heavenly rest

Looking at the wider portfolio, the need to update the Westin and Sheraton brands was obvious but Starwood Hotels, particularly Barry Sternlicht, also wanted to create clear points of differentiation.

For the Westin, it was a case of going back to the basics and concentrating on what really matters for the majority of its (largely business) customers – getting the best possible rest. To do this they wanted to find and offer the best bed. Unable to find a supplier who could deliver what they required, Starwood Hotels ended up creating a bespoke bed themselves. These signature pieces or 'Heavenly Beds' were custom-created by the in-house team and became such a success that Starwood Hotels not only took the concept to their other brands, but, bowing to popular demand, also let customers buy the bed. Through www.westin-hotelsathome.com and subsequently www.sheraton-hotelsathome.com and www.whotelsthestore .com, Starwood Hotels quickly, and almost accidently, became one of the biggest bed retailers in the United States and has even started to expand globally. A simple change, the Heavenly Bed has now inspired a host of imitators such as the Marriott Bed and www.shopmarriott.com.

Beyond innovation

One of the major factors of Starwood Hotels' success is its ability to deliver better service. As one executive said, 'innovation will only get you so far, service is the differentiator. In a hotel you don't want average service.' Rigorous training has been critical as well as a focus on hiring people with the right attitude – 'we can train aptitude.' Employees are encouraged to show their personality and actively promote their brands. They are also involved in the recruitment of the right sort of people to join the team – some even hand out business cards with 'I think you've got the W vibe, if you want to leave your current job come and talk to me' to people who have given them great service in another business.

New concepts

As well as continued enhancement of its core brands, Starwood Hotels has also introduced new ones such as Aloft and Element.

Research showed that both business and leisure travelers were looking for a modern, fresh hotel experience at the mid-scale price point – essentially style without the frills. Aloft was designed to be a highly sociable, tech-savvy destination, inspired by Starwood Hotels' W hotels incorporating sleek urban energy with a more limited service. It has raised the bar in the select-service category, offering urban-inspired, loft-like guest rooms, enhanced technology services, landscaped outdoor spaces for socializing day and night, and an energetic lounge scene. It provides a particularly compelling case study given its status as the fastest launching debut brand in the history of the hotel industry with more than 50 hotels opened in the first three years.

Based on the Westin DNA, Element is Starwood Hotels' most recent brand launch, and is reinventing the hospitality sector's approach to sustainability. Element is the first major hotel brand to mandate that all properties pursue LEED certification from the US Green Building Council. Every Element property is a high-performance building where sustainable practices reduce waste and conserve resources. All rooms feature energy efficient appliances, lighting and water facilities, recycling bins, low volatile organic compound paint on the walls and recycled carpets. Starwood Hotels has developed an 'eco-chic' hotel while still retaining a cool modern design.

Over the past few years, Starwood Hotels has also grown its portfolio both through the acquisition of the business-oriented Le Méridien brand and properties and, at the high end, the addition of more properties in its Luxury Collection, which complement but are not part of the St. Regis brand. Worldwide they now have over 80 luxury hotels, including Helsinki's traditional Hotel Kamp and the US Grant in San Diego, focused on delivering highly individual bespoke experiences. Together, The Luxury Collection, St. Regis, and W portfolios combine to make Starwood Hotels a leader in the luxury hotel space.

Starwood Hotels' sharp focus on delivering such brand experiences is fueling growth. Simon Turner, president of global development, sees that: 'through the value that we bring to owners with our world-class brands, global systems and experienced in-market teams, developers are increasingly turning to Starwood Hotels, resulting in our achieving more than our fair share of executed deals globally in the segments where we operate.'

2: Financial Flexibility

Despite this success, having a clearly articulated identity is not enough. At its heart, the hotel business is highly capital intensive and has traditionally involved huge investments simply to run existing brands never mind to develop new ones.

Five years ago, adopting the approach pioneered by Holiday Inn, Starwood Hotels shifted its strategy from owning hotels, to franchising, managing, and brand building. In 2005 20% of Starwood Hotels' profits came from franchisee fees and today they comprise 60%, getting close to their target of becoming over 80% fee-driven. In selling off their properties the group has created a new business model based on long-term contracts and minimal capital requirements, with the fee business generating predictable and sustainable income streams.

According to van Paasschen this approach protects the company from the ups and downs of the property market. 'In good times it allows us to grow more quickly. In hard times our income stream is less volatile as we are less dependent on revenues than the owner.' It hasn't been an easy journey, however, and in 2010/11 the company made the executive decision to cut costs dramatically in order to further reduce its debt levels. Many non-strategic assets were sold including the Bliss brand and St. Regis retail space.

In parallel with cost-saving measures van Paasschen has insisted on riding out the downturn by opening more hotels, his strategy was for Starwood Hotels to 'own the upswing' and added 'We are probably at the bottom of the cycle, and if you add fresh inventory you can enjoy the ride up.'

Given the growing importance of the East as an economic powerhouse, expansion in the hotel industry in general is now increasingly being driven by Asia. To help ensure that the right decisions are made van Paasschen believes that 'in order to understand a market from a consumer point of view you have to buy the proverbial groceries there' – so he mandated that his exec team spend all of June 2011 headquartered in Shanghai. This immersive technique gives senior leadership a first-hand understanding of their fastest growth market, where, in 2011, they opened a hotel every two weeks.

3: Managing Global Scale

The third and final pillar of Starwood Hotels' growth strategy is that of scale. This relates to global expansion, leveraging collective buying power and the ability to connect customers, properties, and management practices around the world.

Clearly being able to buy in bulk gives Starwood Hotels, alongside any global organization, strong negotiating power in terms of pricing and distribution, but scale provides the challenge of delivering consistency of experience across all of the brands. To do this Starwood Hotels created a set of brand propositions and brand identities for each chain brand underpinned by guidelines identifying the common standards all hotels in the portfolio must adhere to.

Each brand is viewed through the guideline lens and then given the freedom to express its own separate identity and characteristics. For example, the Sheraton brand went on to develop a greater sense of connection to remove the stress of travel and increase the customers' sense of belonging.

In order to gain from the scale of its customer base, Starwood Hotels led the industry with its Starwood Hotels Preferred Guest (SPG) loyalty offer, launched in 1999. Annoyed by airline loyalty programs that gave out miles but made it hard to redeem them at peak times, Sternlicht created SPG to be hassle free with no 'blackouts' – an industry first. With SPG, customers were able to redeem points instantly at any time. SPG immediately gave Starwood Hotels a USP that it exploited across all its brands, and one which took Marriott over four years to replicate.

The Winning Combination

Across its brands, Starwood Hotels has been able to make guest experiences both memorable and consistent. Whilst some companies have created hotel chains that look and feel identical, but can also seem a little dull and characterless, and others have created individual properties where the customer experience is highly memorable, but have been unable to replicate this globally, Starwood Hotels manages to do both.

But what are the unique features of the business that make Starwood Hotels more successful than its peers? Employees point to the culture. Although a franchise model has challenges such as maintaining alignment between the interests and priorities of the hotel owners and operators and those of the brands, Starwood Hotels has been able to build and sustain a culture that determines how employees run the hotels, interact with guests, and deliver the experiences that cuts across any barriers. As van Paasschen says: 'In the hotel business, branding is not so much about marketing as customer experience . . . It's a balance of creativity and operations, right down to training, design, where we value-engineer, how we invest, the way we select staff – there's a secret source in all that stuff.'

More Than Points

The other factor mentioned by both employees and guests at Starwood Hotels is that of customer loyalty. Yes, SPG, the world's most award-winning guest loyalty program clearly plays a part but it's not just points. Starwood Hotels also manages to deliver something that brings people back time and time again.

Perhaps the W is still the hero here but other brands have similar impact. Even though each property is different and provides varied public and private space experiences, there are core elements from staff manners and hotel vocabulary to room fragrance and quality of facilities that encourages guests to try other locations out. They know that every W will be different but they are confident in assured service and a memorable stay.

Future Challenges

From its beginnings as an investment opportunity for Starwood Capital, Starwood Hotels has evolved under different leadership into a global franchise management company delivering rapid growth across many customer segments, around the world.

Looking forward, as competition from existing and new players intensifies, the company will undoubtedly face new challenges. Alongside the need to weather industry ups and downs many see that Asian growth, particularly in China, will be the next great test. There are pros and cons around rolling out more hotels under established Western brands, creating new Chinese brands for the domestic market, or even developing Asian-oriented brands in other countries to accommodate the fast-growing international Chinese tourist market. Given that the concept of service and brand are important and implicit elements of modern Chinese culture, how well Western-focused brands continue to profitably exceed guest expectations will be a fundamental growth challenge.

Inditex

Best known by its Zara brand, Spanish company Inditex is a finely tuned retail engine that gives customers around the world exactly what they want before anyone else. Now one of the world's largest fashion retailers, it is a pioneer of fast fashion offering stylish, affordable clothes through brands including Zara, Pull & Bear, and Massimo Dutti. Inditex's super-efficient supply chain process delivers new designs in less than three weeks compared to the industry average of six months, and does it at a lower cost than its competitors. Daniel Piette, fashion director at Louis Vuitton, notably described Zara as 'possibly the most innovative and devastating retailer in the world.'

From its origins in 1963 when Amancio Ortega started a small company in Spain manufacturing women's clothes, Inditex (or Industria de Diseño Textil, which translates as Textile Design Industries) has grown to encompass over 100 companies operating across textile design, manufacture, and distribution, and is the world's second-biggest fashion retailer after The Gap. With an average revenue growth for the past five years just shy of 15% and, over the same period, net profits more than doubling to over €1.7 billion it now boasts stores in over 400 cities worldwide.

Competition in the Fashion Sector

Outside the high-end luxury segment, competition for the mass market is today fought on two levels: getting the basics at the right price and providing customers with the latest styles as quickly as possible. With the industry average design-to-store time of six months, Inditex and its main competitor, H&M, are pioneers of fast fashion, regularly achieving less than three weeks. More than anyone else, they have focused on getting the latest designs to their customers as quickly as possible.

José Luis Nueno, professor of marketing at the IESE Business School in Barcelona and regarded as one of the world's leading experts on the retail industry, sees the Inditex approach as the role model for the future of retail:

With the certainty that variety will lose out to speed and cost, we can foresee a world in which Zara and H&M are more successful than Gap and Neiman Marcus and the Aldi model wins over the Wal-Mart one. Hypermarkets and department stores will lose out to discount stores and the speed merchants. This is clear. The shape of retailing has changed and the consequences over the next decade will be driven by a clear-out of the also-rans.

Sources of Competitive Advantage

While Inditex could just be seen as a very slick global logistics machine, there are many other things that it does well. These include the way its designs are created and materials are sourced, how it works with suppliers and subcontrac-tors, the way its stores are designed, how its people communicate and are rewarded, and, above all, how its customers are served. Underpinning all of this is the effective use of technology targeted on where it can make the most impact. And it is the combination of these different capabilities that make it a successful growth story.

Embedded design

In many fashion companies, the design teams are found in studios in the hot spots of London, New York, Paris, and Milan or, more commonly for the mass-market offerings, in a central facility where they are left to create the next trend. Often designers are split into teams looking after different seasons of clothes – defining the varied winter, spring, summer, and fall collections – and in several companies looking after all ranges of women's, men's, and children's clothes. Not so for Inditex.

Firstly, each of the eight chains within the group has a team of scouts and design-ers solely responsible for identifying the latest trends and producing relevant designs for their brand. Like their competitors, they go to fashion shows, scan the world's media, and spend time watching and observing people, but they also connect directly with staff in the company's stores to hear what they are picking up about the latest trends. This means that Inditex has several thousand people all sharing where they think the market is going – and they do this twice every week.

Secondly all the 200 or so designers are based in the core production facility in La Coruña in Northern Spain. They are immersed within the same environ-ment where their designs are being made, packed, and shipped, and so are implicitly connected to the core business interacting with manufacturing, testing out ideas, discussing price points and styles with sales teams, and seeing which designs are being dispatched. The same designers work on collections for the current and forthcoming seasons so they can update the designs based on feed-back from the stores and incorporate this into the next round of products.

Thirdly, for optimum focus the teams are split into three groups – one for women's lines, one for men's, and one for children's. Although a single team is often thought to be more efficient, Inditex makes a point of running three teams in parallel with distinct operations and separate sales, procurement, and planning resources as they believe that, although more expensive to operate, it speeds up information flows and allows the supply chain to be more responsive.

Integrated supply chain

The success of the Inditex supply chain is based on three fully integrated components: secure materials supply; strong subcontractor relationships; and speedy product distribution.

Secure materials supply

Inditex runs a highly integrated vertical supply chain all the way through from raw materials supply to its retail stores. This means economy of scale and, by having control of the whole system, its model of just-in-time manufacture, supply, and integrated design and marketing can excel.

Fabric supply is secure because for Zara over 40% is sourced from a wholly owned subsidiary, Comditel, for which Zara accounts for 90% of sales. Most is purchased un-dyed to allow for faster response for any midseason color changes. The company then works with Fibracolor, a dyestuff producer part owned by Inditex, to ensure efficiency. The other 60% of fabrics come from a range of over 250 suppliers, none of which however account for more than 4% of total production to minimize dependency and encourage maximum responsiveness – from a reputational basis keeping Inditex as a happy customer is a priority for many.

Strong subcontractor relationships

While H&M has largely operated a business model based on outsourced production, Inditex has far greater control of the supply chain. More than half the clothes are cut and the materials collated in its own factories. Subcontracting is generally carried out locally – Inditex has over 500 sewing contractors based near its main factories, most of which work exclusively for one or other of its brands. The working relationship is very close and Inditex monitors operations for quality, legal compliance, and timing before all sewn items are sent to the factory for inspection, automated ironing, labeling, and wrapping prior to distribution.

Overall, most commentators see that Inditex has largely resisted the industry-wide trend of moving production to low-cost countries. Whilst true for its fast-turnaround products, it has however moved production of the basic standard designs to cheaper locations.

Speedy product distribution

All Inditex products, no matter where they have been made, pass through the company's 50,000 square meter distribution center where automated systems are used to ensure that the right pieces are shipped to the right destinations at the right time. Given that on average most garments come in half a dozen colors and a similar number of sizes, Zara's system has to deal with around 300,000 new stock-keeping units (SKUs) every year, the vast majority of which are only in the center for a matter of hours. It's all about small steps to increase efficiency, for example by putting all garments on hangers in La Coruña so they can be hung directly in store.

Throughout Europe store supply is by trucks that run on a bi-weekly schedule enabling most outlets to receive garments within 24 hours of an order. On average each store receives around 12,000 garments a week and many of these will only be available for a couple of weeks before being replaced. For the rest of the world, all products are shipped direct by air meaning that US stores get order fulfillment in 48 hours and Japan in less than 72. Although companies may see this as a high-cost luxury, Inditex manages to keep airfreight costs down to about 1% of the selling price of garments.

Flexible stores

The retail stores operate 'as both the company's face to the world and as information sources' for the business.

Store layouts are designed to encourage fast visits. There is no need to mooch in a Zara store if you don't want to – all the latest arrivals are clearly visible so that a quick in and out lunchtime browse and shop is easy. In fact, frequent customers even recognize that clothes on plastic hangers are faster fashion items than those on wooden ones and so hunt them out first.

Managing inventory to avoid disappointing customers whilst minimizing the level of unsold stock is a key driver of profitability and Inditex's policy is 'big store, small backroom.' Whereas many companies keep significant stock to ensure that all sizes are available, Zara aims to minimize stock levels. Indeed 'Zara makes a virtue of stock-outs. Empty racks don't drive customers to other stores because shoppers always have new things to choose from.' Because Zara stores receive regular small shipments they don't need to carry much inventory and so risks are minimized – unsold items account for less than 10% of stock compared to an industry average of 17–20%. This means that, in comparison to peers, Inditex consistently puts less than a third as much of its products into discount sales.

For ten years customized handheld PDAs have been used in every store to allow the retailers to send information directly to Spain about what is selling, what is not, and why not. Augmented by weekly phone calls with the central sales and procurement teams, this PDA network helps provide the hard data upon which many of Inditex's hourly decisions are based.

Culture as a differentiator

Unlike Benetton, which sells its products through franchise operations, Inditex keeps control of its shops and encourages store managers to focus solely on being as efficient and profitable as possible. And to ensure that the results benefit the entire operation, Inditex have built a culture that encourages autonomy, fast decision making, continuous improvement, and retaining the best people – this is what insiders see as the key ingredient that sets Inditex apart.

Pablo Isla, CEO of Inditex since 2005, explains:

We take small decisions and improve every day. Everything in our company is bottom-up. This has a lot to do with our entrepreneurial spirit. The first person with a big entrepreneurial spirit is the store manager. One of the characteristics that the managers mention is the autonomy they have.

Store managers feel like the owners of their stores. In particular, they value the freedom they have with the orders. We value this autonomy because it is critical for us to retain talented people in the business.

To ensure the cultural commonality, managers constantly visit stores to reinforce the team spirit and discuss performance with staff. Face-to-face contact is paramount for the company and the CEO sees that his 'main objective is to make sure that there is no disconnection between the stores and headquarters.'

An average Zara store has about 70 employees, 60% of whom are part-time sales associates, but lots of attention is focused on retaining staff through flexible scheduling and actively promoting employees internally: over 90% of store managers are promoted from within the organization. And all staff are involved in the business – as well as being part of the design scouting processes, employees are regularly briefed on all areas of production. As a result, Inditex has far lower staff turnover than most other larger retailers.

Leadership Transition

Since its origins in 1963 Amancio Ortega has been the heart and soul of Inditex. It was his background in manufacturing, not retailing, that evidently influenced the company's priority in maintaining control of its supply chain. While other companies set up and run by retailers have a different view, Ortega's focus on the security and speed of the supply chain has been critical to the company's success.

When Pablo Isla took over as CEO in 2005 and Ortega became chairman the two worked hand in hand on maintaining the growth of the business. But within a few years, Isla was starting to make some changes that he saw were necessary to keep Inditex at the fore of the sector. From tweaks to store replenishment and opening schedules to launching an online offer with full product range availability, in his own way he has fine-tuned the Inditex engine. Ortega has now taken a complete step back and has also handed over the position of chairman to Pablo Isla. However, no one sees any risk here. As Reuters puts it:

The passing of the baton to Isla is unlikely to be followed by radical changes at the cash-rich company which has become the largest clothes retailer in the world in terms of sales.

The Winning Formula

It is not hard to see why Zara specifically and Inditex generally are so widely praised for their retail efficiency. Taken in isolation the supply chain capabilities could be seen to be replicable by others. However, when you knit together the logistics, the rapid design, the vertically integrated supply network, and the hyper-effective store operation, not to mention the can-do culture, few see that Inditex' growth machine is going to falter any time soon.

As competitors have adopted some of Inditex's practices and sought to emulate the efficiencies, CEO and chairman, Pablo Isla, sees that the company has to speed up. So Inditex has been upgrading its systems and introducing new approaches to become even more efficient. 'There has been a clear change of mentality in the company,' he said in a *Wall Street Journal* interview. 'We now see the automatic replenishment of basics and the introduction of new software to schedule part time staff based on sales volume at different times – so there are more salespeople available at peak times such as lunchtime and early evening while still shaving 2% off the overall hours that staff work.'

Other improvements include having the logistics teams bring the packed merchandise off the trucks and directly onto the selling floor so that sales staff do not waste time unpacking. The machine is being constantly fine-tuned to further optimize performance and take out waste.

The Future

Going forward, Professor Nueno sees that retailing as a sector is in constant evolution and the blueprints for the future are clear:

Back in the 1950s William Starbuck developed one of the few ideas in retailing to have lasted: Every retail model is substituted by a more efficient one. This has been the case for the last 50 years and I see no reason for change in the future. As the success of discount supermarkets like Aldi demonstrates, variety will be substituted by budget. As the continued growth of fast-fashion chains such as Zara and H&M reveals, providing a limited but fast-changing product range is more profitable than holding a broad portfolio to cover the full range of potential consumer choice. We have now entered a world in which the distinction between prediction and following of trends has become blurred.

And Professor Nueno highlights two key competences as being critical in the future – speed and scale:

The most important capability for any manufacturer seeking a decent margin will be the ability to produce faster than the diffusion of a trend. Scale will dominate over choice.

And these just happen to be what Inditex are good at.

Key Insights – Starwood Hotels and Inditex

Despite very different origins – Starwood Hotels in capital management and Inditex in textile manufacturing – by focusing on the exceptional consumer experience, they have both developed the combination of resources that enable them to achieve operational effectiveness, industry-leading financial performance, and high customer satisfaction ratings.

Although the financial growth stories vary significantly, Inditex and Starwood Hotels in their different ways deliver the same thing – an exceptional consumer experience time after time. Both of these companies are highly proficient not only in developing and delivering exciting new products that their customers want, but also in successfully entering new markets with highly efficient operations. Although their models are different in terms of hotel franchise and store ownership and management, both are able to directly influence how they are run and so be intimately involved with their customers.

This achievement is based on combining highly efficient business processes, real-time consumer feedback, optimized levels of capital intensity, and a strong supporting culture beyond the company – across the supply chain. Technology for both is an important enabler to be used to enhance the business activities and to improve the connectivity between business offerings and customer expectations and experience.

Whilst the precise nature of supply chain relationships differs, with Starwood Hotels operating a franchise model for hotels and Inditex having strong partnerships with suppliers and greater ownership of many aspects of operations, what is clear is that both companies have been able to make these 'value nets' completely aligned around the overall objectives of delivering exceptional consumer experiences effectively and efficiently. And through focusing on innovation ahead of the market they have provided customers with something that they didn't know that they wanted.

Inspirational leadership has also been successfully passed from the founders to the next generation – both companies have shown with their leadership transitions from Ortega and Sternlicht to Isla and van Paasschen that continued business success can be achieved. While the new CEOs have added their own stamp and sought to optimize elements of the mix, they have also been keen to sustain the key elements that provide the DNA.

In addition, both organizations have also been able to use their cultures as a means to attract and retain the best staff and build the brand. Hotels and retail both suffer from high levels of staff churn and often leading companies end up training many of the sectors' workforces. However, through their focus on giving responsibility and autonomy to employees and clear career progression opportunities that are better than many alternatives, Starwood Hotels and Inditex have been able to nurture and keep the best talent.

They have also been able to achieve extremely high levels of customer loyalty. Their customers really are fans. Starwood Hotels' guests feel actively part of the Starwood Hotels community and many are keen to try out new experiences from the company while Inditex' customers show by their actions how focused they are on the brands. Visiting Zara stores four times more often than peers' and knowing which products are new in by the hangers they are on provide clear evidence of this.

Starwood Hotels

Growth Impact

Second-largest global hotel group
by market value while only eighth
largest by number of rooms

Distinctive Competence

Driving high customer loyalty from delivering
consistent and memorable guest experiences

Underlying Capabilities

Building great hotel brands	Financial flexibility	Managing global scale

Inditex

Growth Impact

'The most innovative and devastating
retailer in the world'

Distinctive Competence

Culture that encourages autonomy,
fast decision making, and incessant
continuous improvement

Underlying Capabilities

Embedded design within production facilities	Integrated supply chain with fast delivery	Flexible high-revenue, low-waste stores

Amazon	KEY DATA
Total revenue (2010)	$34.2 billion
Average revenue growth p.a. (2005–2010)	30.7%
Net income (2010)	$1.2 billion
Average net income growth p.a. (2005–2010)	27.9%
Revenue per employee (2010)	$1.0 million
R&D investment (2010)	$1.7 billion
R&D intensity (2010)	5.1%
Average share price growth (2005–2010)	46.1%

Google	KEY DATA
Total revenues (2010)	$29.3 billion
Average revenue growth p.a. (2005–2010)	47.6%
Net income (2010)	$8.5 billion
Average net income growth p.a. (2005–2010)	83.2%
Revenue per employee (2010)	$1.2 million
R&D investment (2010)	$3.8 billion
R&D intensity (2010)	12.8%
Average share price growth (2005–2010)	36.4%

CHAPTER 9

Amazon and Google

Expertly using data to get ever closer to customers

Amazon and Google are two of the largest and most successful companies in the consumer internet space. Both have helped construct and reshape the industry, delivering new services and capabilities that improve the way consumers engage with information, with companies, and with each other. Both have created new categories while disrupting others, support thousands of other businesses, and extract value from mind-boggling amounts of user data. Both are still led by their brilliant, billionaire founders, who it turns out all attended Montessori schools in their youth – a system that strongly encourages students to think for themselves, rather than accept the status quo. And both companies have seen extraordinary and consistent, mostly organic, growth over the past decade in revenues and user metrics. Yet these two companies have taken very different routes to success, and have markedly different approaches towards innovation and growth.

Google is obsessed with solving hard problems around information access and management. It built a search engine that was markedly better than anything available at the time, bringing order to the chaos of the web. It taught people that mess was OK, as long as Google was on your side. Users flocked to the site, and Google monetized them by reshaping the advertising world, providing a business model for a whole generation of new companies. The users, and the petabytes of data they trail in their wake, are in many ways commodities to Google – sources of input into a relentlessly analytical machine. Nuances of human life, emotion, and meaning are expressed, captured, digitized, and monetized.

Amazon takes a different approach. It uses data as an input to get closer to its self-imposed goal of being a user-centric company. Top down, rather than bottom up, Amazon more closely resembles a 'traditional company' than the more decentralized Google. It moves more deliberately and has executed its strategy with remarkable consistency since alighting on the opportunity of internet commerce. It had no *prima facie* reason to own the segment, but through a tight focus and years of investment in infrastructure, has now built up a remarkable position. Although retailing is Amazon's day job, its real business is customer satisfaction. Its most notable acquisition has been www.Zappos.com, a company so obsessed with customer happiness that it spawned its own social movement based on the founder's autobiography, *Delivering Happiness*.

As each company has taken a different route to its leadership position, so each faces unique challenges to continued growth. What is clear is that they have already had a very profound impact, and it's likely their next steps will continue to shape the business landscape in the years to come.

Amazon

For Amazon, Every Day is Day One

Before he set up the company, Jeff Bezos, Amazon's founder and CEO, analyzed the nascent internet market and was struck by its annual growth of 2300%. He concluded that books were the most promising online category: the space was fragmented, had a standardized product, and customers didn't need to inspect the product before buying. After highlighting 800% revenue growth in its first year as a public company in 1997, Amazon's first Letter to Shareholders included the following:

But this is Day 1 for the Internet and, if we execute well, for Amazon.com. Today, online commerce saves customers money and precious time. Tomorrow, through personalization, online commerce will accelerate the very process of discovery.

We have a window of opportunity as larger players marshal the resources to pursue the online opportunity and as customers, new to purchasing online, are receptive to forming new relationships.

In today's environment where startups 'pivot' (change their business model and approach) on a regular basis, the clarity of this sentiment, and the faithfulness with which the Amazon team has held to this vision, is impressive. It is fitting therefore that in every Annual Report since then, the company has attached the original letter as an annex. In many ways it is still Day 1 for the internet, with many big opportunities – such as comparison shopping – still a potentially lucrative and unsolved consumer problem. However, as the Amazon 2010 Report points out, it is also still Day 1 for Amazon – an approach that demonstrates it is not in thrall to its history and existing capabilities but prepared to reinvent itself to meet its customers' needs.

The formula has worked well so far. Sales from 2000 to 2010 grew at a compound annual rate of over 30% – and in the second quarter of 2011 at over 50%, putting it on course for annual revenues of over $40 billion. This has meant expanding across multiple product categories as the company fulfills its aim to sell anything that could be sold online. But books have always remained central as we can see by Amazon's recent expansion into the Kindle e-reader products and services. This has required new capabilities and people with new skills and attitudes; however, the love of the books category has remained remarkably steady.

Customer Centricity – Price, Choice, and Service

Jeff Bezos repeats the mantra of 'low prices, wide selection and fast & convenient service' at every opportunity; for example in this interview with Charlie Rose in 2007:

You know, the interesting thing, what we have discovered is every time we have entered into a new country, we find that on the big things, people are the same everywhere. They all want low prices. You never go into a new country and they say, 'Oh, I love Amazon, I just wish the prices were a little higher.' They all want vast selection, and they all want accurate, fast, convenient delivery.

Online retail businesses tend to have high fixed costs and low marginal costs. They involve significant investment to build websites, establish warehouses, implement and manage logistics systems, and design product recommendation algorithms, and thus require a large user base over which to spread the costs. This created a need for growth and long-term thinking that pervades the company. Starting out Amazon struggled to match the buying power of large book retailers such as Barnes & Noble, and instead harnessed the efficiencies of the internet – avoiding staff costs and high-rent real estate charges for stores. As it has grown it has been able to apply increased price pressure on suppliers to generate discounts.

As Amazon moved beyond books it found itself squaring off against the king of retail, Wal-Mart, resulting in price wars with both companies offering deeply discounted mass-market titles.

One of the most contentious tools in Amazon's armory, used to keep prices low, is its ability to avoid levying sales tax in US states where it doesn't have a physical presence. The idea is that consumers self report tax for out-of-state purchases with their annual returns, though in practice few do. Recent legislation in California has brought this simmering debate to a head, with many state legislatures and bricks-and-mortar stores waging battle to remove this advantage. In October 2011, *The Economist* described the coming showdown as 'more complicated than the Boston tea party, but potentially as colorful.' With warehouses, distributors, design centers, and affiliates all over the United States, battle is waging over what constitutes a physical presence. However, whatever the outcome, Amazon has already benefitted for many years and used this advantage to help build its infrastructure and cement its brand values in consumers' minds.

From the start Amazon has been able to avoid the physical limitations of shop shelf space and has operated a network of suppliers working as virtual storerooms. This model has been expanded with Fulfillment By Amazon (FBA), which allows third parties to advertise their inventory with Amazon, and utilize the same infrastructure such as customer service and shipping. On top of this, Amazon's pioneering use of customer reviews and recommendation algorithms has made navigation and selection considerably easier than in a physical store. As a result 30% of the products now sold on the Amazon website are from third parties.

Amazon's success as a customer-centric company is testimony to its single-minded pursuit, against many obstacles, of great customer service. As banks and utility companies have found, running an online business is no guarantee of satisfied customers, in fact often the reverse.

There are many barriers to delivering great customer service online – customers can't visit stores, see and touch the products, or interact with sales people. The key to delivering great service online was, paradoxically, using more, not less, technology. Bezos notes, 'In the physical world, retailers will continue to use technology to reduce costs, but not to transform the customer experience. We too will use technology to reduce costs, but the bigger effect will be using technology to drive adoption and revenue.' To construct a product detail page for a customer, the Amazon software 'calls on between 200 and 300 services to present a highly personalized experience for that customer.'

Instead of attempting to replicate traditional sales experiences, Amazon simply created new ways to communicate and in so doing also exposed the weaknesses of traditional retail – for example by championing the concept of outsourcing the reviewing role to customers, Amazon managed to lower staff costs and increase service quality.

Other ways that Amazon has used the power of an online platform to improve service include the ability to 'Search Inside The Book' which required convincing publishers that providing more online access to their products would boost, not cannibalize, sales. Publishers saw the results, and signed up in droves. Amazon Prime ('free' two-day shipping for a fixed annual fee) addressed two of the downsides of online shopping – unknown delivery time (often 5–7 working days) and the disincentive of additional shipping fees. Finally, 1-Click® Shopping was a patented invention which further lowered the barriers to commerce – customers could now choose a product and have it shipped to them in one click. This idea even resonated with the customer experience gurus at Apple, who liked it so much they licensed the technology.

New Products and Services that Embody Amazon's Approach

Amazon often talks about two types of innovation – incremental and 'clean sheet' initiatives. Bezos sees that:

Ninety-plus percent of the innovation at Amazon is incremental and critical and much less risky. We know how to open new product categories. We know how to open new geographies. That doesn't mean that these things are guaranteed to work, but we have a lot of expertise and a lot of knowledge. We know how to open new fulfillment centers, whether to open one, where to locate it, how big to make it. All of these things based on our operating history are things that we can analyze quantitatively rather than to have to make intuitive judgments.

Amazon Web Services (AWS) and the Kindle are two 'clean sheet' initiatives that are driving new growth.

While an extension from books to other online commerce items seems fairly logical, Amazon's shift to selling access to its own computing resources gave pause for thought. Some wondered how a consumer book retailer could turn its hand to business-to-business enterprise services. The answer of course is that Amazon didn't particularly feel restricted to books. It had built up an impressive infrastructure and spare capacity to cope with peak demands (such as the Christmas season), so why *not* sell it?

AWS allows the company to offer services such as storage and processing power to other companies and developers. This is having a transformative effect on the industry, as businesses can outsource, rather than own, their infrastructure, instantly expanding capacity when needed. It means they can focus their attention on differentiating the customer-facing aspects of their products and services.

Amazon's existing database of millions of stored credit cards, together with an infrastructure that is already accessible to partners, provides a very real opportunity for Amazon to play a defining role in the business of selling and renting digital services as well as physical products. The addition of free movie streaming for customers of its Prime service and its cloud-based music offers are first steps that indicate the company is aggressively going after this opportunity.

The Kindle is an e-book reader introduced in 2007 that uses wireless to allow users to access and download e-books, magazines, newspapers, and online content. Again, the Kindle was a radical product, especially from 'just' a retail company – although this time observers who had witnessed Amazon's existential dexterity were more accepting. Indeed as book lovers Amazon had a reasonable claim to be in this business. Bezos, the product's champion, said, 'The world changed and if we wanted to be the future of books, we would have to learn to build a hardware device.'

The Kindle's promise is, 'Every book ever printed in any language, all available in less than 60 seconds.' This is a smart way of applying metrics to customer delight: it forces the delivery team to think in a holistic way about networks, content owners, and device capabilities to deliver the necessary experience to the user. In fact, it is rumored that insiders are held to a 30-second target. Bezos went on to describe the Kindle's role, highlighting the level of granularity that they were observing (and improving) associated with the seemingly simple job of reading:

We're not trying to create an experience. We want the author to create the experience [. . .]. Our job is to design a perfect device for reading. [. . .] Our job is to provide the experience so you can get books in sixty seconds, so you can carry your whole library with you, so you don't get hand strain, so the device doesn't get hot in your hand, so that it doesn't cause eye strain, so that the battery life lasts a month so you don't get battery anxiety.

The device lets users search the books, make notes, keep bookmarks, see what others have bookmarked, and look up unknown words. Its third iteration offered improved battery life, greater storage of up to 3500 books, and the ability to lend titles. Amazon developed 'Whispersync' to keep each device almost magically in sync, seamlessly finding the place where the book was last read on a different device. One of the more radical features was that they included lifetime wireless access built into the price of certain models.

By May 2011 the Kindle provided readers access to almost a million books. Its impact has been to accelerate a growing shift from physical books to digital books, and places Amazon at the forefront of this trend. The impact in the market has been significant. Although Amazon doesn't discuss the Kindle's revenues, it does say that customers now purchase more electronic books than print books. And perhaps more significantly, a quarter of the emails that Amazon customer service received in response to the Kindle after its release contained the word 'love.'

Much of the company's success has clearly come from organic moves that have led to growth, but Amazon has also made a number of smart acquisitions. After buying happiness-obsessed shoe company www.Zappos.com, Amazon left it alone, respecting the different cultures and resisting the urge to extract 'synergies.' It has made selected investments, such as Living Social – a social commerce service that provides 'daily deals' and has launched its own 'deal of the day' experiment in parallel (My Habit). This allows them bandwidth to experiment as well as to allow innovation to happen outside the company walls.

Future Challenges

Moving forward, many see that Amazon will, at some stage, eclipse Wal-Mart as the world's biggest retailer – certainly the recent economic conditions in the West have served to drive more people to lower-cost direct-to-home services. But future competition is not just about scale. Core elements of the Amazon proposition need to be maintained and improved, for example its recommendation engine, which, despite its leadership position in the industry, appears clumsy and simplistic at times.

A focused Growth Champion that is both adaptable and resilient

Amazon recognized that one of its biggest weaknesses was the perceived lack of customer service in online commerce. By making this its primary objective, Amazon has successfully turned this potential weakness into a strength. It has proved itself a Growth Champion due to the size and scale of its growth, the clarity of its vision, and its ability to reinvent itself. The company now accounts for a third of US e-commerce and is growing twice as fast as online commerce in general. It has also been growing fast internationally: almost half its revenues now come from international sales.

While moving first from books to music and then to other online retailing activities such as cosmetics, clothing, and cars can be all considered incremental innovation, the AWS businesses and the Kindle are entirely different industries – enterprise services and consumer technology hardware, respectively. Traditional retailers, booksellers in particular, were disrupted by Amazon's online efficiencies; it seems likely that this retail engine will also disrupt other outlets.

AWS and the Kindle are expected by analysts to meaningfully contribute to bottom-line results – no easy feat when just delivering 10% growth rate requires additional revenues of over $4 billion annually. A steadfast focus on customer-centricity, coupled with an operational approach that is resilient, yet adaptable, has proved to be a successful recipe for Amazon.

Google

With its launch in 1998, Google changed the face of the internet. Instead of jumbled portal pages brimming with human-derived categories, Google provided a new way in to the web – a blank page with a simple search box. Search was no longer an appendage to a portal; it *was* the portal. Cognitive overload was relieved with Zen-like simplicity, and the web pages it offered up seemed almost magically accurate. For many this represented the first step of a journey in which Google was to become increasingly central to their lives. In May 2011, Google reached a milestone, becoming the first company in history to have over a billion visitors to its sites in a month, according to www.comscoredatamine .com. Google has had a remarkable propensity for solving users' problems, and a unique business approach that can offer inspiration for those looking to grow and monetize an online service business.

The Company Aims to Solve Three Really Hard Problems

The Google mission is to 'organize the world's information and make it universally accessible and useful' and that requires overcoming three challenges.

First, finding information. Although content on the web is growing at an exponential clip, some estimates suggest that only 20% of information in the world is online, the rest is in books, company filing cabinets, on TV, and so on. Indexing the web's billions of pages is a relatively trivial matter compared with finding information not on the web today, and Google is leading the charge. This ambition has driven the acquisition of YouTube in order to access video content and the Google Books project, which began scanning libraries around the world. The second challenge is to make this information accessible over multiple channels. The first two billion people who went online did so primarily via fixed wires and a personal computer; however, the next two billion, most of whom will be in today's developing countries, will connect via their mobile device. This explains the importance of the company's Android mobile operating system, and the acquisition of Motorola Mobility. Finally, Google wants to make information 'useful.' This means going beyond the simple keyword search query to discover what the user actually means. As former CIO Douglas Merrill put it, in an interview in 2007, 'Our goal is to have the result to be not what you asked for, but what you *should* have asked for.'

A Unique Ability to Interpret and Monetize Data

Google is a data-driven technology company, whose core competences are technical rather than service oriented. A number of these competences are unique to Google, hard to replicate, and have a major impact on improving the quality of the end-user experience.

Google's major breakthrough was its Page Rank algorithm that created meaning from links between websites. Now, in addition to Page Rank, Google's search engine uses around 200 factors that determine the relevance of results. These include search terms, synonyms, and website quality. Massive quantities of user data and query logs allow Google to intelligently guess what was meant by a certain request, and improve the experience with spelling correction, or more recently Google Instant – where results are displayed in real time as the user types the letters of their query.

As a result of its search capabilities Google has created new platforms for innovation. Not only does it extract meaning from data it also gives it commercial value. The ability to create value out of search – not only for itself but for other organizations prepared to pay for the benefits that this provides – puts it on the frontline of innovation in the online world. The company sits at the center of an ecosystem, which means that it has visibility of a large amount of data generated by its products such as Google Ad Words, which allows companies to bid for keywords and appear next to relevant search results; and Ad Sense, which allows online publishers to earn revenue by displaying relevant ads on a wide variety of content. Content creators can now get meaningfully paid for the work they are doing.

Processing Complex Auctions in Real Time

The company's Ad Words product was a breakthrough innovation. Google created an auction infrastructure that auctioned all of the keyword slots at the same time, *the instant that a search was made* – billions of times a day. The price the advertiser would pay was determined by an innovative second-place auction – whereby the person who won would pay one cent more than the second-placed bidder. Also the visibility of the ad reflected its attractiveness to previous viewers – making it harder for irrelevant offerings, or those with little user interest – to gain the best positions. This was a novel feature that included the user in what used to be a simple transaction between advertiser and publisher.

Participative Product Development and a Culture of Freedom

Google's two founders, Sergey Brin and Larry Page, are strong advocates of user-centric design. Google makes considerable use of A/B testing where new ideas are tested out on a fraction of users and the results are collected and analyzed. Many of Google's services have been in 'beta' for a number of years – nearly finished but not quite. Users have been encouraged to help refine pretty much all of the add-on products from Google Finance and Google Scholar to Maps, Mail, and Picasa. For Google 90% or so has been good enough to go public, knowing that users will help finish things off and suggest the adjustments needed. Participative product development is very much part of the core Google strategy.

Google famously allows many of its employees 20% of their time to work on their own projects. Other companies have explored similar approaches – 3M developed a 15% rule in the 1950s – but none have become as well known, or with as many documented successes such as Gmail, Google Suggest, and Google News. Company lore has it that research scientist Krishna Bharat conceived Google News after the September 11, 2001 attacks, as he struggled to follow news across his 15 favorite websites. He created a project that aggregated news from these sites, and shared it with other employees. Management picked it up and this became Google News; one of Google's most popular offerings today and one that his team still manages.

Google's vice president of consumer products, Marissa Mayer, told a Stanford University audience that during a six-month period of analysis, 50% of the products and features that Google launched actually came out of this 20% time. However, the power of this idea probably comes mostly from the way it epitomizes a culture of trust and freedom. As Mayer explained:

The key isn't that it's 20%, or 1 day a week, it's that our engineers and product developers see that and they realize this is a company that really trusts them, that really wants them to be creative, and really wants them to explore whatever it is that they want to explore. And it's that license to do whatever they want that really ultimately fuels a huge amount of creativity and a huge amount of innovation.

Three Examples of Innovation: Gmail, Android, and Google Books

Gmail, created by Google developer Paul Buchheit as an internal project, launched on April Fool's Day, 2004, and offered so much storage many considered it a hoax. By April 2011 Gmail had attracted 220 million users worldwide. The company is now offering email among a suite of products targeting the enterprise segment, competing directly with Microsoft. The product was radical when introduced, not just because of the storage, but because it was a very sophisticated, fast and easy to use web experience that was easy to use. It also introduced the idea of selling adverts to users based on the content of their emails. Although some predicted that users would reject this 'privacy invasion,' concerns quickly faded, and another star product was born.

As internet access increasingly goes global, Google has needed access to mobile devices. Andy Rubin, Google's vice president of mobile, came to the company after Google bought his previous mobile company, Android, and used that as the basis for a new operating system. According to Nielsen in Q4 2011, 60% of those who purchased a new handset in the United States bought a smartphone (i.e. one with advanced internet and multimedia features and able to download applications), and Android's share of that was 52%. Rubin announced on Twitter in June 2011 that Google was activating 500,000 devices a day – up from 100,000 at the same time in 2010. Google's bid for Motorola Mobility for US$12.5 billion is another signal that mobile will be one of the main growth drivers of the future. Buying Motorola seems to be an acknowledgment on Google's part that it must control the experience from software to hardware in order to deliver the best experience. It is also recognition that as a newcomer in the mobile space, it doesn't have the deep patent portfolio of its competitors, which may result in the need to pay large license fees on every device. It can now create Android phones to its exact specifications and take advantage of the latest advances in the operating system, in the same way that Apple does. When CEO Larry Page says that buying Motorola will 'supercharge' Android that is probably what he means.

The objective of the Books project was to unlock the data hidden in books, and make them part of the searchable universe. The background, as outlined in Stephen Levy's book, *In the Plex*, is typical Google: a bold idea from one of the founders, rejected by other smart minds as impractical, that was tested to generate data. Levy describes Page and Mayer working together with a scanner in the office one night, figuring out how long, and how much money, it would take to scan all the books in the world. The Book project became one of Google's most contentious projects. Without right-holders' permission, the company proceeded to digitize thousands of books, which then turned into a major public relations disaster, as the company was seen as out of touch, and exploiting struggling authors. Eventually, they reached an agreement with the publishers and Google Search now offers access to millions of books. With characteristic precision, Google estimated in 2010 that there were 129,864,880 unique books in the world, and by October 2010 had scanned 15 million of them.

An Innovation Approach that is Part Montessori, Part Michael Moritz

Google's approach to innovation can be thought of as two separate processes – 'left brain' and 'right brain' – that balance each other out. It starts with an anarchic and unfocused celebration of creativity and individuality, which the founders ascribe in part to their education in the famously creative Montessori school system. This meets a highly analytical, data-driven process that reviews the portfolio, culls losers, and doubles down on winning ideas. In this way the company operates more like the famed venture capitalists Michael Moritz and John Doerr

– two titans of Silicon Valley investing, both of whom joined Google's board with their $25 million venture investment in 1999.

An article by Peter Sims in the *Wall Street Journal* suggested, only half joking, the existence of a 'Montessori Mafia' – due to the large number of some of the creative and successful alumni such as Amazon founder Jeff Bezos and Wikipedia inventor Jimmy Wales. Page and Brin, readily credit their schooling: 'We both went to a Montessori school, and I think it was part of that training of not following rules and orders, and being self-motivated, questioning what's going on in the world, doing things a little bit differently.' There's a sense of irreverence and fun at Google that is most palpable in a visit to the Mountain View headquarters: open meeting areas, free food, bright colors and games adorn the offices, and a dinosaur skeleton greets visitors outside – a daily reminder of the desire not to follow the herd and become extinct.

The other side of the Google brain is more systematic. Chairman Eric Schmidt, in an interview with the McKinsey Quarterly in 2008, says Google aims to be a 'systematic innovator at scale.' By this he means, 'we can systemize the approach – we can actually get our groups to innovate. We don't necessarily know this month which one [will succeed]. But we know it's portfolio theory. We have enough groups that a few [innovations] will pop up.'

Google's innovation approach has allowed it to maintain a sense of freedom and autonomy for its employees even as it has scaled to a head count of over 20,000. However, this is business creativity as an extreme sport; not necessarily appropriate for the many companies that need more structured hierarchies, don't have such a flexible business model, or have less expertise.

Anti-trust and Privacy Backlash

As Google has grown, handling over 70% of searches in some countries, it has attracted some criticism. Despite the 'Don't be evil' mantra, Google has made a number of missteps. It faltered over privacy of user data, sharing a user's most regular contacts on Google Buzz, and the capturing of personal information over unsecured networks by the Street Maps team. In the current rush to use social networks and enable users to share broadly, there may be further tension. In a quote, later clarified as a joke, Eric Schmidt told the *Wall Street Journal*, 'Every young person one day will be entitled automatically to change his or her name on reaching adulthood in order to disown youthful hijinks stored on their friends' social media sites.' He also told the *Atlantic* magazine, 'We know where you are. We know where you've been. We can more or less know what you're thinking about.'

Required: Improved Social Skills

After Larry Page formally took the CEO title, he reportedly mandated that 25% of the annual bonus check for all Google employees would depend on how well the company does in its social efforts. Google's senior vice president in charge of social told *Wired*, 'We're transforming Google itself into a social destination at a level and scale that we've never attempted – orders of magnitude more investment, in terms of people, than any previous project.' The idea of Circles, a key feature where users create subgroups, would appeal to Google management: let the users do the difficult job of categorizing their life and observing this taxonomy – data that could be useful in any number of ways.

To many observers, Google's strategy has been hard to discern: sandwiched between the lofty goals of organizing the world's information and the reality of many disparate consumer services. In sum, Google's strategy can be thought of as extending the breadth and depth of its interactions with people. A broader reach comes from a plethora of services built off its core search and advertising platforms that share a common goal of increasing users and page views. And deeper engagement comes from using an internal innovation marketplace for ideas, together with data analytics, to make the services ever more relevant, efficient, and personalized. Google's challenge will be to ensure that its algorithms and business model stay relevant in an increasingly fragmented, yet increasingly social world.

Key Insights – Amazon and Google

While Amazon innovates in a more traditional way, with incremental and major initiatives being driven largely by the corner office, Google's approach is flatter, less hierarchical. Google's innovation model is more like a seesaw, balancing individuals' zest for freedom to experiment with an actuary's zeal for the numbers. Both approaches have delivered breakthrough results and changed their industries to benefit consumers and their business partners.

Amazon's approach requires a particular confidence to understand the mind of the customer, and place large bets – such as in the infrastructure build out – to become the basis for future growth. This confidence is evidenced by the focus and clarity of mission, and the way that a new skill set can be protected and developed if it comes with top-down blessing. It's easy to imagine there were plenty of book lovers at Amazon, though less likely that people pushing e-readers would have got much attention without support from the top.

Google's more disparate approach risks shareholders' ire, as it can appear unfocused. Its democratic approach may limit new ideas to those the company is already good at, and those its employees like. Also its approach favors new services that can instantly garner online customer data, which may not be realistic in many sectors. A bundled device and service like Amazon's Kindle is expensive and slow to produce, requires complex outsourcing contracts, and needs a marketing campaign targeting to a more traditional, slow-to-adopt demographic. This is not the stuff of 20% decentralized projects, but of daily CEO involvement and sponsorship.

Despite their relative youth, both Amazon and Google function as 'grown-up' companies, and youthful exuberance is no longer acceptable to the public as an excuse when things go wrong. Amazon fights hard – and some would say dirty, such as in the ugly spat over sales tax – but it has done a good job at conveying the impression that it is doing so on behalf of its customers. Google's errors, by contrast, often result in harsher backlash from a media and public in awe of its prowess but still not entirely sure about its motives.

So while both companies offer differing approaches to competing and winning in the online space, together they offer a rich source of learning that can be applied across a variety of industries. In a world awash with data, those companies that find new ways to make sense of it, create greater insights into stakeholder needs, and develop credibility and trust will be well positioned for growth.

Amazon

Growth Impact

A massively efficient and high-revenue
business model owning the online retail space

Distinctive Competence

Delivering evident customer satisfaction via
proprietary technologies and partnerships

Underlying Capabilities

Customer centricity	Clean sheet innovation	Adaptability to accommodate change

Google

Growth Impact

The world's leading and most
profitable information organization

Distinctive Competence

Participative product development supporting
incessant adjacent sector disruption

Underlying Capabilities

Solving users' problems	Interpreting and monetizing data	Processing complex auctions in real time

Narayana Hrudayalaya	KEY DATA
Number of operating theaters (2011)	24
Number of major cardiac operations per day (2011)	30
Share of cardiac operations in India (2011)	12%
Average cost of cardiac operation (2011)	$1800
Number of countries sending patients(2011)	73
Number of telemedicine centres (2011)	500
Total global medical tourism revenue (2010)	$50 billion
Global deaths due to cardiovascular disease (2010)	30%

Novo Nordisk	KEY DATA
Total sales (2010)	DKK 60.7 billion
Average sales growth p.a. (2005–2010)	13.2%
Net income (2010)	DKK 14.4 billion
Average net income growth p.a. (2005–2010)	19.6%
Sales per employee (2010)	DKK 2.0 million
R&D investment (2010)	DKK 9.6 billion
R&D intensity (2010)	15.8%
Average share price growth p.a. (2005–2010)	31%

CHAPTER 10

Narayana Hrudayalaya and Novo Nordisk

Reinventing healthcare

Novo Nordisk and Narayana Hrudayalaya have both outpaced their larger competitors in the healthcare sector by changing the way they work with the broader ecosystem. They have pioneered different approaches to business model innovation – Novo Nordisk through building a world-leading interconnection of drug delivery and education; and Narayana Hrudayalaya by completely reinventing surgery for scale. Both have delivered the goods in this highly competitive arena. They have become the benchmarks for the future but have done so with different emphases from each other.

For many years the world's healthcare systems and most of the participating organizations have been less interested in healthcare and more focused on sick-care. Dealing with patients after they have had an accident, caught a disease, or fallen into ill health has been where the vast majority of money has been spent and so where many companies have prioritized their activities. Consequently after years of investment and progress, we now have multiple high-technology systems capable of repairing our bodies and extending our lives for pretty much as long as we, or our healthcare system, can afford the bills.

Now that there are more of us on the planet, and on average we are living longer, the system is starting to undergo stress. Add in increasingly unhealthily lifestyles, and it is not surprising that the incidence of many chronic diseases and the associated costs are spiraling. The United States clearly cannot afford to maintain a system where 80% of spending is focused on the final year or so of life, and many other countries with high dependency ratios due to imbalanced population demographics are also struggling to meet healthcare costs. Also emerging countries face the need to deal not only with the challenges of endemic diseases but also the lifestyle challenges of increasing wealth and urbanization including increasing incidence of diabetes and heart disease.

It has become clear that the business models that supported the growth of big pharmaceuticals and their counterparts in medical devices cannot continue. Nations and individuals need to get control of their healthcare spending and liabilities and, although issues like Medicare in the United States receive lots of political attention, little true progress has been made in fixing the system. As Jack Lord, CEO of Navigenics and former CEO of Humana said at the start of the 2010 Future Agenda program, 'The next decade is not likely to be the time for change, but instead a time that "stressors" on the healthcare system become progressively evident.'

Within this context a select number of companies have been seeking to change the system and reinvent healthcare. In this chapter we are profiling two that have not only made the greatest impact, but have also become successful growth businesses. Focused on different issues with different innovations, Narayana Hrudayalaya and Novo Nordisk have used radical thinking to change the health-care status quo. From its base in India, Narayana Hrudayalaya has used a combination of business model and process innovation to lower the cost of cardiac surgery and in doing so has revolutionized the access, volume, and reach of its facilities to become one of the fastest-growing healthcare businesses in the world. Novo Nordisk, on the other hand, has not only taken the leadership in developing drugs for diabetes, but has also extended its focus to preventing the disease just as much as treating it, and so has led the way in the sick-care to healthcare migra-tion which many now recognize is an imperative for the whole sector.

Narayana Hrudayalaya

The Indian healthcare industry has growth at a rapid pace and, with revenues of over $50 billion annually, is now the country's second-largest service sector employer, providing jobs to about 4.5 million people directly or indirectly. It is forecast to grow at an annual rate of around 20% and so double its size to $100 billion by 2015 and $280 billion by 2022. Apollo Hospitals was among the first to start the trend of corporate-run hospitals in India, and others have followed. Today the healthcare industry in India is moving rapidly towards becoming highly organized with increasing efficiency of healthcare delivery. Narayana Hrudayalaya is a major player in this market and has become one of the star organizations in terms of the impact it is having.

Dr. Devi Prasad Shetty was Mother Teresa's cardiac surgeon and is the founder and chairman of the Narayana Hrudayalaya Group. His vision is 'to enable every man, woman and child to have access to high tech healthcare within the next 10 to 15 years, including in the poorest regions of the world.' With over 5000 beds in India and an aim of growing to over 30,000 in the next five years, Narayana

Hrudayalaya is well on the way to being one of the leading healthcare businesses in the country. Add on opening facilities close to the lucrative US market in 2012 and expansion into many other Asian and African countries and future ambitions are significant.

As of 2011, Narayana Hrudayalaya is only 10 years old but has quickly grown to become Asia's largest cardiac care center and the world's largest cancer hospital. Narayana Hrudayalaya Health City in Bangalore, spread over 25 acres, and the Rabindranath Tagore International Institute of Cardiac Sciences in Kolkata, are the group's two heart hospitals. Together, they perform about 12% of heart surgeries in India. Worldwide, the Narayana Hrudayalaya Group also performs the largest number of pediatric heart surgeries, providing cardiac care to children from 73 countries. From Dr. Shetty's perspective, 'The first heart surgery was performed over a hundred years ago; however, today, only 8% of the world's population can afford it. Similarly, most of the modern healthcare interventions are not accessible to nearly 90% of the world's population.' The Narayana Hrudayalaya Group is committed to changing this and is driving growth through innovation to bring healthcare to everyone.

Dynamics of Innovation

The average cost of open-heart surgery in the United States is between $20,000 and $100,000 depending on the level of complexity. Narayana Hrudayalaya's flagship hospital charges, on average, $2000 for the same, if not better, service. In 2009, the *Wall Street Journal* reported that 'Narayana's 42 cardiac surgeons performed 3174 cardiac bypass surgeries in 2008, more than double the 1367 the Cleveland Clinic, a U.S. leader, did in the same year. Narayana's surgeons also operated on 2777 pediatric patients, more than double the 1,026 surgeries performed at Children's Hospital Boston.' Compared to the US benchmarks, Narayana is both cheaper and delivers higher volumes.

But what about the quality? Does volume compromise the quality of patient care? It would seem not. According to the *Wall Street Journal*, Jack Lewin, CEO of the American College of Cardiology, sees that 'Narayana hospital has used high volumes to improve quality: For the simple reason that doctors are getting more experience.' The large number of patients passing through Narayana Hrudaya-laya's facilities allows individual doctors to focus on one or two specific types of cardiac surgeries and so develop particular skills. 'This is simply not possible in relatively smaller hospitals in India and other countries, including the US.' Narayana Hrudayalaya has not only become the best place to have heart surgery but it has also become the go-to facility for all aspiring cardiac surgeons globally. Nowhere else can you get so much experience and develop your expertise so quickly.

How is this achieved? The answer is process innovation wrapped up in some interesting business model innovation. Dr. Shetty's view is that 'Japanese companies reinvented the process of making cars. That's what we're doing in health care: What health care needs is process innovation, not product innovation.' Focusing on reinventing the whole surgical procedure, eliminating inefficiencies, and optimizing quality has enabled the company to reap the benefits of economies of scale. By driving up volumes, including that of sophisticated heart surgery, the group has succeeded in driving down the cost. 'It's all about numbers. Because we do a large number of operations our overheads are distributed over a larger number of patients. Because we implant the largest number of heart valves in the world we get heart valves at a lesser price.' The company has looked at all aspects of the flow and costs of each type of cardiac surgery and everything that can be improved has been optimized.

Volumes create the potential for enormous savings, as Narayana Hrudayalaya is able to cut costs significantly by buying medical equipment directly from manufacturers. Medical equipment also has higher utilization rates, typically used 15–20 times a day, 3–5 times higher than a comparable hospital in the United States. With healthcare being such a high capital-intensive business, Narayana Hrudayalaya has shown innovation in breaking through the high capital cost structure. It does not pay for laboratory machines that cost as much as $40,000. If manufacturers want to supply the organization, they have to contend with making a profit from consumables used by the equipment in return for leasing the machine free to the hospital. Given the volumes involved, few manufacturers have refused this option. In addition, building hospitals capable of profits at such low prices also requires innovative thinking. Low-cost construction techniques, often including prefabrication, enable Narayana Hrudayalaya to build each 300-bed hospital for US$6 million in less than six months.

Adopting a pricing model similar to that used by Avarind Healthcare, India's leading eye-care organization, Narayana Hrudayalaya has also introduced differential pricing with poor people paying less than the rich and overseas customers paying a different rate still. Indeed the success of the business has been such that many foreigners now regularly travel from Europe and the United States to India for operations and, alongside cataract operations, cardiac surgery is at the forefront of this shift. As the overall package costs for flights, hospital stay, and surgery are between 5% and 10% of US prices, the savings for individuals and national healthcare systems are significant. Not surprising then that, given the quality and cost dynamics, a growing number of insurance companies now promote medical tourism as a good option to their customers. In 2010 over one million US citizens went to India for healthcare. As one patient from Atlanta put it, 'I was expecting something extraordinary and that's exactly what I got. The expertise, the team player approach – all of this is unusual in the US.' By 2012 Deloitte forecast that the number of US medical tourists to India will top 1.6m and by 2013 the overall Indian medical tourism is expected to be worth over $2 billion.

The new 2000-bed Narayana Hrudayalaya facility opening in the Cayman Islands shows how the company is working with governments to further enhance the opportunities from US medical tourists. By having highly efficient hospitals at locations nearer to the main markets, flight costs and times are significantly reduced and the benefits for patients even greater. At the same time the Caymans get world-class facilities for locals who no longer need to travel to the United States for their operations. Alongside expansion in India, this 'closer to the market' approach is driving much of the company's other expansion plans.

The Narayana Hrudayalaya Difference – Leading Cardiac Expertise and Eliminating Waste

Although other Indian companies are successfully driving down the cost of healthcare by focusing on reinventing processes for the 'bottom of the pyramid' market, none have achieved the level of success as Narayana Hrudayalaya. Partly this is down to the area of primary emphasis and partly due to the culture of incessant optimization.

By choosing cardiac surgery as its core area of focus, with the volumes of patients it has passing through its facilities, Narayana Hrudayalaya has been able to build up world-leading expertise and do so at a profit. Even though it charges 40% of the average cost of coronary artery bypass surgery at other Indian private hospitals, Narayana Hrudayalaya's volume ensures that the business's margins are very good. High utilization of the best equipment and specialized surgeons ensure that the company is seen globally as well as nationally as the pre-eminent facility for cardiac surgery. Although cost is important and the business model allows this to be attractive at all levels, the high-quality recognition is paramount.

The second distinctive competence in optimizing the process is a combination of analysis and culture. While the initial reinvention of the processes surrounding the preparation, cardiac operation, and aftercare resulted from a different way of thinking, ongoing optimization is focused on incremental elimination of wasted time and resources. For example, the company operates a Physician Accountability system, which every evening sends each doctor an SMS that gives a breakdown of their individual profit/loss statement. 'Most hospitals, including in developed countries, often display a careless attitude to conserving resources as patients are charged for consumables. Narayana does not believe in such waste, even if it comes to stitch thread left on the spool.' Every doctor is individually focused on maximizing his effectiveness whether this is in the quality and speed of operations or the resources used in the theater.

New Growth Platforms

As well as expanding its core cardiac surgery facilities across India and other markets, Narayana Hrudayalaya is also involved in other high-growth areas including cancer treatment, neurology, organ transplant, orthopedic and reconstructive surgery, vision and dental care, tissue bank and stem cell research. A key catalyst in adding new specialties has been the development of the health city concept – a conglomeration of hospitals in one campus. Health cities further support volume and scale in treatment, and lower the cost of healthcare – with all the care, support, and labs being shared across many specialties. There are currently five Narayana Hrudayalaya health cities in India, with many more under construction or in planning.

Narayana Hrudayalaya is also innovating its approach to different segments of the market. It has established a unit to work directly with large corporations providing a single point of contact that handles all aspects of healthcare for corporate clients. Although a common feature in other industries, for many in the healthcare sector this is another step forward in optimization and simplicity.

Two other developments are also worth noting:

Telemedicine

McKinsey estimates that the global mobile health business will soon be worth over $50 billion a year and India is one of the primary markets. Making healthcare accessible to all in a vast country like India, with its varied geographic and social-economic regions, is a huge challenge. The Indian Space Research Organization (ISRO) has done pioneering work by partnering with leading healthcare providers and various state governments in making healthcare accessible in the rural and remote parts of the country. With the satellite communication now being supplemented by high-speed mobile broadband and wider penetration of simple mobile connectivity, advanced medical services are able to reach previously inaccessible areas.

Narayana Hrudayalaya is a partner in a major program that kicked off in remote areas of India and which is now being extended to other regions. While ISRO delivers the IT access, Narayana Hrudayalaya and participating hospitals provide the infrastructure and resources to maintain the system. This telemedicine network has matured into an operational system and now covers 332 hospitals – 299 rural health centers connected to 33 specialty hospitals located in major cities.

Narayana Hrudayalaya and the Asia Heart Foundation have also partnered to create a network of Intensive Care Units and telemedicine centers providing

24-hour support in treating patients and rendering specialty outpatient consultations.

As Dr. Shetty points out, 'the beauty of telemedicine is that it makes ordinary people do extraordinary things – ordinary rural healthcare providers, using tele-medicine, have treated patients suffering with myocardial infarction, ischemia, and unstable anginas successfully with assistance from senior cardiologists in the hub hospitals located in the larger cities.'

Micro health insurance

Another area of interest for Dr. Shetty and Narayana Hrudayalaya is the potential transformation that India will go through in the arena of healthcare insurance. Similar to the change that the United States went through in the 1970s with the growth of the insurance industry, Medicare, and Medicaid, he predicts 'govern-ments in emerging countries, including India, will play a significant role in providing access to health insurance to the masses within the next ten years.' He sees this as a key enabler to fulfill his vision of providing high-tech healthcare for all.

The Narayana Hrudayalaya Group is already innovating in this sector through micro health insurance. It partnered with the Karnataka state government about eight years ago to launch Yashaswini, a micro health insurance product, targeting India's rural poor farming community, at a staggering price of just 5 rupees, or 11 cents, a month. They have demonstrated the efficacy of micro health insur-ance for 1.7 million farmers and now cover nearly 3 million farmers today.

Nearly a third of Narayana Hrudayalaya's patients are enrolled in this insurance plan, which reimburses the hospital $1200 for each cardiac surgery. That is about $300 below the hospital's break-even cost of $1500 per surgery. The hospital makes up the difference by charging $2400 to the 40% of its patients in the general ward who aren't enrolled in the plan. An additional 30% who opt for private or semi-private rooms pay as much as $5000. Today, Yashaswini is the world's largest self-funded health insurance plan, and is being studied by the International Labour Organization and the World Bank for applicability worldwide.

Future Growth

Narayana Hrudayalaya is increasingly seen as the global poster child for integrated business models and process innovation. In a sector steeped in legacy procedures and cozy relationships between providers, the company has brought about systemic change. Focusing primarily on the needs of the patient and rewriting the rulebook on healthcare expense, it has developed and refined an approach to cardiac care that is now spreading quickly into other areas. What is more, having created a solution at the bottom of the pyramid that delivers as good results as you can find at the top, Narayana Hrudayalaya has almost single-handedly kick-started mass medical tourism for serious healthcare services.

Going forward, others are clearly out to mirror Narayana Hrudayalaya's success and many challengers will emerge not only from India but also from other countries. However, the healthcare market is huge and growing and so, even if new entrants do arrive on the scene, the potential for a leader in the field such as Narayana Hrudayalaya is unlikely to be diminished. The anticipated success of the nearby offshore facilities in the Caymans will be pivotal in opening up greater access for the wealthiest healthcare system in the world – the United States – and may well lead to similar models close to other high-income markets. However, what may be more transformational will be the moves into other Asian and African countries where Narayana Hrudayalaya's philosophy, approach, and model can potentially deliver far greater change.

Novo Nordisk

The pharmaceuticals sector generates revenues well in excess of $350 billion a year. Companies like Pfizer and Johnson & Johnson are the biggest hitters, each turning over more than $50 billion, but others such as Merck, Eli Lilly, and Abbott are not far behind. However, as an industry, the business model that drove growth has proven to be unsustainable, with most companies facing significant patent expiry cliffs. The ambition is to create the next blockbuster, or more recently, the exploration of targeted medicines with specialized prescribers – small markets but high prices.

Companies within the sector have tried a variety of different approaches to rekindle the business model of old, but without great success. GSK, for example, introduced Centres of Excellence for Drug Discovery, based on trying to mimic the success of biotech start-ups. Eli Lilly developed the InnoCentive open innovation model to put challenges out on the web and get experts from around the world to solve them, for a fee.

However, the company that has been doing the most to change the industry is, in many eyes, Novo Nordisk. Today it is challenging how we think about diabetes, and rather than just providing drugs to manage the disease, it is investing in reducing diabetes altogether. For a pharma company this looks like eating its own lunch. If it is seeking to prevent diabetes, what does this mean for its diabetes business?

Novo Nordisk has been at the forefront of looking beyond the typical drug horizon. It was exploring the patient role as far back as the 1980s when it developed its pen-like preloaded injection systems. These offered a much more convenient model of delivering insulin compared to the traditional hypodermic, allowing easy delivery in 30 seconds versus the minutes and complications of the needle.

Whilst other companies were focused on enhancing the drug, Novo Nordisk looked at the patient experience and how to deliver a better clinical outcome – which resulted in improved uptake and treatment compliance and the company taking 40% of the market.

Innovation and Growth

Innovation is the lifeblood of pharmaceuticals companies in a way that some other industries don't experience. With patent expiry an issue for all major companies, they can pretty much expect to lose their market, so growth is therefore about innovation processes that favor big bets. Where Novo excels is in both maintaining a very healthy portfolio that has driven consistent growth, and in going broad on looking at diabetes. Rather than focus all its energy on the molecule pipeline, it has developed devices and applications, and beyond that looked at engaging thousands of interested parties in an exploration of diabetes prevention.

Novo Nordisk has a clear statement of intent – 'Our aspiration is to defeat diabetes by finding better methods of diabetes prevention, detection and treatment.' This drives the innovation agenda and the growth agenda.

Diabetes is a major and growing disease area linked closely to the rising obesity challenge. Today diabetes affects over 285 million people and may impact over 430 million by 2030. Whilst most efforts have focused on treatment, Novo Nordisk, to its great credit, has stepped beyond the lucrative market of drug sales to help people be aware of and act to reduce their likelihood of becoming diabetic. As CEO, Lars Rebien Sørensen, sees it, 'only by offering and advocating the right solutions for diabetes care will we be seen as a responsible company. If we say "drugs, drugs, drugs," they will say; "give us a break!"' Novo Nordisk has made it an express purpose to solve diabetes, 'we could solve the problem of diabetes in my lifetime – even if that sounds strange as this is where we make our living. But if it can be done, we must be the ones to do it. With all our technological progress it must surely be possible to cure diabetes, and with all our knowledge and expertise it would be a crime if we did not try to find the solution. After all, being there for our patients is our express goal, and we know that their greatest wish is good health. So we must – and indeed want to – do our utmost to solve the riddle and then we'll have to find another way of making our living.'

It is difficult to find a comparable statement of intent in the industry or indeed elsewhere. It drives the sense of purpose within Novo Nordisk and has led to stellar financial performance, experiencing strong growth for over 10 years, with insulin delivering over 75% of total sales for the company. In insulin, with over half the world market, they are the reference point and the benchmark for the sector.

In achieving its growth success over recent years, executives in Novo Nordisk cite three key areas where they believe the company is operating ahead of its peers. These are: the clarity of its mission and sense of purpose; a deeper and broader focus on patients' needs; and innovative and meaningful engagement of stakeholders around the key issues and challenges.

The Novo Mission

Novo Nordisk is a company with a typically Scandinavian sense of a company's role in society, characterized by its use of the triple bottom line approach of economic viability + social responsibility + environmental soundness. While this notion is used by quite a few companies, in Novo Nordisk it lines up well with what is called internally 'The Novo Nordisk Way of Management,' which preceded its adoption of the triple bottom line approach. A set of guidelines and beliefs about how the company should be, it starts with a clear vision – 'Novo Nordisk is changing diabetes' – then describes the underpinning values and the structures and approaches that manage and ensure Novo Nordisk respects its core principles.

For Novo Nordisk this formalizes the commitment to lead the fight against diabetes including the effective prevention, early diagnosis, and optimal treatment to improve the health of patients. In other pharmaceuticals this might be seen as a bit of PR, but in Novo Nordisk it has clearly driven the direction over the years. At a drug level it has meant the extension of the portfolio into more advanced insulin treatments, looking earlier up the chain of insulin treatment to tackle pre-insulin and pre-diabetic conditions, and the development of anti-obesity related drugs that help reduce food intake and manage weight: 'By better controlling obesity we can reduce the likelihood of people developing type-2 diabetes.'

The 'Novo Nordisk is changing diabetes' vision has acted as a clear cultural reinforcement and given employees a way of managing and understanding the nature of the decisions they need to make. It is also set up to create choice and local decision making, not a hierarchically imposed way of answering questions, so it does not strip out the complexity, but rather empowers individuals to make sense and give direction to their choice.

Customer Focus

Beyond the direct molecule level Novo Nordisk has also led the development of innovative delivery mechanisms such as the recently launched Flex Pen and the NovoPen Echo, designed specifically with children in mind. What makes this of particular importance is less the specific technology that sits around it, than the fact that Novo Nordisk looked beyond the typical horizon of a drug manufacturer and explored the wider patient experience. The Flex Pen is designed to make self-injection easier and so helps improve compliance to insulin treatment and reduces the risk of complication. With this move the competing solution became irrelevant as a simple pre-loaded pen device removed many of the complications associated with regular injection using hypodermics.

The ability to see the challenge, to cross from drug design to patient interface is a clear outcome of the Novo approach. Thanks to the insight around the pen the company became the 'diabetes care company' instead of an insulin supplier and this shifted the focus away from the direct cost of insulin.

Further out still from the classic drug delivery approach has been the proactive development of tools to help physicians. In 2010 Novo launched the first ever insulin-dosing guide app that allows physicians to look up dosing guidelines and blood glucose goals for patients via their iPhone.

The ability to define a clear mission that resonates with the cultural context of the company has been critical to driving innovation and growth. It is easy to imagine such a broad and inspirational ambition being dismissed as 'management speak,' but something about the culture and history of the company, the evolving capabilities and success of its workforce, and its heritage in Denmark have contrived to turn a simple phrase into a clear, compelling, and guiding ambition.

Engaging Stakeholders

The broad 'Novo Nordisk is changing diabetes' vision also led to a series of far-reaching programs that look at how diabetes can be contained. This started back in 2001 with the company recognizing the need to engage the broader community (GPs, nurses, other healthcare professionals, and patients) in how diabetes care could be improved. This led to the DAWN study (Diabetes Attitudes, Wishes, and Needs), the largest diabetes study of its kind ever conducted, involving more than 5400 people with diabetes and 3800 healthcare professionals. Initiated by Novo Nordisk, in collaboration with the International Diabetes Federation, its most significant insights were that people with diabetes suffered from different types of emotional distress and poor psychological well-being, which are major contributing factors to the problems of diabetes management. The findings were notable, but what is more important is the Novo Nordisk response. In order to increase internal understanding of the findings Novo Nordisk set a target to get 60% of all its employees in relevant areas to discuss the study with a person/people with diabetes within the first year.

The DAWN initiative brought about a different understanding of the diabetes ecosystem, most significantly the need to treat the person as much as the disease. This gave rise to a series of new approaches including a program of training providing primary care physicians with understanding and skills about the psychological aspects of diabetes treatment and care, which is integrated into the structures of many countries' healthcare procedures.

The organization has built up a bank of goodwill both in its engagement in the approach, and also in its strong ethos of support for the healthcare community. People are drawn to the company, have a strong sense of their commitment to the cause, and so contribute more fully and with greater willingness. Arguably they also seek to collaborate and share more fully with Novo Nordisk than with other pharmaceutical companies. The overall impact is that the company is able to get better insight more quickly than others, and with its higher ambitions, create outcomes that are more thoughtful and impactful, thus reinforcing people's perspectives that this is the healthcare organization to work with.

The Novo Nordisk USP

Novo is not the first company to engage with stakeholders, focus on the customer, and have a clearly articulated vision. It might be the first drugs company that has brought this mix together, and is almost certainly the first to apply it with such clear impact – a continuously growing revenues performance over at least a decade, dominance in its chosen field of specialization, and a patient/healthcare professional credit bank second to none. As Lise Kingo, chief of staff, sees it, 'we are seeing increasing evidence of a clear correlation of actions as a responsible and sustainability driven business and our performance, measured by conventional yardsticks such as operational profits and return on investment in capital.'

At a purely financial level Novo Nordisk has demonstrated an ability to continuously grow its business, delivering against internal targets of 15% growth from operating profits. Its performance from this perspective is one of the best in the industry, not least because it is driven not from one or two super blockbusters, but from a plethora of products. Its success has been built upon its ability to define a therapeutic area in its broadest sense and look for ways to impact on it. Where it stands out as a Growth Champion is in how it extends beyond the remit of other pharmaceutical companies and has taken on a mission to significantly impact diabetes prevention – and not necessarily through drugs.

It is exploring a space which is created by a social desire for wellness combined with the economic reality of burgeoning healthcare costs and significant economic deficits. Whilst other companies are still talking about 'three blockbusters a year' Novo is tackling a bigger challenge with a much more diversified set of tools.

Looking Ahead

Although in a very strong position, Novo Nordisk does have a number of future challenges to deal with. Foremost of these is that it is very 'one-therapeutic' dependant. The company could potentially be exposed to a significant external breakthrough in diabetes that would threaten revenues. Novo is addressing this in two ways. Firstly by spreading the portfolio and expanding up the diabetic intervention chain, looking at pre-insulin treatments and obesity more generally. Secondly it is also expanding into the diabetes prevention space outside of drug delivery.

Another major challenge concerns rising total healthcare cost. For all pharmaceutical companies there is a day of reckoning around how will this be managed. Novo Nordisk is perhaps more insulated than most because of the growth of diabetes in the developing world coupled with the rising wealth of those countries. However, it also has to consider how treatment will be paid for and how choices can be made easier for the healthcare authorities.

The third challenge is in innovating around the broader impact that the company is having. The approach adopted from DAWN onwards is in many ways the answer to the previous two challenges. As Novo develops effective answers to diabetes prevention this firstly renders increasingly irrelevant the questions of insulin innovation, and secondly is likely to be a very palatable answer to health-care authorities – cost of prevention is likely to be lower than cost of chronic treatment by orders of magnitude. As Novo explores this path, from a growth perspective the challenge it faces is the kind of business models it builds off the back of it. It is likely that this will look very different to the business of running a drug development company.

Key Insights – Narayana Hrudayalaya and Novo Nordisk

Narayana Hrudayalaya and Novo Nordisk are understandably attracting attention as governments and healthcare organizations look for future models of the sector. Both are seen as pushing boundaries not only in terms of strategy and business models but also in terms of philosophy and purpose. Narayana Hrudayalayas is built on the premise that we can use our talents and resources more effectively in serving the poor and providing them with quality healthcare. Novo Nordisk sees that healthcare is more than just sick care and so has become as much focused on education and prevention as it has on improving the cure and dealing with chronic disease. Although neither is necessarily pushing the boundaries of technological innovation in their spaces, what they are doing is using appropriate technology within the context of a bigger, and maybe higher, sense of purpose. And their stories resonate beyond their sectors.

With increasing media coverage every year, the Narayana Hrudayalaya story is spreading well beyond healthcare. *Wall Street Journal*, *Financial Times*, and *The Economist* articles as well as coverage on the BBC and CNN are all showing how the approach taken in India around cardiac surgery has lessons for others. Lessons not only for those inside the healthcare sector but also for any company seeking to reinvent its marketplace, transform service, and do so with a profit-able and sustainable model at its heart.

Novo Nordisk has made a seismic shift – from focusing resources on treating the outcomes to addressing the causes of diabetes and considering the entire

Introduction

The Growth
Agenda

Nestlé
PepsiCo

Audi
Samsung

Reckitt
Benckiser
P&G

Starwood
Inditex

Amazon
Google

Narayana
Novo
Nordisk

Rolls-Royce
ARM

BASF
Shell

Tata
Bharti

LEGO
Apple

The Growth
Challenge

user experience. And it has not tried to go it alone but, in recognition of the scale of the challenge, has engaged, involved, and collaborated with multiple stakeholders and so created a 'coalition of the willing.' In a world of many complex challenges Novo Nordisk may provide lessons for us all to consider, whether in relation to wellness, sustainability, security, education, financial systems, and beyond.

The future for all companies in the healthcare sector will look very different over the next decade as the challenges of balancing healthcare expectations and healthcare costs come to the fore. The best answers to those challenges may lie in the sorts of spaces that Narayana Hrudayalaya and Novo Nordisk have started to occupy, and of all the companies in the field, it is difficult to imagine better-placed organizations to find out the answer to the challenge.

Narayana Hrundayalaya

Growth Impact

India's leading healthcare provider
well positioned for wider global impact

Distinctive Competence

Highly efficient healthcare delivery through
integrated process and business model innovation

Underlying Capabilities

| Process optimization | Eliminating waste | World-leading cardiac expertise |

Novo Nordisk

Growth Impact

Sustained growth from leading in
addressing a clear global challenge

Distinctive Competence

A total healthcare view encompassing drugs,
devices, and preventative diabetes education

Underlying Capabilities

| Leader in diabetes treatment | Patient focus throughout organization | Engaging stakeholders to reduce diabetes |

Rolls-Royce	KEY DATA
Total revenue (2010)	£11.1 billion
Underlying service revenue (2010)	£5.5 billion
Average revenue growth p.a. (2005–2010)	11.1%
Net profit (2010)	£543 million
Revenue per employee (2010)	£259,000
R&D intensity (2010)	4.7%
Average share price p.a. (2005–2010)	21.5%
Order book (2011)	£59.2 billion

ARM Holdings	KEY DATA
Total revenue (2010)	£406 million
Average revenue growth p.a. (2005–2010)	19.1%
Net profit (2010)	£85.9 million
Average net profit growth p.a. (2005–2010)	29.9%
Revenue per employee (2010)	£215,000
R&D intensity (2010)	50%
Share of cellphone market (2011)	95%
Average share price p.a. (2005–2010)	37.6%

CHAPTER 11

Rolls-Royce and ARM

Technology partnerships for growth

Rolls-Royce has been successful in changing the business model for engine supply by developing a service case business that delivers more contribution than its core high-tech product business across the whole market. While in the world of semiconductors ARM has become the essential hidden ingredient in every major smartphone as it is rapidly making the business of IP-based revenues very much its own.

Much of the innovation and growth agendas in many sectors is focused on technology access and utilization. Whether talking about new formulations and biotech in the chemicals, food, and pharmaceutical industries, new communication platforms in telecoms, or new electric drive systems in the automotive world, ensuring that you have access to the latest technology developments to incorporate into your products and services is a key strategic issue. While in a few sectors such as banking and travel, the balance of consumer focus to technology focus may shift one way or another, in most arenas today, from fashion to FMCG, technology has as important a role as ever.

Most companies have traditionally supported internal R&D functions, whether they are the large research labs run by the likes of Samsung, IBM, or Pfizer, or smaller initiatives, the rationale of owning your own technology platforms has been a mainstay of many an innovation strategy. However, the costs of supporting this type of investment are both large and risky – the famed VHS vs. Betamax format war and the more recent HD DVD vs. BluRay standoff in the consumer electronics sector are testament to this. Even if you develop a 'better' technology platform than the competition, you are not guaranteed ultimate market success.

As a result, there has been a gradual shift for many companies towards technology licensing and open innovation programs as a means of accessing others' technologies that have already been developed and proven. While the likes of Procter & Gamble have taken a broad view on where they will access new technologies from, others have been more focused; high-technology intensive sectors in particular have moved towards specific and deeper technology relationships between organizations. In the pharmaceutical world, in a bid to gain access to the best new molecules, companies such as Novartis have developed biotech development partnerships with over 400 academic institutions. As we shall see, in the aerospace sector, Rolls-Royce has been even more selective on who it is partnering with and why. In the consumer electronics sector Philips has developed a significant income stream from licensing its technology to others; and in the mobile arena, with platforms such as Bluetooth, Ericsson has been able to lead hundreds of companies towards a common view and helped create new communication standards. ARM, on the other hand, has now pushed these two concepts to new levels and created a business model focused solely on licensing incomes, but one that is also de facto setting the standards in the smartphone industry and having increasing influence in the PC/laptop/tablet device arena.

Both Rolls-Royce and ARM have taken the principles of technology partnerships found elsewhere and moved them into new paradigms where they can access technologies and provide new platforms to their respective ecosystems in a highly effective and focused manner. Although taking different approaches, both have generated significant growth, invented new business models, and are now among the leaders in the field.

Rolls-Royce

Rolls-Royce plc is growing very well. It is a global power systems company headquartered in the UK. It is the world's second-largest maker of aircraft engines and also has major businesses in the marine propulsion and energy sectors. In the past five years it has nearly doubled sales to over £11 billion and spends just under £1 billion on R&D. It has a large forward order book of over £59 billion for engines across the civil and military aviation as well as in the marine and energy sectors. It supplies the likes of Airbus and Boeing, as well as many of the world's commercial airlines and governments, and, as a result, it has built very close relationships with them. While this partly keeps its future sales in healthy shape, more recent attention has been on its technology and innovative business model.

Media commentary in recent years has focused primarily on the latter of these two and in particular the TotalCare service that Rolls-Royce provides to its customers. Changing from an old model of selling engines and then, several years later, spare parts to one of being a service provider, where Rolls-Royce provides airlines with 'power by the hour,' this has now become the standard approach across the aviation sector. The company is still developing and selling high-performance engines, but the means by which customers access and pay for the product has changed and is now wrapped up in a different service model. With over half of Rolls-Royce's revenues and around 70% of its profits coming from the TotalCare service business model, it has proved to be a wise move. It is not difficult to understand that this shift is what many companies find interesting about Rolls-Royce and has been a primary area of focus for bilateral discussions over the past few years.

However, while TotalCare is evidently a great success, it, and the rest of the Rolls-Royce business, still relies on the company producing great products that are higher performance, more efficient, and increasingly more compact. Whether for airlines, military, marine, or energy customers, the expectation is that new engines and turbines will be far more effective in terms of energy and material consumption than previous generations. Given the high levels of technological sophistication of the products, demanding requirements around systems integration, and increasing expectations around product support, Rolls-Royce and peers such as General Electric have developed key capabilities in many of the related areas. The barriers to entry into this market are therefore very high but the competition between existing players is extremely vigorous with multi-billion dollar contracts supported by close customer support relationship the name of the game. Over the next 20 years, the aviation industry is forecasting 137,000 new engine sales worth over $800 billion for the commercial sector – largely driven by Asian growth – and around $160 billion worth of engines for the military sector plus aftermarket services of up to $270 billion. Add in projected demand for over $200 billion of marine power systems and $70 billion of turbines for the energy sector plus aftermarket support of another $175 billion and you can see why competition is intense. Pivotal to success in these markets is therefore technology leadership.

Research and Technology Partnerships

Gone are the days when a company can do all the research into new materials, manufacturing processes, and design concepts in isolation. Especially in the high-tech world of aerospace, collaboration has been a core element of innovation for many years. In 2010 Rolls-Royce invested over £900 million on R&D and two-thirds of this was focused on improving environmental performance, in particular reducing emissions through the acquisition and development of new technologies. Products such as turbine blades are incredibly complex structures and components: a typical blade today involves 70 different suppliers and over 30 university research facilities. Hamid Mughal, executive vice president – manufacturing engineering and technology, sees that 'manufacturing products of this complexity requires an in-depth scientific understanding that can only be achieved by comprehensive and collaborative research.'

To gain access to the relevant technology, Rolls-Royce operates a decentralized research and technology (R&T) operation where the majority of the group's R&T is conducted in a global network of funded University Technology Centres that complement internal development programs. These academic partnerships are funded as long-term strategic relationships that keep Rolls-Royce directly connected to cutting-edge academic research capability. They also provide access to skilled people and enable recruitment and retention of highly qualified and motivated staff. In addition, a new network of collaborative Advanced Manufacturing Research Centres is helping to develop innovative manufacturing technologies that focus on understanding how to reduce the time and costs involved in component production.

Given the multiple areas of interest the company has for new technology application and acquisition, Rolls-Royce looks at its needs over three time horizons of 5, 10, and 20 years as part of what it calls its Vision Programme:

- **Vision 5 – Applying technology.** Vision 5 describes the technologies that Rolls-Royce currently has available 'off-the-shelf' that will be incorporated in new products, such as the aero Trent XWB gas turbine, while some existing engines will be modified to incorporate these proven technologies. Vision 5 is designed to ensure that current products remain market leaders in every aspect of performance, reliability, and cost.
- **Vision 10 – The next generation.** Vision 10 embodies technologies currently at the validation stage that are due to be commercially available in the

medium-term 10-year time frame. The next generation of market-leading Rolls-Royce products will rely largely on Vision 10 technologies.

- **Vision 20 – Exploring new ideas.** Vision 20 technologies target future generations of products in a 20-year time frame. These are at the strategic research stage – emerging or as yet unproven – but will ensure that Rolls-Royce is prepared for future market developments by focusing its extensive research base (including universities and institutions) on the technology requirements of future generations of products.

Together these help provide a framework for internal project focus as well as how the associated interaction with external bodies can be formulated. Examples of the sort of environmentally focused projects being undertaken include the 'Fishtail' propulsor program and the 'silent aircraft' concept.

The 'Fishtail' propulsor program in the marine area is being carried out with Clavis Technology in Norway. Engineers are seeking inspiration from nature to create 'energy converters' that are less harmful to the environment by exploring one of the most efficient hydrodynamic systems in the world – that of fish, and in particular the tuna. As can be imagined, a propulsion system based on the motion of the fishtail poses enormous engineering challenges in areas such as structural design, materials, weight, and actuation. For example, the tuna fish exhibits remarkable acceleration and speed using very little energy, showing a level of efficiency well beyond anything currently achievable using man-made devices. The 'fishtail' propulsor program has been successfully demonstrated on a full-scale vessel.

The development of the 'silent aircraft' concept is in the civil aviation area. In this program a 40-strong collaborative research team from Cambridge University in the UK and MIT in the US have been working on a low-noise, fuel-efficient aircraft, designed to carry 215 passengers for journeys of up to 5000 miles, with noise estimated to be less than 63 dBA (equivalent to urban road noise at 50 km/h and 10 m distance) outside the perimeter of a typical airfield, and fuel consumption 25% less than for current aircraft. The engines use 'shape changing,' variable geometry exhausts, allowing the optimization of engine performance for low noise during takeoff and low fuel burn at altitude.

Managing Long-Term Collaborations

To complement excellence in technology and innovation, the associated key distinctive competence that Rolls-Royce has developed over the last few years is the ability to develop and manage long-lasting collaborations and partnerships with suppliers and customers, and even competitors in both pre-commercial and commercial areas. In all areas of the business from research through to customer service support, the company has been adept at developing and maintaining global partnerships that have resulted in mutual technology leadership.

Internationally, the most important group of research partners is the network of University Technology Centres (UTCs). In the late 1980s, Rolls-Royce adopted a policy which focused its basic academic research with selected university partners. Since then, the group has established a global network of 28 UTCs, with the first formal collaboration being signed in 1990. Initially UTCs were established in the UK (where there are currently 19), but in more recent years the network has been extended to the United States, Norway, Sweden, Italy, Germany, and South Korea. Each UTC addresses a key technology and collectively they tackle a wide range of engineering disciplines – from combustion and aerodynamics to noise and manufacturing technology. This strategy of developing long-term relationships with selected universities has provided close contact with world-class academics, and given access to a wealth of talent and creativity to help develop and protect future capability, providing access to skilled people and enable recruitment and retention of highly qualified and motivated staff.

As well as directly supporting research via this global network, Rolls-Royce also has the opportunity to match government grants, such as those provided by the Research Councils in the UK and other international government agencies, in order to fund the development of leading-edge science and technology. In addition to supporting university research, the company has forged relationships with a number of international, world-class research centers in the United States, Germany, Japan, China, and the UK. Each center has a specific expertise and collectively they complement the activities of the UTCs. Simon Weeks, head of aerospace research & technology, sees that 'key to the success of Rolls-Royce's relationships with the varied UTCs has been the small teams who look after the underlying process which form the contractual rules of engagement and so leaving the capability teams in the organization to focus more on the content side of the partnerships.'

Although other companies have university partnerships for technology development, what sets the Rolls-Royce approach apart is the depth of the collaboration. Rather than just using universities as one of many sources of potential new technologies that the company may or may not bring into the fold, Rolls-Royce has effectively outsourced the long-term R&D in defined areas to specific institutions and migrated some of its internal resource into these institutions. The UTC approach has effectively extended and embedded the company's R&D capability into nearly 30 universities around the world whose facilities are, in turn, incentivized to focus primarily on Rolls-Royce as the route to market for their developments. According to Weeks, 'Rolls-Royce has adjusted its research effort with the result that there is very little competition between the academic UTCs and the internal teams. As the UTCs now include Rolls-Royce personnel who direct much of the research, they look after the early stages of development so the company can focus its internal capabilities on the latter stages to commercialization.' Other organizations that have tried to emulate the UTC approach have failed to recognize the significance of this split.

Each UTC has a different area of strength and hence they all play a part in the overall future technology portfolio for the company. So, Cambridge focuses on materials such as nickel-base alloys that have been specifically developed for operating in gas turbine engines at temperatures in excess of 1500°C; in the area of computational hydrodynamics, the Chalmers UTC, founded in 2002, studies the flow around and the design of marine propulsion systems elements such as propellers or water jets; and the University of Genoa concentrates on the development of advanced solid oxide fuel cell systems. In Singapore, partnerships with A*STAR (Agency for Science, Technology and Research), as well as Nanyang Technical University and the National University of Singapore, have been complemented with a joint venture with a local consortium of industrial partners to develop a new power system based on solid oxide fuel cell technology. With these and other projects, the view is that 'with the UTC model Rolls-Royce have succeeded in breaking down the traditional barriers between academia and industry

– so now there is a collective focus on developing the best technologies to address the challenges.'

Impacts

Much of the recent success for Rolls-Royce has been on the watch of CEO John Rose, who retired at the end of March 2011. He was chief executive for 15 years, during which time he led the transformation of Rolls-Royce into a world-class company operating on a global stage. On retirement he commented:

We have continued our programme of investment, funding world-class facilities in all major geographies, providing capacity for future growth, contributing to improved productivity and delivering products with operational lives which may well extend to half a century. We remain confident in our ability to double revenues in the coming decade through organic growth alone. However, we also have the management and financial capability to accelerate growth through acquisition and partnership.

The long-term disciplined application of our strategy has created a broad portfolio of products, services and capabilities that ensures a wide range of options for future growth. The expected doubling of revenue over the next decade is underpinned by a record order book, which gives good visibility of the future, and a strong balance sheet which enables us to invest in the people, technology and capability that will enhance competitiveness.

Going Forward

Delivering over 1600 engines a year and with a healthy order book, Rolls-Royce is clearly in a good position. With new CEO, John Rishton, now at the helm, Rolls-Royce's continued growth will depend on a number of factors. These include continuing to establish long-term supplier and customer relationships that allow the group to differentiate its products and services; a steady focus on improvement in operational performance, for example through maintaining manufacturing facilities at the leading edge; and maintaining sustained investment in technology acquisition through collaborative programs and funding of UTC and

Research Centres. For a company focused on the long term, both from a technology development as well as commercial relationship point of view, Rolls-Royce has to balance this with ensuring continued success in the short term. Constant appraisal and fine-tuning of the varied business and partnership models is an essential part of the mix. With an expected doubling of revenues over the next decade, the company is confident but not complacent: Fast-growing global markets and a large installed base provide the growth opportunities, but keeping ahead of the competition and winning with the leading technologies is critical.

ARM

Every iPhone runs on an ARM-designed chip. In fact 95% of all smartphones, most tablet PCs, including the iPad, Samsung's Galaxy, and Motorola's Xoom, and over 10% of laptops globally use ARM chips because they are faster and use less energy than many of the competing designs from the likes of Intel and AMD. There are constant rumors that Apple will in fact switch to ARM as its sole platform for all Macs and the company is aiming to have 50% of the global mobile PC market by 2015.

What is particularly interesting about ARM, and of great concern for its competitors, is that the company doesn't actually manufacture anything. It has no factories, relatively few employees, and yet it leads the semiconductor world in developing the latest technology platforms for a growing majority of consumer electronics products. ARM makes its money by conducting leading-edge R&D from its HQ in Cambridge and then licenses the designs that emanate from this to as many companies as possible around the world. Instead of ARM bearing the cost of manufacturing, a network of partners of the world's leading semiconductor manufacturers does that. In an industry where technology licensing has been an interesting revenue contributor for several companies for a number of years, ARM has made it the business model. With a pipeline of innovative new products coming to market, 2010 revenue growth was over 30%, profits more than doubled, and revenue per employee was over £215,000.

Tracing its history back to the 1980s, the seed that became ARM was the first ARM (Acorn RISC Machine) chip developed by the R&D team at Acorn

Computers, previously famous for creating the BBC Microcomputer. In 1990 ARM Ltd. was spun out of Acorn and, with backing from Apple and VLSI technology, created as an intellectual property licensing company. Twenty years later with revenues of more than £400 million, over 740 licenses for ARM design chips had been granted to a host of major manufacturers. The company is now the world's leading semiconductor intellectual property supplier with its products at the heart of an increasing array of digital products from phones and laptops to cameras, digital TVs, and even washing machines.

The Business Model

The longevity of ARM's partnership relationships is based on considerable research and development investment and expertise in developing this licensable core processor technology: R&D spend in 2011 was £250 million, double that of 2008, and involved some 1200 people in staff currently growing at 10% p.a. If this was translated to the licensee partners' R&D spend, every semiconductor company would need to allocate between £80 million and £240 million every year to develop equivalent leading-edge technology. It would represent an additional annual cost to the semiconductor industry of some £32 billion. By designing once and licensing many times, the costs spread over the whole industry, thus helping to make digital consumer electronics cheaper.

ARM's business model is based on partner companies paying an up-front license fee to gain access to a design followed by a royalty on every chip that uses it. A single license is the starting point for the applications development associated with many different ARM powered chip designs, with the result that, in 2010, ARM partners shipped over six billion ARM powered chips. ARM receives a royalty, typically based on a percentage of the chip price, for every chip sold by the semiconductor company containing ARM technology. It takes an average of 3–4 years from the time the semiconductor company signs the license until they start to pay royalties. ARM's partners are able to re-use ARM's technology in different chips going into a broad range of end markets. Each new chip starts a new stream of royalties.

As ARM's partners are the world's largest semiconductor manufacturers, their regular royalty payments have become a highly reliable cash flow and, given the broad base of partners and end markets, ARM has diluted dependency, and is not overly reliant, on any one company or consumer product for future profits and cash. Of particular note is the shareholder value created through this model: Since 2004, ARM has returned over £400 million of cash to shareholders through a mixture of share buybacks and dividends.

Market Dynamics

Although it has been around for half a century or so, the semiconductor market is in pretty constant evolution. Technology is continuously improving, as most famously captured by Moore's law – the number of transistors that can be placed inexpensively on an integrated circuit doubles approximately every two years. In addition the structure of the relationships between companies is also steadily shifting. On top of that there is rapid convergence of core mobile and computing products and hence technologies, as well as faster migration of new platforms into other sectors from automotive to domestic appliances.

In terms of industry structures, there have recently been key periods of con-solidation with the likes of Intel acquiring Infineon's wireless business and the merger between NEC and Renesas. Mostly undertaken to increase market share but primarily reduce cost of manufacture, some of these have provided oppor-tunities for ARM to license its designs to the merged entities as a means of adopting a common technology platform across the whole business.

In terms of convergence, smartphones are getting smarter and laptops are getting smaller and more portable, and there is a continual introduction of new mobile computing products. This is creating many opportunities for technology to migrate both ways between smartphones and laptops. Consumers are demand-ing more portable products that provide continuous connectivity with their social and business networks, which are simple to use and have an all-day battery life.

ARM-based chips for mobile computing are significantly lower cost and lower power than other products available based on the Intel 8086. Due to the extended 'life between re-charge,' in early 2011 a number of ARM's partners announced chips that are suitable for major growth markets such as mobile computers, including tablets, e-book readers, and netbooks. In addition the ARM partner community is working with software companies and original equipment manufacturers (OEMs) to ensure that a complete ecosystem of PC-class software is available, and that shared experience in developing portable consumer products will enable a new generation of low-cost mobile computers.

Growth Drivers

In recent years the growth in ARM's revenues has been driven by three key areas – within and beyond mobile applications and also in new technology outsourcing.

Growth in mobile applications

As mobile devices, such as smartphones, become increasingly sophisticated they require more semiconductor chips within them. Many of these chips contain ARM technology. As the number of chips per device increases, and as the value of each chip increases, so ARM's royalty per mobile device grows. Between 2006 and 2010 the royalty ARM received per mobile device increased by more than 60%.

Growth beyond mobile applications

ARM technology is being increasingly used in applications such as digital TVs, hard disk drives, washing machines, and many other products that require smarter chips, and that are making our lives easier, safer, and more energy efficient. As more products embrace the digital options for future platforms, many see an increasing and divergent range of new applications for new chips.

Growth into new technology outsourcing

ARM is also applying its business model to other technologies that the semiconductor industry is looking to outsource. The company is already seeing success in licensing physical IP that focuses on manufacturing processes and graphics technology, where these technologies add incremental royalty per chip and so further increase ARM's added value per device.

Choreographing Communities

While ARM's business model and internal technical capabilities in developing the best chip designs in the world can be considered as part of the company's distinctive competence, a major pillar is its ability to build, support, and manage multiple communities, some of which overlap. ARM's customers are the community that many would see as the most prominent. Given the licensing business model, ongoing interaction with the multiple licensees of ARM designs is a core platform for the company and its influence and reach across the sector. However, there are also other communities that ARM helps to organize and choreograph.

ARM has built up an extensive community of third-party technology providers and designers, called the ARM Connected Community. This has been designed to facilitate the networking opportunities for the member companies in an effort to increase design, win opportunities and shorten the time-to-market of complete ARM powered solutions. There are currently more than 800 companies within the Community spanning the semiconductor supply chain. This Community not only serves to enable the uptake of ARM technology, but also as an extensive competitive advantage and barrier to entry for IP companies providing technologies in the same areas as ARM. It is also part of an extensive R&D community comprising hundreds of semiconductor companies that license ARM technology and build it into their products.

The Future

Over the past five years, Intel's share price has stayed largely flat while ARM's has gone up by over 350%. The ARM business model is clearly working. The company has set the goal to overtake Intel's dominance of the mobile PC market so that ARM-based processors will be in more than half of all tablets, mini-notebooks, and other mobile PCs sold by 2015. Chips based on its technology already power most of the leading tablets including Apple's iPad, Samsung's Galaxy Tab, and Motorola's Xoom, and the company has licensed designs for use in chips made by companies such as Samsung and NVIDIA, in anticipation that growing consumer interest in tablets will translate into a big jump in its market share. ARM is fast becoming the processor of choice in smart phones and tablets.

At the end of 2011 ARM had about 15% market share in mobile PCs. By 2015, ARM's goal is that this will rise to over 50% of the market.

ARM will have, however, its work cut out. Google's influence over the mobile market via its Android platform and its Motorola acquisition is a potential threat. Steve Taylor, director of solutions marketing at ARM, sees this as a major challenge, but one for which the company already has plans:

A threat to the current licensing model is that as players like Google come on the scene with their android phone, the business model of licensing the same processor design to many silicon suppliers may be an Achilles heel. The challenge is that, whilst the basic design is similar, the added value created by each chip manufacturer means that when the Google Android manufacturer comes to design the software, if the chips are sourced from a number of suppliers, there is an added level of complexity in adapting the software to each supplier's chip, which increases the cost of the final product. This has resulted in Google's Android manufacturers specifying only one supplier, a situation that, in the future, would favour the vertical integration business model adopted by Intel.

In response to this challenge, ARM has set up a pilot partnership with a number of organisations, including four silicon processor providers, under the banner of a not-for-profit organisation, Linaro, to see whether by establishing a Linux 'kernel' that will allow a certain amount of software standardisation, this will encourage the likes of Google to source processors from more than one supplier.

The new Linaro business model is based on the four processor manufacturers and ARM putting between £1.5m and £3m into this partnership, plus a number of engineers (reputed to be circa 100) with the goal of collaborating to design chips for the Google Android based on sharing non-differentiating work, whilst ensuring any differentiation will not contribute to extra software development for the Android manufacturer.

The model has been running for 12 months and the Linaro partnership should be able to tell whether this new business model can work within the next year. Of course, with Linux being open source, any differentiation will have to be in non-technical areas, such as market responsiveness and partner-ship management, both of which are critical skills of ARM.

These and other potential developments, including a fight back from AMD and Intel, and the probable creation of similar types of business are clearly challenges for ARM – but ones that it is confident of addressing. The great advantage for ARM is that it is in essence a very small team and has a flexible business model with no major physical assets or liabilities. As such its nimbleness in the market, its deep partnerships, and the ecosystems that it is part of can all quickly adapt to new shifts as and when they occur. The close relationship with Apple is a great asset and one which many see getting closer in the future. If Apple moved com-pletely to ARM designs, it would be able to unify its mobile and laptop platforms and simplify into one ecosystem. As this bears fruit and Microsoft's interest also rises, some see that ARM may well be the next big UK-based acquisition for a deep-pocketed US firm.

Key Insights – Rolls-Royce and ARM

Although neither organization is unique in adopting technology partnering as the core element of their innovation and growth strategies, both Rolls-Royce and ARM have refined generic approaches to build specific capabilities that are setting them apart from the mainstream. They have used their respective technology partnerships, and the associated ecosystems that have been developed, as the core of their current business relationships and their future business devel-opment. They have changed the underlying business models in their sectors and made the purchase decision for customers both strategically compelling and financially attractive. In achieving this, they have also both been flexible and willing to experiment. As one Rolls-Royce executive shared, 'TotalCare wasn't big from the start.' The company saw an alternative approach and was willing to give it a go and then provide the support to make it the *modus operandi*. The same is true for the UTC partnerships and also for ARM's business model. Neither company is therefore wedded to the past but rather they operate at the leading edge of technology in their respective fields and are both willing to, and expect to, adapt to take advantage of whatever future challenges come their way.

Rolls-Royce

Growth Impact

Secure 10-year product order book with guaranteed high-margin service revenues

Distinctive Competence

Managing deep, focused long-term research and technology partnerships

Underlying Capabilities

Leading-edge materials technology development	Power-by-the-hour business model	Managing successful strategic collaboration

ARM

Growth Impact

Dominance of smartphone chip design with growing influence in adjacent categories

Distinctive Competence

Choreographing communities and partnerships based on technology sharing

Underlying Capabilities

Design not production focus	The essential hidden ingredient	Partner licensing networks

BASF	KEY DATA
Total revenue (2010)	€63.9 billion
Average revenue growth p.a. (2005–2010)	10.3%
Net income (2010)	€4.6 billion
Average net income growth p.a. (2005–2010)	37.8%
Revenue per employee (2010)	€585,000
R&D investment (2010)	€1.49 billion
R&D intensity (2010)	2.3%
Average share price growth p.a. (2005–2010)	17.2%

Shell	KEY DATA
Total revenue (2010)	$368 billion
Average revenue growth p.a. (2005–2010)	8.7%
Net income (2010)	$20.1 billion
Average net income growth p.a. (2005–2010)	8.0%
Revenue per employee (2010)	$3.79 million
R&D investment (2010)	288%
R&D intensity (2010)	$1.0 billion
Average share price growth p.a. (2005–2010)	4.8%

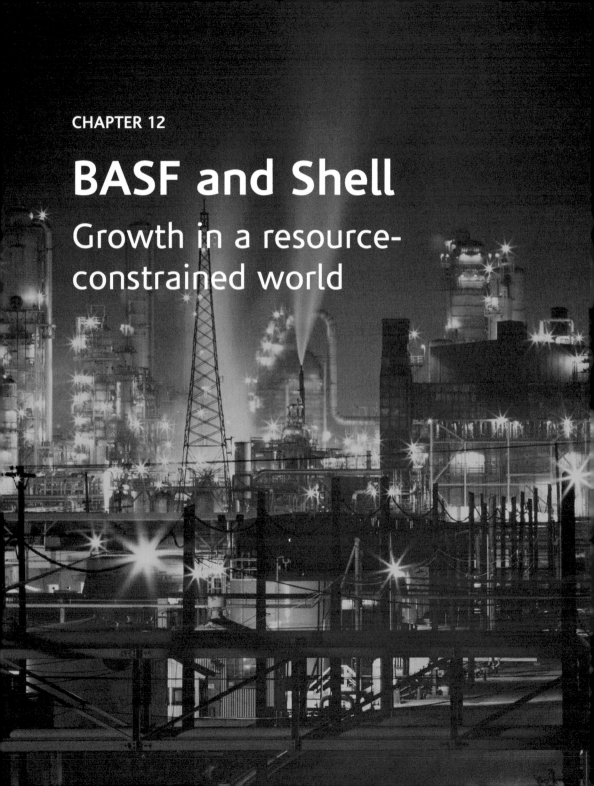

CHAPTER 12

BASF and Shell

Growth in a resource-constrained world

In a resource-constrained world, both BASF and Shell have led their respective sectors by significantly changing their sources of material supply to lower carbon whilst keeping an innovation edge over their competitors and maintaining constant growth across the board.

Over the past decade, and the last five years in particular, the green agenda has moved mainstream. There is growing awareness of the stress that is being put on limited resources and as a result we have seen an increase in political, media, and regulatory pressure to encourage organizations to do their bit to address the problem. Most companies are now looking to develop a more eco-efficient and therefore sustainable approach. Whether the focus is on carbon, energy, water, food, waste, land use on the environmental side, or a host of social issues this has brought a new perspective into the core of the business world.

While some consumer-facing organizations, such as Nike, SABMiller, and Uni-lever, have used sustainability initiatives as part of a wider customer engagement platform, others have been making changes to the way they run their operations out of the public spotlight. This is particularly true in the business-to-business space, where changes have been initiated either from the demand side with the likes of BMW and Wal-Mart putting tighter environmental restrictions on the companies who provide them with goods and services, or on the supply side where organizations such as Du Pont and General Electric through its 'ecomagination' program have started to proactively change the mix of products and materials they are making available to their customers.

In a world where population growth and economic development highlight the risk of 'peak everything' particular focus is now placed on reducing dependency on finite resources such as oil-based products, better management of water consumption, and decreasing waste. Although this has placed major challenges on corporate supply chains and business models, it has also provided oppor-tunities for proactive innovation to identify and develop new growth platforms. In the energy and chemicals industries, the two organizations that have focused on these opportunities, made the most notable shifts towards improving their environmental efficiency, and maintained their growth performance have been

BASF and Shell. In this chapter we examine how this has been achieved, what key changes have taken place, and the lessons for others seeking to do the same.

BASF

The chemicals industry is the backbone of pretty much anything we physically use or consume, be it directly through the development of specific properties (e.g., aroma, texture, strengthening) or indirectly through the use of treatment processes that alter the product on its journey. However, after years of using oil as a basic component of many of its products, the industry is now facing challenging times. Growing concern and increased regulation around environmental issues combined with rising oil prices mean that the innovation focus has to shift toward the use of alternatives, particularly for the chemicals that are now no longer permitted. Most evident of this change has been the use of biology to help chemistry. The industry started looking at enzymatic routes over two decades ago, and today this is a key part of any chemist's toolkit: identifying new raw materials with significant green credentials, faster routes to market, and a whole new take on chemical synthesis.

The industry has been very effective at spotting and developing complementary technologies, taking positions in them, and allowing them to blend together into new, evolved offers. What is particularly interesting about this is that it covers an uncharacteristically broad sweep of related worlds and technologies than other, supposedly more innovative, sectors struggle to do. Emblematic of this approach, both as an innovator and a chemicals company, is BASF, the world's leading chemical company. As a long-term partner to most industries and with a product portfolio ranging from chemicals, plastics, performance products, and fine chemicals to crude oils and natural gas, BASF has a finger in many emerging technology pies.

Open about its growth ambitions, BASF clearly defines and shares its challenge for the next decade. It is currently targeting revenues for 2020 of €90 billion, and capital expenditure in the run in to 2015 of over €12.5 billion. The company states how it will do this: 'we earn a premium on our cost of capital,' 'we help our customers to be more successful,' 'we form the best team in the industry,' and 'we ensure sustainable development.' This focus on having a clear line of sight between future perspectives, strategy, and delivery has meant that BASF has consistently grown as a business (apart from everyone's slump in 2008). Between 2000 and 2010 revenues doubled from €32 billion to €64 billion and profits rose from €4.1 billion to €11.1 billion.

Traditionally BASF has grown in areas associated with its core market, for example, moving into animal nutrition as a result of its work in agricultural products and into petrochemicals because of its involvement in supporting exploration in oil and gas. Success in these adjacent areas is testament to the benefits of the company's core innovation model or 'verbund,' which elegantly combines products, process, technologies, and business models.

In addition to growing its own business base, BASF is not averse to the occasional high-profile deal – but there has to be a reason. For example, the purchase of Cognis for €3.1 billion has reduced BASF's dependence on commodity chemicals and opened the door to new areas which enjoy higher margins and more stable demand. BASF is now the world's biggest supplier of cosmetic ingredients and the third-largest supplier of food additives such as vitamin E. Dr. Jürgen Hambrecht, chairman of BASF's board of executive directors, was right when he observed, 'the combination will broaden our portfolio of specialty chemicals and boost innovation for our customers.'

But there is much more to the company than the endless push for greater efficiency and the occasional high-profile acquisition. BASF's strategy focus is based on how to continue to grow with a responsible perspective, and from this, how to innovate in a world of constrained resources. This creates the rationale for the way the company interacts with the world, and is followed up by significant investment in reducing its environmental impact.

The results so far are impressive. Across the business BASF has reduced its own greenhouse emissions per metric tonne of sales by 61% from 1990–2002 and is on its way to a further reduction of 10%. Whilst production of BASF products creates 90 million tonnes of CO_2, use of such products saves customers 287 million tonnes of CO_2: an impressive 3:1 ratio. So, all the evidence suggests that for BASF eco-efficiency really is key.

Innovation and Sustainability

BASF's success is characterized by a focus on creating resource-efficient product lines and using integrated production sites. The largest of these is located in Ludwigshafen and currently employs around 33,000 people. The sites are characterized by co-location of a large number of individual production lines (producing a specific chemical), which share an interconnected material flow. All production lines use common raw material sourcing and feed back waste resources, which can then be used elsewhere (e.g., sulfuric acid, carbon monoxide). The incentives for this approach are not only that it is resource efficient but also that it is energy efficient. In addition, the high cost of development establishes a high entry barrier for competitors trying to enter the market for volume chemicals.

In addition to streamlined processes BASF has focused on innovation to help increase efficiency across the board. It has built a whole structure designed to encourage innovation, which looks like the A–Z guide to innovation practices. Its scouting business looks at emerging trends; its ventures group takes stakes in new technologies; its technology platform structure carries out research and applied science in a number of nascent sectors outside the business such as white biotech and nanotechnology; it even has a process to capture any incremental innovation ideas from the shop floor. From transport to herbicides to super absorbents for diapers the company is constantly exploring ways to increase efficiency and, at the same time, decrease environmental impact.

BASF considers five 'Growth Clusters' as areas for innovation. These are: energy management; raw material change; nanotechnology; plant biotechnolgy; and industrial or white biotechnology. 'By creating our Growth Clusters, we have identified the important topics of future relevance that will contribute to solving urgent social issues,' explains Dr Andreas Kreimeyer, research executive director. 'But it will only be possible to address the challenges of the future through international and interdisciplinary cooperation. We therefore increasingly attach importance to cooperating with outstanding partners from science and business. With everyone contributing their own strengths, we advance much more rapidly and create sustainable success.'

The interest in environmental issues is not new. Since it first appeared on the corporate radar, BASF has used its technology investment and strategy to constantly drive a shifting portfolio that positions itself around the ways of addressing the environmental challenge. Indeed, the development of eco-efficiency analysis back in 1996 directly led to BASF becoming the world's first company to produce a detailed corporate carbon footprint report over a decade later in February 2008. This contrasted the CO_2 emission savings achieved with BASF products and processes with the emissions from raw material extraction, production, and product disposal, and showed that BASF products could save about three times more greenhouse gas emissions than the entire amount caused by their production and disposal.

Stimulating Growth Performance

BASF has stated that it aims to generate €8 billion new sales by 2015 from product innovations that have been on the market for less than five years. Having successfully delivered €6 billion in the five years to 2010, it looks promising, and the R&D budgets have been ring fenced to help deliver this ambition.

BASF invests significantly to understand the mega-trends that will affect its businesses and identify the key challenges it needs to think about. For example, given the expected growth of urban populations, the company begins by considering 'how can we create a liveable environment in the cities?' and goes on to 'what will buildings look like in the future?' and 'which materials will be needed?'. This means the organization can clearly see how insights translate right the way through to specific products for the market, whilst also reflecting the underlying environmental positioning.

Pragmatically this translates into exploratory projects. Teaming up with the University of Nottingham, BASF's showcase, affordable, environmentally friendly housing, blends low construction costs with low environmental impact, and achieves a sustainability rating of 4 stars – or in other words a 44% improvement against the Target Emission Rate as set by the 2006 Building Regulation Standards. The design uses a whole variety of BASF materials including Insulated Concrete Framework – two layers of polystyrene, with a gap between them filled with concrete, which provides a cost-effective and quick construction material with high insulating properties for the ground floor, through to roofing coated with BASF Plastisol topcoat to provide solar heat management.

As new products hit the market they are explicitly positioned within the broader framework of the company's sustainability ambition. For example BASF's new light stabilizer, Tinuvin XT 200, extends the life of agricultural film combining an economic improvement with the benefits of UV protection. 'Greenhouses are increasingly being used to help secure the world's food supply. This innovative light stabilizer is particularly beneficial for greenhouses, which are often built inexpensively using plastic film.'

BASF Future Business GmbH

The most high-profile part of the organization tasked with identifying and nurturing new growth platforms is BASF Future Business GmbH. This was set up in 2001 and is an owned subsidiary of BASF. Its mission is to open up business areas with higher than average growth opportunities that sit outside the core BASF business. Starting with a critical scouting role the Future Business group looks at social and ecological megatrends to pick out what opportunities best suit the company strategy, and then goes on to develop these. It gets involved in anything from initiating internal research projects, co-sponsored with the existing businesses, to ventures that take positions in emerging technologies that may eventually be integrated back into BASF. As a separate business it works by commissioning work within the BASF research labs on an operational basis, and developing its own portfolio of technologies and investments, which it then passes on (when and where appropriate) into the mother company.

This strategy has been successful so far. For example, BASF Future Business recently signed a development agreement with Interface Biologics (IBI), a privately held Canadian-based company working in biomedical polymer products. The companies will collaborate in the development of new polymeric formulations with anti-microbial and anti-thrombogenic properties. By joining IBI's technology with BASF's proprietary anti-microbial platform, the aim is to develop new materials that can substantially improve the safety and performance of medical devices.

Dr. Thomas Weber, managing director of Future Business, highlights the need to keep the innovation culture alive. 'We strive to keep the spirit of innovation alive in the long term. We do so even in times of crisis – we may strive even harder then!' It is less about product success and more about the learning curve for the business: 'a project that has been successfully completed is obviously a success for each individual involved. However, the rewards given to individual employees do not hinge on what they have achieved, but rather how they did it.' This mix of defined culture and business investment provides the encouragement and confidence to the Future Business group to keep searching for new ideas and striving to make ideas a reality.

Coupled with the BASF Future Business GmbH is the company's 'Verbund' principle. This is a highly integrated manufacturing, process, infrastructure, and waste management procedure. It represents entire interlocking value chains. This means the byproducts from one plant can be used as starting materials for another (including process inputs such as waste heat). This leads to reductions in emissions, logistics costs, higher yields, and lower resource consumption. 'Despite an 86% increase in our product volumes since 1990, the Verbund structure has succeeded in reducing the company's absolute greenhouse gas emissions by 27%. Indeed the reduction in specific greenhouse gas emissions, i.e. per tonne of product sold, is as high as 61% in some sectors.' This awareness and understanding of process design, integration, and cross-value is second to none.

Eco-impacts

As a result of its environmental focus BASF has shifted its portfolio from basic chemicals to a mix of high-end, high-tech chemicals, with a further R&D evolution into areas such as white biotechnology, nanotechnology, and plant biotechnology. From a business perspective this has led to an overall shift in the portfolio with 36 acquisitions, 24 divestitures, and 8 joint ventures. As a result the emphasis on specific areas of technology and development has driven the change in the overall company performance, allowing it to enjoy an increasing profit margin and evolve its revenue base to be more relevant and leading edge.

A good example of this is BASF's Green Sense Concrete. This uses different materials, often waste from other processes, and a mix of additives to create a concrete that has improved setting, strength, and durability. The potential impact of this can only be truly understood when you consider that the concrete manufacturing process currently represents 5–6% of global CO_2 emissions.

At times this also translates into improved processes in BASF's more traditional businesses. For example, as early as 1990 it switched from chemical synthesis to a biotechnical process in the manufacture of Vitamin B2, an important human supplement. This has been refined over the years, leading to a reduction in resources of 60%, CO_2 reductions of 30%, decrease in waste by 90%, and lowering of production costs by 40%.

The chemicals industry has seen a decline in R&D spending since 1998 from around 3.4% to around 2.2%. At the same time the industry has found itself at the wrong end of a consumer push for green. On the other hand, the challenges open up interesting opportunities for alternative energy, water, emissions, agricultural yield, and high-performance materials.

Of all the companies in the sector, BASF was one of the earliest to spot and act on these changes, and has become a champion of growth. The longevity of its vision and its introduction of eco-efficiency analysis has allowed it to really understand the tradeoffs between economic and environmental impact. The approach came by scientifically considering the potential impact of these kinds of challenges. From the original insight, through the metrics to the evolving portfolio, BASF has been able to demonstrate an admirable mix of strong growth coupled with reduced environmental damage. At each stage it has also led the market, so achieving better sustainability targets and hitting improved growth targets.

Future Challenges

Over the next decade the key challenges for BASF are less likely to be technological than organizational. BASF has earmarked key capabilities already by loading up their Growth Cluster platforms, so we can expect continued investment and evolution of offers coming from nanotechnology, white biotechnology, and so on.

Particular questions for the organization from a people and culture angle, however, include: Given that China is such an important growth market, how does a primarily German-focused leadership team ensure sustained understanding of the emerging issues? How can BASF be a global magnet for emerging talent and maintain its insightful grip on how the key challenges to industry will play out? And, how will BASF continue building its already burgeoning reputation in societal and ecological imperatives?

Shell

The economic development and energy demand of energy fuels are expected to double over the next 20 years. For more than 100 years the fuel of choice has been hydrocarbon based – coal, oil, and gas – and an enormous energy system has developed to supply the world's energy needs. Although renewable energy supplies are now part of the global mix their promise has some way to go before they can replace existing hydrocarbon supply as well as meet new demand.

Not only are 'easy' and 'cheap' resources running out but also we are increasingly aware of the environmental impacts of energy. Despite this, technically challenging energy reserves such as tar sands and shale gas are on the radar for many countries and companies keen to secure future reserves and ensure 'energy security.' The challenge for the energy industry is how to meet demand growth in the short, medium, and long term in a way that balances the need to keep the lights on and the necessity to protect our planet.

The Deepwater Horizon disaster in 2010 was a stark lesson to everyone involved in the industry: companies need to earn the right to participate in energy projects on the basis of their ability to address and manage environmental and technological issues in a safe and cost-effective manner.

Operating in its current form for over a century and with a history going back to 1833, Royal Dutch Shell, more commonly known as Shell, is the world's second-largest energy company with operations in over 90 countries in oil, gas, and increasingly biofuel businesses. It has been at the forefront of much of the development of the energy sector, has had a few reputational challenges over the years, but is now taking a lead in shifting the supply of energy for the 21st century towards a more sustainable and environmentally sensitive mix. Although far from being zero carbon, due to some major strategic moves in selecting future growth platforms, of all the international oil companies, Shell has moved to the forefront of bringing about a lower carbon world.

Shell's Growth Ambition

Over the years, Shell has developed a reputation for looking forward both for emerging issues and challenges and also in planning its future, which appears to be based on delivery of major new projects: 'For the next wave of growth, to 2020 we have over 30 new projects on the drawing board which will generate new options for the medium term, for the integrated energy company of the future.'

The Link Between Innovation and Growth

Innovation is at the heart of addressing the energy challenge and delivering Shell's growth ambitions. Today CEO Peter Voser sees that: 'Our commitment to technology and innovation continues to be at the core of our strategy. Our key strengths include the development and application of technology, the financial and project-management skills that allow us to deliver large oil and gas projects, and the management of integrated value chains.'

Whilst innovation is a clear part of Shell's current growth strategy, there was a period during the early 2000s where the company could have lost its way. Things came good in 2006 when a small group was put together under the sponsorship of Corporate Strategy to look at the 'Future of Energy' and the 'Role of Research' within the organization and to make specific recommendations to senior management for the best way forward in a rapidly changing world where low carbon was the clear direction.

These two pieces of research – 'the most impactful studies I have seen in getting the attention of our leaders' according to the head of strategic planning at the time – led to innovation and technology being put back at the heart of strategy and a renewed focus on technology-led growth.

Introduction

The Growth Agenda

Nestlé PepsiCo

Audi Samsung

Reckitt Benckiser P&G

Starwood Inditex

Amazon Google

Narayana Novo Nordisk

Rolls-Royce ARM

BASF Shell

Tata Bharti

LEGO Apple

The Growth Challenge

As a direct result, the, new role of chief technology officer (CTO) was established to oversee the development and implementation of a group-wide Technology Strategy and chief scientists – experts in key sciences and technologies – were appointed in order to raise the profile of Technology within Shell, to act as external ambassadors, and as focal points for addressing many of the emerging challenges facing the energy sector. Technology became central to business strategy and communications with internal and external audiences.

The Key Role of Foresight

Shell Scenarios are widely used, not just within the business but also by other companies and governments worldwide to better understand how uncertainties may develop and identify the associated challenges and opportunities. Foresight (Scenario Planning) has enabled Shell to spot potential opportunities early and to be prepared to act on them: 'At Shell we have been using scenarios for 30 years to inform our planning and help people understand the possible futures that confront us.'

Recognizing that change often comes from developments outside a sector, in 2004 and 2007 Shell's GameChanger and Scenarios teams initiated an additional program called Technology Futures that brought together a unique mix of people from different companies and countries to collectively map out the major probable developments in different fields from food and transport to IT and business. From this Shell was able not only to identify a host of potential opportunities and threats but also, using technology scouts, to build an early warning system to keep the company aware of ongoing changes.

These programs fed into the development of the 2008 Energy Scenarios, which highlighted: the growing gap between demand and supply for conventional oil and gas; the inability of renewables to ramp up fast enough to fill the gap; the opportunity to develop large-scale technological solutions for bringing new 'unconventional' sources of supply to market; and the ever increasing environmental stresses. These insights significantly influenced the many portfolio investment and divestment decisions taken by Shell in recent years and have helped to provide focus for innovation and research.

Additional Distinctive Competence

Alongside the culture and practice of using foresight, which is unquestionably an area where Shell leads the pack, there are three other capability areas where the company believes it has an edge over its peers. These are:

- Technology – development and application of technology to access resources and get products to market.
- Scale – large-scale projects requiring engineering, project management, and financial skills.
- Integration of value chains – from exploration to market.

The combination of these capabilities gives Shell its distinctive competence – 'the ability to provide integrated solutions at large scale utilising technological breakthroughs.' On top of this, Shell's growth platforms are reinforced by its strategy of portfolio management to fund capital investment enabling it to finance projects at a scale beyond the scope of most of its competitors.

Consistent investment in such projects over recent years has enabled Shell to develop a growth portfolio that is seen by analysts as sector leading. For example, Ed Crooks, energy editor at the *Financial Times*, sees that 'six years after it was first set out, Royal Dutch Shell's strategy is about to pay off.' More than any other energy major, Shell is the one that has placed some good bets that are now paying dividends. Although every investment has its own challenges – think of Sakhalin Island in Russia and the political and environmental problems – there are a growing number of successes that are now driving the company towards a lower carbon future.

Impacts

The results Shell gains from its distinctive competences are best demonstrated by looking at two of Shell's new businesses developments. One, Biofuels, aims to help meet demand for lower carbon mobility fuels whilst the other, Floating LNG, will unlock supplies of gas for power generation.

Biofuels – growth through partnering

In an energy-scarce world, the opportunity to 'grow' rather than 'drill for' oil has become a major area of focus for many companies over the past few years. The likes of Cargill and ADM from the food sector are now new players in the energy game. However, using corn or sugar for fuel has become a highly contentious issue as competition for land between food and fuel has led to deforestation and price spikes for food.

Shell's 2004 Technology Futures program highlighted the potential for second-generation land-based biofuels and marine-based algae supplies to address these concerns. Already a major trader in biofuels, Shell started a number of partnerships to develop and bring to market these more sustainable alternatives to oil-based transport fuel.

Whilst these partnerships are promising longer term options, it became clear that the technologies would not mature fast enough to contribute towards filling the short-term need for biofuels driven by government mandates. So Shell has been looking towards Brazil for help. Professor Edgar de Beauclair, of the crop production department, São Paulo State University sees that, 'Sugar cane is the most efficient plant we know in converting sunlight into energy.' And in Brazil the byproducts from turning sugar cane into ethanol are recycled as organic fertilizer and plant waste, which is then burned to produce power for the processing mills and the national grid.

Shell have partnered with the Brazilian company Cosan to form Raízen – a joint venture which will distribute biofuels through a combined network of nearly 4500 Shell-branded service stations. Ethanol made from Brazilian sugar cane produces 70% less CO_2 than petrol and the sugar cane to ethanol process used by Raízen is the most efficient in the world. Although not perfect, it is a much better option than current alternatives.

Shell brings expertise in global distribution, retailing, and technology partnerships in advanced biofuels, while Cosan adds to the venture its experience in the commercial production of low-carbon biofuels. And according to Mark Gainsborough, Shell executive vice-president alternative energies, this has potential to deliver future growth. 'We expect the development of advanced biofuels to benefit from Cosan's feedstock and its expertise in large-scale biofuels production. This has the potential to accelerate the future commercial viability of cellulosic ethanol.'

'This is a turning point in the search for alternative energy sources,' says Rubens Ometto Silveira Mello, Cosan's chairman. 'Raízen is one of Brazil's largest companies and is ready to offer international markets a clean, renewable and economically viable solution.'

In the biofuels market, Shell has chosen to play an interesting role. As a key part of the lower carbon fuels strategy it is choosing partnerships with smaller companies to fill knowledge and capability gaps and matching this with its ability to scale and integrate. Shell is not trying to bring the technology in-house as it will be superseded over time but rather use its complementary assets and skills to greatest effect.

Floating LNG (FLNG)

Energy reserves are often located far from the markets and developing innovative solutions to getting energy to markets at a reasonable cost is therefore a major ambition. Although not zero carbon, natural gas is significantly lower carbon than oil and coal and Shell has been at the forefront of developing new technologies for bringing more gas to market.

Whilst oil in liquid form is relatively easy to ship and transport by road, shipping gas requires it to be in the form of liquefied natural gas (LNG) – gas chilled to $-162°C$ in order to turn it into liquid and shrink its volume by 600 times – which is then shipped closer to markets then turned back into gas for use in power generation. Whilst LNG is not new – Shell has for decades been a pioneer in LNG – it has taken more than 10 years of R&D to get to a Final Investment Decision on a potential game changer: Floating LNG.

Shell explains the rationale: 'Moving the production and processing out to sea where the gas is found is a major innovation that brings huge new energy resources within reach. It also avoids the potential environmental impact of constructing and operating a plant on land, including laying pipelines to shore and building other infrastructure.'

'This is groundbreaking technology developed by Shell,' says Neil Gilmour, Shell general manager FLNG. 'It has the potential to change the way we produce natural gas.' To provide some idea of the size of the project a scale model of the vessel alone is 8 meters long and weighs 4.5 tonnes. Once complete, the facility will be longer than four soccer fields laid end to end, will weigh roughly six times as much as the largest aircraft carrier, have a storage capacity roughly equal to 175 Olympic swimming pools, and will contain five times more steel than used to build the Sydney Harbour Bridge. Whilst the project is 100% Shell owned, the skills to design and build the vessel reside in two other companies, Technip and Samsung, who have entered into a strategic partnership with Shell to deliver this and future FLNG projects.

These projects highlight Shell's ability to not only do things on a grand scale and make the big business deals that characterize much of the energy sector. It also shows how the company is willing to invest in major opportunities, leverage its technology expertise, and collaborate with others who have complementary competences. Floating LNG brings together Shell and experts in ship design and construction and Biofuels combines the manufacturing skills of Cosan with Shell's marketing and technology expertise.

Both projects utilize technologies that have been around for some time but bring them into the 21st century at scale helping to deliver energy security with a higher level of eco-efficiency than can be achieved by the available alternatives. Whilst the projects are clearly not zero carbon, they help to responsibly meet growing global demand for energy.

Looking Ahead

Such future growth platforms allow Shell to maintain its position as a leading energy provider, but also nudge it towards a lower carbon energy mix. Whilst we wait for renewable energy to achieve the scale needed, this shift to lower CO_2 hydrocarbons for the world's rising energy demand will play an important role in addressing energy constraints.

Going forward, as with other energy companies, the pressure to find and gain access to more reserves is the primary challenge. Shell is focused on a strategy of leveraging its current distinctive competences in order to gain access to resources and markets through local partnerships. Increased partnering with national oil companies is clearly a primary avenue for this but expect also to see more ventures around alternative fuels. Whatever the supply source, managing the cost of energy production will also continue to be a key issue as will further driving down the environmental impact of energy both operationally in use, in the car, home or factory, and also over the full cycle from extraction to end use.

Key Insights – BASF and Shell

In a world of increasingly constrained resources, both BASF and Shell highlight that growth is still possible. Through taking the long view on the right way to go and planning the steps forward that will balance satisfying market demand with the sustainability imperative and the need to run a successful business, both highlight some common issues:

Looking to the future ahead of peers and acting early

- BASF has done this in the whole environmental space, but also was an early mover into biosynthesis routes and has now built a platform in white biotech.
- Shell has seen the long-term opportunities in advanced biofuels and the near-term demand for LNG, has partnered with the best, and is leading the sector.

Aligning growth strategy and future opportunities

- BASF has done a great job of building a few federating principles around its ambition and role in the world, which it has translated into specific targets and ways of analyzing/filtering innovations so there is a clear line of sight between everything it does and everything it wants to be.
- Shell, more than any other energy company, has taken the long view and shares through its scenarios the 50-year perspective on energy options. Although not in control of how others choose to move, it is placing multiple

major bets that ensure that whichever way the world shifts, Shell will be a major player in the energy sector.

On top of this they also have separate areas of focus:

- Understand the consumer – BASF is not a consumer goods company, but it does a far better job than many FMCG companies in defining a sense of purpose and impact for end consumers, which it then translates into reasons to buy. This makes the link between supplier and consumer for the intermediate customer really easy. Backing this with all the necessary support around chemical trail, environmental impact and so on makes buying BASF a very easy choice.
- Leverage capital – Shell has access to large financial reserves and uses aggressive portfolio management to fund organic growth – shifting the portfolio to new growth markets and new technological solutions.

These two companies, operating in different sectors but linked through a legacy dependency on oil, have both taken eco-efficiency a major step forward. While the end ambition that they have set for moving towards a zero carbon future is a good way off, both are making good progress to lower carbon options. Innovation, partnerships, and foresight are coming together in Shell and BASF to deliver bold changes in the next few years and bigger ones in the future. Achieving this, while also continuing to maintain growth and market leadership positions, is a major feat.

BASF

Growth Impact

Leading sustained growth from the front in the chemicals sector

Distinctive Competence

Managing continuous growth while simultaneously improving its products' environmental impact

Underlying Capabilities

| Integrated manufacturing, infrastructure, and waste management | Highly efficient process development and implementation | Valued foresight informed innovation |

Shell

Growth Impact

Sustained revenue growth and lower carbon reserves replacement

Distinctive Competence

Providing integrated solutions at large scale utilizing technological breakthroughs

Underlying Capabilities

| Undertaking and using foresight to steer strategy | Developing and applying technology | Managing large-scale projects | Integrating value chains |

Tata Steel	KEY DATA
Total revenues (2010)	INR 12,236 Crores
Average revenue growth p.a. (2005–2010)	75%
Net income (2010)	INR 8856 Crores
Average net income growth p.a. (2005–2010)	88%
R&D investment (2010)	INR 76 Crores
R&D intensity (2010)	0.06%
Average share price growth p.a. (2005–2010)	41%
Tata Steel Group production	23.5 million tonnes

Bharti Airtel	KEY DATA
Total revenues (2010)	INR 594 billion
Average revenue growth p.a. (2005–2010)	41%
Average revenue per user (2010)	INR 194 per month
Net income (2010)	INR 60 billion
Average net income growth p.a. (2005–2010)	31%
Number of customers (2010)	220 million
Number of countries (2010)	19
Average share price growth p.a. (2005–2010)	29%

CHAPTER 13

Tata and Bharti
Leapfrogging from India

Today a good proportion of the world's disruptive innovation is coming from emerging markets and much of it is changing the balance of power across a variety of sectors. Many companies are focused on exploiting the opportunities in high-growth markets and applying what has become termed as 'frugal,' 'reverse,' or 'cost' innovation – redesigning products and processes to eliminate up to 80% of costs and so provide for the masses at the bottom of the pyramid – but that also work very well for those at the top. The majority of the action is taking place in India where Tata Motors is selling the Nano 'people's car' for INR 150,000 ($3000); Bharat Biotech retails a single dose of its hepatitis B vaccine for 20 cents; and Bharti Airtel provides one of the cheapest wireless telephone services in the world.

In 2006, emerging markets' challengers on the global stage were a novelty. Lenovo had recently purchased the PC business of IBM and China NOOC had made an unsolicited and ultimately unsuccessful bid for Unocal. Just five years later it's all changed. Global challengers from emerging markets are the norm, and many are taking a different route to growth than the established players. The new challengers are leap-froggers, moving quickly to build leading-edge international operations. Significantly, alongside strong organic growth, they show an appetite for inorganic growth via mergers and acquisitions that marks them out from their Far East predecessors on entering the world stage.

As *The Economist* recently pointed out, 'Over the past decade the world's corporate pecking order has been disturbed by the arrival of a new breed of plucky multinationals from the emerging world. These companies have not only taken on Western incumbents, snapped up Western companies and launched exciting new products; they have challenged some of the West's most cherished notions of how companies ought to organise themselves.'

'In some ways these groups look like throwbacks to old-fashioned Western conglomerates such as ITT. But in other ways they are *sui generis*: much more diversified and readier to blur the line between public and private. A growing number of them are proving that they can compete in global markets as well as in sometimes rigged local ones. The Boston Consulting Group lists the rise of diversified global conglomerates as one of five trends that will shape the future of business.'

Tata and Bharti are both major Indian conglomerates that have demonstrated a hunger and ambition for global leadership in their sectors. As well as driving significant organic growth in their domestic markets, they are using big acquisitions as a key part of their global strategies. They recognize the need to reach beyond India to sustain rapid growth; they have access to capital; they are partnering to build world-class capabilities, fast; and they have built management teams with a global outlook. While acquisitions and partnerships are enabling both companies to expand their footprint, they are not only strengthening their competitive position globally but are also ensuring continuing growth through simultaneously managing innovation and operational efficiencies.

Tata

Perhaps the most significant of all the Indian conglomerates now playing on the global stage is Tata. A longtime major force in India, the Tata Group is quickly establishing a global presence. Tata is a diversified conglomerate, successfully present in businesses as diverse as consumer products, energy, engineering, information systems, communications, services, and materials. Taken as a whole, the Tata Group is a global player with several of its companies important multinationals in their own right.

In 2010, group revenues were 3.2 trillion rupees ($67.4 billion) with profits of 82 billion rupees. With nearly 100 companies in the Tata Group, on July 21, 2011, the combined market capitalization of the 28 listed ones crossed the $100 billion mark. As *The Economist* views it; 'Just as Tata played a leading role in nation-building from its foundation in 1868, creating India's first Indian-owned steel plant, power station, luxury hotel, domestic airline and sundry other firsts, it is now one of the stars of India's globalization. The group has also projected a new type of company onto the global stage – more diversified than Western firms, more engaged in the life of the community and, if its employees are to be believed, better equipped to prosper in both developed and developing markets.'

Tata has developed its portfolio domestically with Tata Motors gaining much of the limelight through its Indica and Nano cars but with steady growth also taking place across all platforms. On top of this, Tata has also been using foreign acquisitions, such as the Tetley Group, Corus, Jaguar Land Rover, and Daewoo Trucks, to both increase its global footprint and enhance its capabilities. Between 1995–2003 Tata companies made, on average, one purchase a year; in 2004 they made six and in the following two years they made more than 20. In all Tata has spent around $20 billion on foreign companies. Today it earns about three-fifths of its revenue abroad and employs more British workers than any other manufacturer.

While each Tata business is run independently, there are common traits. As well as many of the interlocking shareholdings and trusts that sit across the 98 separate companies and give such significant financial firepower, many recognize that there is a clear Tata culture that has been marinating for 140 years and is now experienced by Tata's global workforce of nearly 400,000 people. Tata Group argues that three things – loyalty, dignity, and corporate social responsibility – define this. To gain insight into how Tata achieves its success we are looking in detail at just one of the Tata Group companies – the largest business in the portfolio – Tata Steel.

Tata Steel

The steel industry is a highly fragmented and cyclical sector. At the same time, it is largely an old industry with legacy practices, facilities, technologies, and mindsets. However, the global landscape of steel production has been trans-formed in the last decade driven by the stunning speed of China's growth in steel production: Between 2001 and 2009 China's share of world steel production rose from 18% to 46%. Today, the continued shift of demand away from the mature Europe, Japan, and North America to emerging markets – not just China but other growing economies as well – is accompanied by other issues that impact profitability, especially volatility in raw material prices.

Tata Steel was established in 1907 and retains its headquarters in Mumbai. In recent years, the company has expanded both within Asia and in Europe through its 2007 acquisition of Corus. Tata Steel has also made a host of smaller acquisitions, joint ventures, and associations. Tata is now among the world's most geographically diversified steel producers, with operations in 26 countries and a commercial presence in over 50 countries. Tata Steel had a turnover of $22.8 billion in 2010, has over 80,000 employees across five continents and, in its own right, is a *Fortune 500* company. Most notably, during a period where the world's steel industry has been under significant pressure, Tata Steel has grown revenue income as well as market value, and through more efficient operations has also tripled its average revenue per employee.

Indian Growth

Up until the late 1990s, Tata Steel was identified primarily with secure employment – 'it had outdated processes, a large workforce and an inward looking mindset.' Through a major re-engineering program the company transformed itself into a globally competitive, low-cost manufacturer of steel.

By 2002, Tata Steel recognized that future organic growth in India would be slow. Although the company was in a strong financial position, large capital projects such as steel capacity expansion were subject to significant delays and there were limited opportunities for growth through local acquisitions. Meeting Tata Steel's ambitions necessitated a move out of India onto the global stage.

Overseas Expansion

In 2004, Tata Steel duly acquired Singapore's NatSteel, followed in 2006 by Millennium Steel of Thailand. These acquisitions gave the company access to six markets in the region, including Vietnam, the Philippines, and Malaysia – all fast-growing economies with attractive long-term potential. More importantly, these first acquisitions allowed Tata Steel to test the waters of M&A, transfer internal best practice from the successful purchase of Tetley, learn how to run a trans-national business, and also understand the cultural issues of integrating larger organizations.

The next acquisition was, however, to catapult the company into the big league and make Tata the sixth-largest producer in the world. The take-over of Anglo-Dutch steelmaker Corus was a logical step in the value chain after its Asian acquisitions. More importantly, the move was in line with the company's de-integration model that involves making primary metal in markets close to raw materials and establishing finishing (value-adding) facilities in the end-user markets. The deal between a large player with a significant presence in value-added steel and a strong distribution network (Corus) and an outfit that is the lowest-cost producer of steel (Tata Steel) offered synergies that make the combined unit far more competitive in the global league table of steel makers.

Two key features of the Corus acquisition and the subsequent journey are notable:

1. *Partnered M&A:* This was a massive leap in scale for the company as Corus was at least three times larger than Tata Steel when it came to revenues and production capacities. However, the same was true of the Tetley acquisition which was twice the size of Tata Tea. In both cases a partnered approach was adopted.
2. *Sustainable innovation:* It was also as much about raising the technological capability and innovation competence of the whole organization as it was about geographic scale on manufacturing and distribution.

Exploring these two features highlights what Tata is doing differently to win.

Partnered M&A

While many Western mergers and acquisitions have become notorious for destroying value, M&A activities being undertaken by many Asian companies are proving to be more successful. Lenovo's takeover of IBM's PC business is one of the most public, but Tata's tea, car, and steel acquisitions are some of the most successful. Whilst the traditional model of acquisition is to put a large integration team into the new company to align people processes and systems with those of the new owner, Tata takes a different approach as explained by Koushik Chatterjee, CFO Tata Steel, in 2009:

We quite genuinely tend to look at an acquisition as a partnership rather than an acquisition . . . we don't send planeloads of people into a new company. Instead, we only send in a few integrators. That's been the key interface.

We also tend to co-create a vision for the enlarged organization rather than just imposing our own. For example, after we closed the transaction for Corus, on April 2, 2007, we worked together for the next six months on co-creating a vision for the enlarged enterprise. If the vision exercise isn't shared or if the process isn't participative, then the acquired organization's willingness to be part of the future action plans and the consequent accountability will be much lower. This approach requires a lot of maturity from the senior leadership as it requires a lot of adaptability to new situations, cultures and sensitivities. It is not easy to do.

And this partnering approach extends beyond creating a shared vision to a concept of shared change, which encourages sharing and adopting of good practices from both partners; accepting cultural differences between Indian and non-Indian companies but thinking and performing as one enterprise. And whilst this approach takes time it results in trust in the partnership and in the whole target-setting process, and trust can be a source of competitive advantage as Mr. Chatterjee explained:

I believe that when we eventually establish that trust, things move faster; you don't have to go around reassuring people. This was demonstrated by our European colleagues, who reacted very fast to the global economic crisis last year, when we realized Europe would be significantly affected. A short-term program, 'weathering the storm' was launched, which gave us very significant savings – over 700 million GBP – in the six months between October 2008 and March 2009. The program continues even today with significant savings forecast for this year too.

Analysts have commented that Tata overpaid for Corus and Jaguar Land Rover and Ratan Tata admits that the group had to reach deep into its pockets to keep some subsidiaries going. However, even the financial crisis has done nothing to damage Tata's growing self-confidence: The big global deals are beginning to repay its patience. Tata Steel's European operations are now in the black and Jaguar Land Rover made £1 billion in profit last year as well as providing Tata Motors with valuable skills.

Sustainable innovation

In a highly fragmented and competitive industry, survival depends on rapid and continuous innovation to create competitive advantage and to profit from emerging opportunities. In this sector sustainable innovation is the watchword and Tata Steel has been playing a smart game.

A major battleground for organic growth in the steel sector has been providing better performing and cheaper products. 'Light weighting' – the process of taking out material but maintaining or increasing performance – is common across many steel-intensive sectors – from automotive and domestic appliances to construction and packaging. As a major player in the European market, Corus was a recognized leader in joint product development in this field and so the acquisition provided Tata Steel with world-class knowhow that it could build on.

With highly volatile raw material costs, securing the supply of high-quality feedstock is an essential ingredient for business success. At the time of the acquisition in April 2007, Corus did not have any captive raw materials. Today Tata Steel Europe has 25% raw material self-sufficiency across the Tata Steel group and the target is 50% self-sufficiency in the medium to long term.

In 2007 Corus undertook a foresight program, 'Sustainable Futures,' which brought together a range of organizations from different sectors to debate the key issues. From this the company gained unique insights not only into the major drivers of change at a global level, such as the need to improve environmental performance, but also which sectors were likely to be the ones where change impacted first.

As a consequence of this, Tata Steel now has some of the leading environmental products in the market and more major platforms in development. For instance, in the part of the business supporting the construction sector, the company launched Confidex Sustain, the world's first carbon neutral building envelope system; and Target Zero, a project providing construction companies with guidance on how to build sustainable low and zero carbon buildings. Tata Steel has also been co-developing a unique low-cost solar energy coating for steel roofs that has the potential to enable the likes of Wal-Mart and Tesco stores to become zero carbon.

In a sector where customers are becoming increasingly aware of the environmental impacts of their suppliers' products, Tata Steel is working to a target of less than 1.7 tonnes of CO_2 per tonne of steel and a single gas recovery project in South Wales will reduce CO_2 emissions by 300,000 tonnes a year – roughly equivalent to the national CO_2 reduction target for Wales.

Both the takeover of Jaguar Land Rover and Corus led to a shift in attitudes and a focus for innovation in the acquired companies. A year after the acquisition, one Jaguar Land Rover senior manager shared that the change of ownership from Ford to Tata was 'like a heavy burden being taken off our shoulders: We are more secure about our future and are being encouraged to build the world's best car brand.' Similarly for a Corus strategy director 'the Tata ownership has changed the mindset from surviving the short-term business cycles of the steel industry to being given permission to think about the longer term.'

Social Responsibility

Alongside big acquisitions and sustainable innovation, the Tata Group is also known for its commitment to creating value for all stakeholders: 'Tata Steel has always believed that the principle of mutual benefit – between countries, corporations, customers, employees and communities – is the most effective route to profitable and sustainable growth.'

Evidence of Tata's role in the community can be seen in Jamshedpur, the home of Tata Steel and perhaps the world's most successful company town. Tata Steel runs almost all the city's institutions including a hospital, zoo, sports stadium, and the local utility company. The city is remarkably well run by Indian standards, with broad avenues, green parks, reliable power, and water that you can drink. Tata Steel gently mocks all this corporate philanthropy with the slogan, 'We also make steel.'

Kirby Adams, former managing director of Tata Steel Europe, added:

The Tata name and philosophy is a unique asset which evokes trust and a sense of common purpose among our employees, our customers, our investors and the communities in which we operate, as well as opening doors into new markets where the Tata brand is especially well-known and respected. Being

Introduction

The Growth Agenda

Nestlé
PepsiCo

Audi
Samsung

Reckitt
Benckiser
P&G

Starwood
Inditex

Amazon
Google

Narayana
Novo
Nordisk

Rolls-Royce
ARM

BASF
Shell

Tata
Bharti

LEGO
Apple

The Growth Challenge

part of Tata Steel has been a tremendous advantage to us in weathering the storm that raged more severely in Europe than anywhere. And it will continue to benefit us as we position ourselves for a return to growth.

The Future

Looking forward, the industry faces many challenges and the top companies will need to innovate further to survive and succeed. Alongside competition from China there are a number of other issues to deal with. Most significant of these will be the continued volatility in raw material prices and moves by suppliers to more dynamic pricing models. Coming at the same time as low demand in the United States and Europe due to the prevailing economic uncertainty, many see further consolidation as a likely scenario. With Brazilian steel producers rapidly becoming the lowest cost producers in the world, thanks to abundant local supplies of high-quality iron ore coupled with low energy prices and low wages, only those companies that have adaptive strategies in place, have a strong innovation engine and healthy balance sheets will do well. Tata Steel qualifies on all three criteria and is in a good position to grow even in an uncertain environment.

At a Group level, as *The Economist* sees it, 'Tata's spread helps it wage two of the hottest wars in modern India: for talent and trust. Tata can compete with Western talent-magnets such as General Electric and Accenture. It is well enough known to appeal to people in the remotest villages. Even the twin strategy of advancing at both the bottom and the top of the market makes sense: it is hard to dismiss Tata as a "cheap" brand when the group owns luxury hotels and fancy consultancies.' Tata's diversified structure has given it a valuable mixture of flexibility and deep pockets. Its Bombay House HQ provides Tata companies with clout when they want to make ambitious acquisitions or when the market turns against them.

Bharti

Founded in 1976, Bharti Enterprises has grown from being a bicycle manufacturer to becoming one of the largest Indian conglomerates. Still very much led by its founder Sunil Bharti Mittal, the group now covers retail, real estate, insurance, and food distribution but is best known internationally for its tele-communications and IT businesses – Bharti Airtel, Bharti Infratel, Indus Towers, Comviva, and Beetel Teletech. Across all the companies in the Bharti group highly effective partnerships is probably the most visible common thread. In the retail area, Bharti Wal-Mart is a joint venture with Wal-Mart; the insurance businesses are all joint ventures with AXA; FieldFresh Foods is a joint venture with Del Monte; and Bharti Airtel is partnering with all the leading companies in the telecoms arena. As with Tata, although each business is run independently, there are similar traits across all and so understanding Bharti's growth success and strategy is best achieved by looking in detail at its largest company – Bharti Airtel.

Bharti Airtel

Bharti Airtel is India's leading telecommunications company and the largest telecoms operator in the world with over 210 million subscribers. As well as providing mobile services across 19 countries in South Asia and Africa, it offers land-line telephone services and broadband internet access in nearly 100 Indian cities and also has a satellite TV business. Launched in Delhi and Himachal Pradesh in 1995 under the brand name Airtel, the company has grown steadily over the years through a mix of organic growth and competitor acquisitions and went public with an IPO in 2002. Already India's largest integrated mobile opera-tor by 2005, Bharti Airtel launched services in Sri Lanka in 2009 and Bangladesh in 2010. In the same year it made a major move on the international expansion journey by buying Zain Africa in a $10.7 billion deal. Bharti Airtel has expanded at a breathless pace in the 16 years of its existence and analysts see that it has displayed remarkable capacity to scale up year on year and to execute its plans with high energy.

Outsourcing Business Model Innovation

For the first few years, Bharti Airtel followed a very similar growth strategy to other mobile operators around the world – buying licenses, building networks, growing support activities such as customer care, billing and network operation, building its brand, offering competitive tariffs and the latest phones, and so steadily gaining more customers. This served the company well, but did not significantly differentiate it in the market or give it any major competitive advantage over its peers.

Bharti Airtel's breakthrough came at the end of 2002, when the management team took the hitherto unprecedented step in the telecoms services industry of outsourcing the technical backbone of the service to global specialist firms in a long-term partnership arrangement. This was followed by four other major outsourcing decisions that left Bharti Airtel focusing just on the things it does best. Manoj Kohli, joint managing director and international CEO of Bharti Airtel, explained this reasoning in an interview in 2008:

When we started our journey in this sector in 1995, we knew that the telecom industry needs deep pockets, it demands huge funding, billions and billions of dollars. We also knew that Indian customers would need to be serviced with affordable prices – very low prices. Now these two things actually didn't connect with each other. On the one hand we sell at very low prices but we invest billions of dollars, so we may not have a viable business plan. So we thought to ourselves, how do we get over this? If we have to succeed in this sector, we said; we need to change the paradigm; we need to invent a new business model. We decided in a meeting in Dec 2002, if we have to sell at the lowest prices in the world, then obviously we must have the lowest costs in the world. There is no choice; it is a necessity. Let us modify and alter the business model according to the needs of the customer. We initiated a huge outsourcing strategy in five big parts.

And those five parts were all significant activities that other companies have distinctive competences in:

- Networks – outsourced to Siemens and Nokia, Bharti Airtel then buys capacity and pays according to usage and capacity utilization.
- IT – hardware, software, services, and people all outsourced to IBM.
- Call centers – outsourced to Indian call centers.

- Towers – rather than each operator building their own towers, Bharti Airtel put its towers into separate tower companies which then share the use and cost of the towers with competitors.
- Distribution – rather than build showrooms and shops in every town and village, the Airtel brand is sold by local entrepreneurs through their retail outlets – one million of them across India.

Overall, what we have done in this new business model is that we have out-sourced all expertise areas to people who are better than us in their areas and we have no problems saying this, that the partners are better than us and kept to ourselves our core competence.

Our core competence is customer management, brand management – brand is so very important to us, people management – motivating our people, financing is our job, and regulation management. These are our 5 jobs that we do. We do those aspects that are our competence, everything else we don't do. Everything else is done by our strategic partners who have better domain knowledge, better skills and capabilities to help us do it. Today, in the global telecom sector, Bharti's business model is looked upon as most unique and most viable and great for all emerging markets.

Outsourcing these five traditional internal capabilities fundamentally changed Bharti Airtel's competitive position. Unlike the great majority of its peers, it could now scale quickly by relying on other companies' infrastructures, resources, and assets. If it so desired, Bharti Airtel could now grow faster and quicker than the competition, but this would only work if it had the right product and brand mix that customers would want.

Partnered Customer-Focused Innovation

Bharti Airtel's entrepreneurial culture and customer-centricity come together to create an organizational culture that is consistently opportunity minded. Again the focus is on partnering with others rather than trying to deliver everything itself, enabling the company to profit from innovation despite its low average revenue per user when compared to other global telecoms operators. As a consequence the company has been able to deliver new services to its customers fast and effectively without the need to invest heavily in building new internal capability.

One typical example is the company's app store which extended reach from just smartphones to the more basic devices used by many of its customers. It is a 'device agnostic platform' so from launch it supported over 500 phones across all operating systems and saw over 2.5 million downloads in its first month of operation. By 2011 Bharti Airtel's app store had over 100,000 applications making it the largest operator-owned app store globally.

Given its large number of rural customers, Bharti Airtel also launched IFFCO Green Card – a unique system that creates localized content and delivers it to farmers in their language of preference. 'A good example is our collaboration with IFFCO which is India's largest fertilizer company. It has 36,000 societies and 55 million farmer members all over India. We picked up a small equity stake in their marketing company so that IFFCO and Airtel are working together in all of these societies. We are providing specialized content that is geared for farmer users, we have developed agricultural content and content in 16 different Indian languages that helps farmers. This works as a win-win for IFFCO and Airtel because the equity of both brands grows in the customer's mind.'

In a joint venture with the State Bank of India, the company is preparing to launch Bharti Airtel money – India's first 'mobile wallet' service providing 24/7 payment and transfer options to its customers. 'If you spot an opportunity early, try to capitalize on it quickly. If you can't do it on your own, look to develop it pro-actively with partners. Partnership should be done early, so that the partner and company can work closely together to make it work. If it is done late, then most of the potential is gone. Partnership only works if there is a match with the DNA, the vision and the values of the partners. If it is not congruent, it does not work.'

The partnered customer focus, rapid innovation to scale, and consistent investment in brand equity building have enabled Bharti Airtel to retain a significant revenue per user advantage in the hyper-competitive Indian market even in regions where operators are market leaders.

Africa

Having honed its business model in India, over the past couple of years Bharti Airtel has been on a spending spree — adding operations in what it sees as other high-growth markets. Sri Lanka and Bangladesh were initial forays but the big acquisition that put the company on the pages of the *Wall Street Journal* and the *Financial Times* was the purchase of Zain Africa's operation in 15 countries. Having failed in an initial attempt to buy South African operator MTN, the Zain acquisition was seen as a good option. It added 42 million customers and moved Bharti Airtel well up the big league of mobile operators.

With an optimized low-cost business model at home, the company believes it can 'bring the benefits of mobile telephony to millions and millions of lower middle class and poor consumers around the world.' Moreover it is confident that it can do this more effectively than any other operator. 'By 2015, Airtel will be the most loved brand in the daily lives of the African people.'

Manoj Kohli sees that 'the acquisition of Zain Africa is clearly amongst the biggest professional challenge that any Indian companies has undertaken in recent times. The big test for us lies in transporting our unique business model and recreating our brand magic across the large population in the new continent and be seen as a global corporation with global best practices. Our partner ecosystem linked through a rich culture of win-win collaboration will undoubtedly be the bedrock of our strategy.'

For Bharti Airtel, Africa presents its own set of challenges as a market. Unlike India, which is one country with several states, Airtel Africa has to contend with 16 different countries – all with different legal, regulatory, financial, economic, and social frameworks. With the Zain acquisition, Bharti Airtel is now playing a more complex multinational, multi-regulator game – one where its ability to manage its multiple partnerships is key. This has involved replication of business structures and processes and re-creation of partner ecosystems. The program commenced in mid-year 2010 when the deal was completed. Bharti Airtel has put in place partnership deals – the first of its kind in Africa – with many of the world's top global ITC corporations, including IBM, Ericsson, NSN, Huawei, Spanco, Avaya, and Tech Mahindra.

Further Optimization

Over the last couple of years the growth of the Indian mobile market has come from prioritizing revenues over margins and all companies have sought to expand their user base to boost profits. With more than 850 million customers, prices for voice have fallen to record lows of half a paisa (1/100th of a US cent) per second. However, as Vodafone and other challengers in India have continued to compete incessantly on prices, Bharti Airtel was the only Indian operator able to recoup its cost on capital last year. Although its return on capital has dropped in recent years from 30% to 15%, the next best competitor is down at 5%. So, to improve profitability, Bharti Airtel is now looking to further streamline its operations. First off is the integration of the African businesses and the merger of its satellite, mobile, and fixed-line businesses in India into one entity. Sunil Bharti Mittal recently said that the company 'had always pioneered new business models that have set industry benchmarks while creating consistent value for our customers, employees and other stakeholders.'

Future Growth

Sunil Bharti Mittal sees future growth continuing to come from both India and other markets: 'The next phase of our journey is set to be another game changer – requiring superior thrust and focused leadership. We continue to win in the Indian telecom market, which is going through a phase of hyper competition. At the same time, we will be developing comprehensive plans for our journey to cover emerging markets beyond India and the South Asia.'

In satellite, broadband, and fixed-line, growth is so far primarily coming from riding and driving the internet penetration wave in India – a country which, with less that 10% fixed broadband access at the moment, has plenty of growth potential. In mobile, the rollout of 3G and 4G is providing opportunities for fine-tuning pricing plans to enhance margins in line with the non-stop growth in consumer numbers. So far only 50% of the Indian population has a mobile and many see that this will quickly rise to over 80% in the next couple of years. In particular, given the company's experience in building partnerships some see that Bharti

Airtel is well placed to take full advantage of the projected rise of data use by consumers.

More mobile expansion in Africa is clearly on the agenda although Akhil Gupta, deputy chief executive of Bharti Group, sees that 'Bharti Airtel first needs to fully exploit the potential in the 16 countries in which it already operates in Africa. We are not going to be greedy. We are not going to rush in to things. We want to get the model right and make sure that we are completely successful here.' Although China led the way in Africa with infrastructure investment via state-supported organizations, Bharti and other Indian companies are keen to ensure that they become as important in future African market growth. Akhil Gupta sees that 'India is ready to put in large investments in Africa. We can match China in investment dollar for dollar and skill for skill.' Two-way trade between India and Africa has now passed $50 billion a year and commentators see that the likes of Bharti Airtel will be at the forefront on future growth.

Financing further investments and acquisitions is coming from a mix of external and internal capital. Most significantly the potential flotation of all or part of the two towers businesses could enhance the corporate treasure chest for future M&A. Analysts estimate that the towers businesses have current value of between $10 billion and $12.5 billion.

Key Insights – Tata and Bharti

Diversified groups are the 'dominant' form of business in many emerging markets. Tata and Bharti are both at the fore of the new Indian conglomerates that have mastered domestic growth and are complementing it with international expansion. In globalizing, both Tata and Bharti have been fast learners, absorbing lessons from within their organizations and their Indian peers. Even though Tata is a far older organization than Bharti, both share some common elements. As well as being run by the founding families and professionals who have been 'lifers' in the organizations, they both reference themselves against the global rather than the local competition.

Although operating in different markets, one very much a business-to-business (B2B) company and the other business-to-customer (B2C), both Tata's and

Bharti's main businesses operate in highly competitive sectors where price is a primary factor. Tata Steel and Bharti Airtel have re-engineered the business model in their sector at home and, in different ways, created highly efficient low-cost growth engines that can match the best the world has to offer. With the frugal innovation mindset at the fore, they have focused first on efficiency and have each leveraged their ability to manage partnerships – Tata for how it manages acquisitions and Bharti in how it runs its business. In addition, both have strong corporate social responsibility credentials – doing rather than just talking about helping the wider society.

Foremost, however, both have the long-term view and focus more on stakeholders than shareholders. They run profitable high-growth businesses but, if needed, will dig into their respective pockets to get through challenging periods in order that they develop the capacity to win in the long term. Tata and Bharti are Growth Champions because they have hunger, ambition, and pride in what they do, which provides the fuel for enterprise growth. These are the energies that create a growth culture and enterprises that seek to grow wealth. In comparison to many of the world's large companies, the likes of Bharti and Tata are distinctive because they still retain their founding spirit, which was to grow wealth for all stakeholders, not just shareholders, and to serve the communities that they are a part of.

Tata

Growth Impact

India's largest company with major multinational brands and operations

Distinctive Competence

Delivering sustained growth and change across multiple sectors simultaneously

Underlying Capabilities

Sharing knowhow across significantly diversified operations	Managing effective partnered acquisition and integration	Delivering social and environmental change

Bharti

Growth Impact

India's leading telecommunications company and the world's fifth largest telecoms operator

Distinctive Competence

Outsourced business model driving growth via frugal innovation

Underlying Capabilities

Partner-based outsourcing	Customer-focused innovation and brand development	Priority on the stakeholder not the shareholder

LEGO	KEY DATA
Revenue (2010)	DKK 16.0 billion
Average revenue growth p.a. (2005–2010)	51.4%
Net profit (2010)	DKK 3.7 billion
Average net profit growth p.a. (2005–2010)	129.1%
Revenue per employee (2010)	DKK 1.6 million
R&D intensity (2010)	1.9%
Number of bricks produced p.a. (2010)	36 billion
LEGO sets sold per second at Christmas (2010)	28

Apple	KEY DATA
Revenue (2010)	$65.2 billion
Average revenue growth p.a. (2005–2010)	42.2%
Net income (2010)	$14.0 billion
Average net income growth p.a. (2005–2010)	117.4%
Revenue per employee (2010)	$1.3 million
R&D intensity (2010)	2.7%
Average share price growth p.a. (2005–2010)	69.6%
Market capitalization (September 16, 2011)	$371 billion

CHAPTER 14

LEGO and Apple

Bringing magic to the everyday

In much of the consumer product mainstream, mediocrity is pervasive. It doesn't matter if it's TVs and kitchen equipment or bicycles and bathrooms, 'average' is everywhere. Differentiation, from a design and performance perspective at least, has become increasingly challenging. Pretty much everyone sources the same components from an increasingly globalized supply chain, and often they even use the same or very similar design agencies. As a result, over and above pricing and margins, few companies have any significant levers to position their product significantly ahead of their peers. For many consumers, choice has become anathema as products blur in the store or online.

However, within this global malaise, a few select companies are pushing the boundaries and bringing out products that delight and excite their users. Some, such as Bang & Olufsen, focus on high-end design and performance at a price, but others are more cost driven. One company in particular has brought world-leading design, intuitive interaction, unique business models, and far better than average performance to the consumer electronics sector. Equally while organizations such as Hasbro and Mattel have focused on filling our children's bedrooms with an increasing range of similar toys and games, another firm has consistently provided a product family that stimulates the imagination and allows kids and adults to make their dreams. These two companies are Apple and LEGO, long-term challengers in their respective markets but now unequivocal leaders.

Apple, the world's most valuable company in August 2011, has easily gained its place in the history books, alongside Microsoft, Sony, and Nokia, as a company that has delivered transformative technology across the PC, music, and cellphone sectors. With seven sets sold every second, LEGO is now the world's third-largest toys and games company and has produced well over 485 billion bricks so far. Apple and LEGO do something that their peers can only dream of: they bring magic to the everyday. Their products are attuned to how we live, and how we want to live, so they are both intuitive to use and prized above all else. People who use Apple products or play with LEGO are not customers, they are fans. Both companies have become the global benchmarks by which others rate themselves, not seeking to usurp their leadership positions but merely to emulate their success.

In this chapter we look at how LEGO and Apple have succeeded despite the challenges that went before them; how their leaderships have set the ambition and led the organizations forward in alternative ways; and how the cultures of these two very different firms have played such a significant role in building world-leading capability, flexibility, and drive to succeed.

LEGO

Everyone who works at LEGO has the same ambition: 'We all have one thing in common – the goal is to put a smile on a kid's face.' Not many of us can say this. Across the whole organization 'everyone buys into what the LEGO Group's purpose is.' With its track record, most would agree that LEGO and its employees are hitting the mark.

Although nearly bankrupt at the start of 2003, the manufacturer of what *Forbes* nominated as 'the toy of the 20th century' has made a remarkable turnaround and done it largely by itself. As Jan Christensen, communication manager at LEGO puts it: 'its 99% our own fault that we were really down low and its 99% our own success that we are back up.' In the past five years or so LEGO has launched new products that have taken it into totally new markets. Revenues have more than doubled while profits have risen by over 1700%. But LEGO is not out to be the world's biggest toy company – just the best.

Founded in 1932 and named from the Danish words 'leg' and 'godt' meaning 'play well' LEGO's first big shift was in 1960 when it switched from making wooden toys to concentrate solely on the now iconic plastic bricks. With the development of DUPLO for younger kids and LEGO Technic for teens as well as a host of kits linked to themes likes cities, pirates and, especially successful, a Star Wars franchise, LEGO became a top 10 global toymaker. Over 36 billion LEGO elements are produced each year and, in theory, everyone on the planet owns 75 bricks. Across LEGO the need to deliver on the company's ambition 'to inspire and develop the builders of tomorrow' is clear to all.

Catalysts of Change

In 2004 LEGO hit a crisis point. Cheaper imitations appeared on the market and video games quickly rose to the top of many Christmas wish lists. If it had not been family owned LEGO would have been bankrupt and it was clear that there had to be fundamental change. A new CEO was appointed – Jørgen Vig Knudstorp – who quickly initiated change programs first to stabilize the company then to build a sustainable platform for growth.

Although the results related to different sides of the business – the supply chain and new product development – both highlight not just how LEGO had to change but also how effective that change was

Redesigning the Supply Chain

One of the reasons the company had lost money in four of the seven years from 1998 to 2004 was due to its outdated, inefficient, and extremely complex supply chain. Having expanded its range of kits and bricks, the company had thousands of different components or 'elements,' as LEGO terms them. To provide all the various components, LEGO had 11,000 suppliers – nearly twice as many as Boeing uses to build its airplanes. Moreover, 'just 30 products generated 80% of sales' and LEGO paid 'as much attention to the thousands of stores that generated only one-third of its revenue as it did to the 200 larger chains that accounted for the other two-thirds.'

By 2004, the company clearly had to change and the whole approach to manufacturing was redesigned under the guidance of the new CEO. It was an emotional time as the move to a global supply chain meant lost jobs in Denmark as some of its production was moved to cheaper locations. In 2005, LEGO started to outsource the management of global manufacturing and five distribution centers across Europe were replaced by two global centers operated by logistics experts DHL. This transformed the efficiency of the supply chain and was one of the key elements that put the company back on track. The other was in how it undertook much of its product development.

Open Innovation and Crowd Sourcing

In 2006, *Wired* magazine featured LEGO's MINDSTORMS NXT program as the exemplar of fan-based innovation and it quickly became the reference point for many other companies seeking to better engage with their customers. The article, 'Geeks in Toyland,' describes how the MINDSTORMS NXT development was uniquely undertaken.

MINDSTORMS NXT was a project to create an updated version of MIND-STORMS – programmable software linked to LEGO Technic that enabled users to build and control robots. It was soon discovered that there were tens of thousands of 'Adult Fans of LEGO' (AFOL) and quite a few of these were hacking into the original MINDSTORMS software. Seeing this as an opportunity, LEGO invited them to apply to be part of a virtual development team. Over an eleven-month period 100 carefully selected candidates worked together to create the new product – a major success for Christmas 2007 and a strong seller ever since. No one was paid – people wanted to be part of this because they loved LEGO and the privilege of being involved in the new product development of such a major platform was more than enough of an attraction.

www.LEGOFactory.com was launched in 2005. By using the online software, 'LEGO Digital Designer,' and a virtual warehouse of LEGO bricks and elements, children around the world were able to design 3D models on their computers, share these designs with others, and buy the bricks to physically make models. Within 12 months the site had over five million visits a month and www .LEGOFactory.com became the world's largest mass-customization vehicle as the components for thousands of different user-generated designs were delivered direct to the home. Re-launched as LEGODesignbyME in 2009, around a new version of LEGO Digital Designer, LEGO has struggled to balance customization with the simplicity needed by users. In January 2012 LEGO discontinued DesignbyME whilst still supporting Lego Digital Designer as a free design software.

What innovation and strategy leaders in companies find so compelling is not only the impact that the associated changes have had in the market, but more specifically the way the organization shifted its way of operating. 'In the old days LEGO had around 100 designers developing its products. Today it has a full-time equivalent team of 300,000 – average age 9' is one often repeated quote.

Internal Innovation

LEGO has not completely embraced the open innovation approach of MIND-STORMS and the focus today is on 'engaging consumers more organically' as part of new concept development in 'a more systematic way.'

Once a week children from local schools visit the company HQ in Billund. Mike Ganderton, creative senior director for markets and products at LEGO, comments: 'We put ideas in front of them and get feedback. The kids play with the products before they are final designs and also get involved with new themes the company is exploring and help to "spin stories" and create narratives that steer the direction of new concepts.' This 'growing element of storytelling' has become a common DNA through many of the recent successes for the company. Especially with the BIONICLE range, providing kids with the means by which to create and share their stories is a big factor in its popularity.

It is not that the kids are in control but more that they are an integral part of the creation process. This allows the company and the innovation teams to really understand what puts the all-important smiles on faces, but also enables them to stay in the driving seat.

Irrespective of what the market and competitors are doing to catch up, LEGO's internal mantra on continuous innovation now ensures that it keeps pushing the boundaries. The founder of LEGO, Godtfred Kirk Christiansen, once said, 'only the best is good enough for children' and today those in the company see that 'kids always deserve the best we can give them.'

Mike talks about 'systematic creativity' that helps the innovation teams mix creativity with problem solving and analytic development. 'LEGO as a core product has always sought to encourage kids to use both sides of the brain' and that is also how the company approaches new concepts. Mike sees that 'everyone in the innovation area is very clear on what we are trying to do – it is about delivering on our mission.' Combining clear objectives, systemic creativity, and early involvement of consumers helps the company to bring only what really works to market.

Experiments Outside the Core

The LEGO organization has had several forays outside the core business focus of toys and games. For many years it has been well known for the chain of LEGOLAND theme parks. However, as focusing on the core was the priority in 2004, the company decided to sell the parks to an expert in the entertainment sector. Since 2005, they have been operated and 70% owned by Merlin

Entertainment, part of the Blackstone Group. Analysts point out that the sale was not only good financially for LEGO at a key time in its turnaround, but also allowed the company to focus more on its core expertise while still gaining revenue from a growing platform outside.

Another venture outside the core has been 'LEGO® SERIOUS PLAY®' – a strategy development technique that builds strategies, literally, using LEGO bricks. Originally created by two IMD professors in the mid-1990s, LEGO sponsored its commercial development and in 2001 set up a new business to train and manage a global partner network of facilitators for SERIOUS PLAY workshops. However, although successful and well regarded by the companies that embraced the approach, it did not really fit with the LEGO organization and in May 2010 the SERIOUS PLAY approach became open source. Now anyone can use this approach as part of their corporate toolboxes. LEGO still sell the bricks for the workshops but have stepped away from the facilitator network.

Five years apart, these two shifts from ventures outside the core are seen by some as indications of the limits of the LEGO organization's capacity to extend its capabilities beyond the core. Others see them as examples of LEGO getting something going, helping to prove the concept, and then handing it over to others better able to scale them profitably. Just as with the decision to move some manufacturing and distribution to organizations more expert in those areas, passing LEGOLAND and SERIOUS PLAY over to others could be seen as belonging to the same mindset.

In-Sector Expansions

Where LEGO has had more 'success' in terms of both creating and internally sustaining new platforms has been in extending its portfolio within the toys and games sector. If the core bricks and associated kits have been the backbone of LEGO for the past half century, the last few years has seen some positive moves to expand the footprint.

Whereas the original MINDSTORMS product developed with MIT was an extension of the LEGO Technic product, the company has moved into new categories within the toys and games sector with products like LEGO UNIVERSE, a multiplayer online game, and LEGO Games. LEGO Games launched in 2009 and shook up a traditional market: After building and playing a game you can rebuild it, change the rules, and make it better.

LEGO continues to bring its unique magic to the industry whilst also generating highly profitable revenue streams for the business.

The LEGO Culture

LEGO seems to have a culture that others would find nearly impossible to replicate. 'One of the pros of family ownership is we don't have to answer to shareholders: We can do things because we think they are right.'

As found in other Scandinavian firms, the LEGO CEO 'is humble and modest' and does not seek to dictate the way forward. But he has 'almost unconditional support and respect' from all employees. The organization is very flat with much value placed on 'everyone being equal' – LEGO likes to highlight that there are only seven layers in the organization from the CEO to a cleaner. Everyone feels that they can approach each other and discuss issues. Access is not a problem.

Being Danish and, despite now having global operations, still having Billund very much as its center of gravity is also a major factor – as Jan Christensen says, 'if people decide to come here and work it is really because they want to work for the LEGO Group.'

Although LEGO has moved from number 5 to number 3 in the toys and games sector in the past few years and commercial success is important, this is not really what drives the organization. Its desire to 'be the best toy company in the world' is a fundamental influence not just on its strategy but also on the culture. As Jan concludes, 'Every successful corporate has a clear purpose. We had forgotten this. The big turnaround was about getting back to the core play experience' and 'Everyone understands the importance in delivering that.'

The Future

There is no complacency in LEGO. After the experience of 10 years ago and the pain of the turnaround, the company knows that it has to keep pushing ahead.

The leadership team has been laying out what the company terms its 'innovation vectors' – the directions that they believe LEGO should move in over the next few years. These include issues such as the further blurring of the real and the virtual worlds in the mind of kids and how to responsibly support this; and the overall sustainability of the product mix and especially its environmental impact.

While to 'inspire and develop the builders of tomorrow' has been the core purpose of LEGO for the past few years, moving ahead the company has a longer term vision to 'invent the future of play.' As yet undefined in terms of outcomes but clear as regards intent, the internal belief is that right now LEGO is the only organization that can really do this.

Building Brilliance

LEGO is the success story in its sector – the definite Growth Champion. It had to change to survive in 2004 but the way it changed has transformed many organizations' views of innovation. It was back in profit by 2006 and the following year was its best ever. www.LEGOFactory.com and MINDSTORMS provided the definitive reference for fan-based innovation of the past decade. However, this was only the start and since then the company has been willing to change more. In Mike's eyes, 'the company is passionate about play and believes it can deliver the best products and experiences for the children of the 21st century. In order to do this it is connecting with its millions of fans, has set itself the ambition of reinventing the future of play and thus has made a commitment to also put smiles on the faces of the children of today's children.'

LEGO is evidently not the most efficient organization around but with its heritage, purpose, ownership, and culture it works – and clearly delivers the goods in terms of impact and returns. Actually, maybe that's what passion can do?

Apple

Apple's history reads like a corporate fairy tale. It was co-founded by the late Steve Jobs in his parents' garage. It went on to launch the world's first real personal computer, becoming the star of Silicon Valley. The then board fired its CEO and the company nearly went under. Next, in search of some enabling technology it bought the company that its former CEO had set up and got him back with the technology he needed for the future. It then reinvented the computer, changed the music industry, changed the mobile sector and, most recently, it reinvented the laptop as a tablet. Succeeding with all this meant it became the most valuable company in the world without a single cent of debt. It continues to produce great products that people love, that they never knew they wanted, which come wholly from its own internal gut feel around what is right without using market research and focus groups.

In the second quarter of 2011, Apple sold 20 million iPhones, 9 million iPads, 4 million Mac computers, and 8 million iPods. Profits more than doubled to $7.3 billion on sales up 82% to a record $28.6 billion. In August of the same year, Apple took over from Exxon as the world's largest company by market capitalization and had more money in the bank than the US government. When Steve Jobs announced his retirement, *The Economist* announced that, 'the minister of magic steps down' and declared, 'no other boss in recent history has embodied and defined a firm as completely.' Other commentators stated that he is not only 'a genius' but 'also the last and greatest media mogul' and 'the only CEO in the world with rock star status.' Steve Jobs's biography was Amazon's best selling book of 2011. You may well have already read it. So what new can be said about this company? The world's most well-known brand, the manufacturer of products that have changed sectors, cultures, and lives: the world's most effective Growth Champion?

The challenge we had is that Apple doesn't give many interviews and few employees say anything about the company on record. Off record, or anonymously on sites like www.glassdoor.com, they may share views, but officially the only way Apple communicates with the outside world is when it launches a new product or shares its plans at the annual MacWorld event. It doesn't woo investors and doesn't do corporate PR. So how do you know what is really going on inside this company that makes it so special and so successful?

It has been said that Apple is innovation objectified in its products and services. Yet this statement belittles the real work that goes on behind the scenes to improve its products, services, and platforms over time. From the days of being the maverick self-styled underdog of the industry with Steve Jobs's mantra of 'it's better to be a pirate than join the navy' to being market leader, the company has still needed to manage the market's and public's evolving perception of its identity and steer its growth adroitly over time.

If you read what is in the public domain about Apple you get two extremes: there is talk about the secretive organization where 'flops are not tolerated' and where the former CEO controlled everything, got 'irate when something that barely worked had been released to the public,' and is an 'infamous thief of other people's best ideas.' An organization that 'we seem to think is entirely different from, say Microsoft. But is not: it's just as ruthless, squeezing out competitors.' Others, however, see a 'phenomenally well-run company' with the 'world's best design outfit' which 'has thrived by sprinkling a little magic on investors instead of sending them to study its cash-flow,' that managed the 'greatest comeback since Lazarus' led by a 'geek with the Midas touch' that 'not only regularly dreams up beautiful, functional and fantastically complex products, but gets them to market in working order, on time, on budget; and has continually done so despite exploding demand.' Apple has given 'people products they didn't know they wanted, and then made those products indispensible.'

As ever the truth lies in-between. Although we don't have any approved quotes from inside the company, from what we know from following it for the past decade, from talking to ex-employees, from discussing Apple with other business leaders, and from some of our own personal experiences of working with the firm, it is evident these two strands coexist to make things both beautiful, functional, profitable, and shipped. In Steve Jobs' early words to his original Mac design team in 1983 'real artists ship.'

Beneath the headlines there is a company entity that is highly distinctive: its ability to attract and retain the world's best talent is testimony to that. Apple's culture was defined by Steve Jobs but is well embedded and as much influenced by its first decade as the last. With people like Jonathan Ive, Tim Cook, and Phil Schiller now taking the company forward, we expect to continue to see a phenomenal sales growth and a healthy product pipeline.

Apple always had a big mission: to design a computer for 'the Person in the Street (PITS); one that will be truly pleasant to use, that will require the user to do nothing that will threaten his or her perverse delight in being able to say: "I don't know the first thing about computers," and one which will be profitable to sell, service and provide software for.' This statement is as true today as it was in 1979.

It is also a company that has stayed in all levels of provision – from operating system to hardware and software and marketing. We agree that 'its secret sauce lies in the integration of devices with software and services . . . that form what tech types like to call an ecosystem that has proved so popular that it is forcing other companies to develop similar capabilities.'

Stay Hungry Stay Foolish

To gain an insight into what motivated chairman and former CEO, Steve Jobs, it is useful to listen to a commencement address given to graduating students at Stanford in June 2005.

There were three core messages in the speech that reveal a lot, not just about the former CEO, but also about the culture of Apple that has built up over the decades.

Jobs talked first about how 'you can't connect the dots looking forward, you can only connect them looking backwards. So you have to trust that the dots will somehow connect in your future.' Urging students to follow their intuition and passion he told a story of how he dropped in on a calligraphy course that, he felt then, wouldn't have any bearing on his future life but looking back found it completely inspired the look and feel, the visual interface of the Mac – a trait that has defined the USP of the company ever since and speaks to the love of detail found in all Apple products:

Throughout the campus every poster, every label on every drawer, was beautifully hand-calligraphed . . . I decided to take a calligraphy class to learn how to do this. I learned about serif and san serif typefaces, about varying the amount of space between different letter combinations, about what makes great typography great. It was beautiful, historical, artistically subtle in a way that science can't capture, and I found it fascinating. None of this had even a hope of any practical application in my life. But 10 years later, when we were designing the first Macintosh computer, it all came back to me. And we designed it all into the Mac. It was the first computer with beautiful typography. If I had never dropped in on that single course in college, the Mac would have never had multiple typefaces or proportionally spaced fonts.

He also shared a view that 'your time is limited so don't waste it living someone else's life. Don't be trapped by dogma – which is living with the results of other people's thinking. Don't let the noise of others' opinions drown out your own inner voice.' And, perhaps most significantly, he gave the advice that he had picked up from the last edition of *The Whole Earth Catalog* in the mid-1970s to 'Stay hungry. Stay foolish.'

Many in Apple see that the way the business behaves is very much a reflection of these views. There is always the flip side with Apple. It may be obsessive about detail and control of the experience, but that does not make it dogmatic –- it also has the nerve to do its own thing and not play by others' rules.

The Apple Magic

When compared with all of the other companies discussed in this book, it is obvious that Apple is currently the 'best' Growth Champion. On all metrics – revenue growth, share price, profits, brand, fans – Apple is the winner and, given the past decade's performance deservedly so. When you talk to other leading organizations the references to Apple as a model are frequent. Using the same distinctive competence lens through which we have been looking at all of the Growth Champions, we see five distinctive areas where Apple, as a business, has put clear distance between itself and the competition and in so doing managed to deliver the results everyone gets so excited about.

Self-belief

While some have commented that Steve Jobs was a notorious micromanager, the reality is that Apple simply believes it is doing the right thing. This comes from a company where the culture is focused on challenge, perfection, and a vision about democratizing technology. In Apple 'innovation doesn't come from coddling employees and collecting whatever froth rises from the surface; it is the product of an intense, hard fought process, where people's feelings are irrelevant.'

Back in 1979, Jeff Raskin, Apple employee number 31, wrote an internal confidential memo called 'Computers for the Millions' thinking ahead to what would have to be done by any company if computers became truly personal: 'If "personal computers" are to be truly personal, it will have to be as likely as not that a family, picked at random, will own one. To supply even our own nation with enough computers to make this happen (over, say a four-year period) we will require, for example, twenty-five companies each producing over a million computers a year.' Actually thinking ahead and reading the possibilities has been a trait of key Apple personnel over time. It has not been all done by magic.

Steve Jobs liked to quote, 'I skate to where the puck is going to be, not where it has been' and said, 'You can't just ask the customers what they want and try to give it to them. By the time you get it built, they will want something new.' The view that Apple defines where the market is going by delivering the future product is found across the organization. Chris Morrison phrases one of Apple's guiding principles as: 'Don't follow your customers; lead them.' As Leander Kahney put it in *Wired*, 'no other company has proven as adept at giving customers what they want before they want it.' When you watch the video of Macworld announcements you see a company that is far from being shy. Apple believes that the products it produces are the best and uses words like 'beautiful,' 'amazing,' and 'awesome' to describe them. This is not seen as marketing overstatement but as what the company really believes.

Control and integration

In 2001 with the launch of the iPod the consumer and technology world began to see the fruits of Apple's change of strategy. In what reads now as a prophetic speech Jobs launched the 'digital hub strategy' placing the PC at the center of the new age of the 'digital lifestyle.' Commenting on the rise of the cellphone, MP3 player, DVD player, camcorder, and handheld organizers, the PC or the Mac was seen to be the connector and enabler for consumers to make, create, and store their digital libraries and lives.

Apple believes that it can deliver the best products by integrating the design and delivery of its products keeping control of the necessary elements of hardware and software. The reason the iPod and iPhone have worked so well with the iTunes software is that they are so implicitly linked together. Tom O'Reilly talked about the future of the net being 'three-tiered systems' – that blend hardware, software, and propriety apps, and sees that Apple is 'the only company that really understands how to build apps for three-tiered systems.'

While Intel and Microsoft sell their products through partnerships and publish roadmaps in advance so that their partners can create the machines to use them, Apple keeps pretty much everything within its tent so that it does not need to tell anyone anything. Apple is almost unique in being vertically integrated – it sees that it 'is the last company in our industry that creates the whole widget,' and, 'as the only company that designs the hardware, the software and the operating system, we stand alone in our ability to innovate beyond the status quo.' Even when a new iPhone is launched at Macworld, the major global telecom operators who will be running the networks and selling it to their customers don't get advance notice on the product.

The company has a major R&D pipeline with a constant stream of patents being filed and discussed in the press as commentators try and define the future lines that Apple may be developing. The website www.patentlyapple.com details many of Apple's patents and recent articles in the press have also started to explore more about what the company has up its sleeve. In 2010 and 2011 it increased its visible IP activity significantly. After a show down with Nokia, not only did it join Microsoft in buying all of Nortel's remaining telecommunications patents, but it also started to prevent Samsung from showing, never mind retailing, its latest Galaxy tablet in Europe. Apple's desire to control the ecosystem it believes it has created is increasingly becoming a public side of the company.

Technology access

Apple doesn't always use the latest technology within its products. In fact many see that it waits until a technology is proven and then wraps it in a simple but beautiful design. For example, as Samsung pointed out, MP3 players were on the market well before the iPod. Apple waited until it had worked out the perfect ecosystem and business model that would enable it to scale a massive profitable business built around a product that was effortless and sublimely intuitive to use. However, it is not quite so simple. When Tim Cook joined Apple he outsourced almost all of Apple's manufacturing operations to Asia. The company also does not make its own technology – but it does have control.

ARM, in which Apple has a stake, designs many of its chips. Apple has used Intel as a supplier and it buys numerous components from producers around the world. What Apple does is to use its position and cash to bring other people's technologies to scale in return for exclusivity and future discounts. Often when a new technology emerges it is expensive to produce because volumes are small and raising investment capital is a major challenge. As shared by an anonymous user on Quora, 'Apple pays for the construction cost of initial facilities in exchange for sole access to factory output for a year or two and then a discounted price thereafter. Not only does this mean that Apple has access to the technology it wants well ahead of rivals but also means that when the technology is available to all, that Apple gets the best deal and so can achieve higher margins.' The outcome of this is that Apple can deliver better performing products more effectively and more profitably than anyone else.

Keeping a tight team

Although Apple has over 50,000 employees, an extremely small team defines the future direction of the company especially in terms of strategy and product design. In 2011 *Fortune* magazine published an article by Adam Lashinsky which described the organizational chart for the Apple leadership team. It highlighted that the whole company is run by a group of around 18 key people and within that group, the CEO, COO, and SVPs of design and marketing are really the ones that make the decisions on what to do and, perhaps more importantly, what not to do.

John Gruber, the technology blogger, summarized what he sees as special about Apple and why it is different from its peers with, 'Apple is a design company with engineers; Google is an engineering company with designers.' There is a lot to be said for this view. At its core Apple has a very clear design-focused development process, the principles of which were shared in a *Business Week* article by Helen Walters in 2008. Most notable in this analysis was the idea of 'paired design' meetings:

Every week, the teams have two meetings: One in which to brainstorm, to forget about constraints and think freely. Then they also hold a production meeting, an entirely separate but equally regular meeting which is the other's antithesis. Here, the designers and engineers are required to nail everything down, to work out how this crazy idea might actually work. This process and organization continues throughout the development of any app, though of course the balance shifts as the app progresses. But keeping an option for creative thought even at a late stage is really smart.

Right from the start, Apple has hired excellent designers who brought new thinking, new materials, and new design language into the company. Hartmut Esslinger, founder of Frogdesign, was the creative input behind the Apple II and the first Mac. He was senior designer at Apple from 1982 to 1989. He recalls being hired by Steve Jobs with a brief to introduce their 'snow white design language' and 'reposition Apple as a California-Global Brand – Hollywood and music, a bit of rebellion, and natural sex appeal.'

Steve Jobs said; 'In most people's vocabularies, design means veneer. It's interior decorating. It's the fabric of the curtains of the sofa. But to me, nothing could be further from the meaning of design. Design is the fundamental soul of a human-made creation that ends up expressing itself in successive outer layers of the product or service.' Apple really does embody this idea from the innards to the interface, the casing to the packaging all wrapped up with intelligent advertising and marketing campaigns as part of the whole.

Steve Jobs highlighted the role of key individuals throughout his leadership, including back in 1998: 'Innovation has nothing to do with how many R&D dollars you have. When Apple came up with the Mac, IBM was spending at least 100 times more on R&D. It's not about money. It's about the people you have, how you're led, and how much you get it.'

One highly significant employee, Jonathan Ive, joined the company in 1992 and has been the design lead behind every major new product since then. In a

2002 interview, he described using a Mac for the first time as a student: 'Innovating was in Apple's DNA. I clearly realised that the first time I used a Mac . . . I remember it very very clearly. There was nobody there to help me and I would never never look at an instruction book . . . I could just use the product straight away. It was a very profound moment. I don't think I had ever had that sense of "wow" with a product before.' From the iMac and the iPod to the iPhone, the Macbook Air, and the iPad, he and his very small team of designers have created many of the icons of the start of the 21st century. Unlike other firms there is virtually no churn. People don't leave because where else would they be able to do what they do? Apple has 'built and retained the respect of the most remarkable design team in living memory, a group that has done more innovation than the rest of the computer industry put together.' Jobs made the comment that, 'Great things in business are not done by one person; they are done by a team of people.' Many see that more than any other organization, Apple has been obsessive in caring for its 'creatives' and nurturing its 'Innovation Elite.'

Apple stores

You only have to enter an Apple store to see teeming and buzzing activity. It's here where you realize just how many generations are using and buying its wares. Seniors, smart suits, parents, teens, and toddlers; people playing, talking, testing, checking their mail, and finding new ways of doing things. Engaging with the staff and engaging with Apple Inc. whether they know it or not. Compare it to any other shop where you might buy a computer or a phone. What do you see there? The salesperson on one side of a counter, and the customer on another. This simple but arresting contrast tells an instant story. Yes, you can buy Apple products elsewhere and many do, but in an Apple store there is always something new you can do with what you have got and people who can tell you or show you what that might be. Apple has created, and continues to evolve, a completely different shopping experience, but one that is hugely profitable. Even though it has lots of space for people to try out products and get advice, according to retail analysts, Apple's Regent Street store in London is the highest sales per square foot facility in the city. It has made an astonishing success of bricks-and-mortar retailing as the rest of the world has been moving online. This experience has been as carefully constructed as any Apple product.

Future Growth

Apple ended Wednesday August 11, 2011 as the most valuable publicly traded company in the world. 'They have an enormous value being the market leader in two of the fastest-growing segments of the industry, tablets and mobile. When you're a leader in two sectors that are growing exponentially, it's hard to ignore,' said Susquehanna Financial Group's Jeff Fidacaro. Over the past five years Apple's revenues have grown at an average of 43% per year and its net profits at an average of 65% – that through a major recession when shops in many countries were closing down. If you had invested $1000 in Apple in 2000, 10 years later it would have been worth $13,294. Where does a company like this go next? On taking over as CEO, Tim Cook wrote a letter to staff that said 'I am confident our best years lie ahead of us and that together we will continue to make Apple the magical place that it is.'

In a 2011 *Fortune* magazine article by Adam Lashinsky, an executive who worked at Apple and Microsoft was quoted as saying 'Microsoft tries to find pockets of unrealized revenue and then figures out what to make. Apple is just the opposite: It thinks of great products – then sells them. Prototypes and demos always come before spreadsheets.'

It's the creative designers and the alliance with consumers that have helped to propel this company into the business stratosphere. Some years ago Steve Jobs hired Joel Podolny, formerly dean of Yale Business School, to create Apple University with an aim to bring to life some case studies to help current and future employees understand how their products were developed and the success achieved. As something done in many other corporations around the world, from an internal knowledge development and culture-building perspective, this clearly has merit. But will they go so far as to share the insights and case studies with the world of business and education? Apple may feel it has sufficiently 'flummoxed the competition' to believe that no other company can copy its ways sufficiently to overtake it. If and how this takes place will be interesting to watch.

Despite the death of Steve Jobs, few see any major changes taking place in what Apple does. To some it is magic, to others it is a perfect combination. It is a company, a business model, and a whole ecosystem that has been designed to work as well as one of its products. It may not be the best at everything but the overall combination is hard to beat.

Key Insights – LEGO and Apple

LEGO and Apple are clearly on top of their game. They are the organizations against which many others benchmark not only their actions but also their aspirations. They are justifiably the companies that get major media coverage but more significantly they are the organizations of whose consumers have most become fans.

Although operating in different markets, with different dynamics at play, it is notable how many commonalities there are between LEGO and Apple. From a business point of view, both came back from the brink, became the challenger, and have gone on to be the recognized leaders in their fields – all within a decade. They are both very confident in their own ability to create the future and almost take it as their responsibility. Just as LEGO feels that people should think 'of course LEGO should be the ones to do that'; Apple's view is that as the only company with the hardware, software, and digital platforms they should be the ones that shift our experiences forward. Equally they have self-belief that what they are doing is the right thing and are pushing the boundaries. LEGO's ambition is to engender the view that its products are 'obviously LEGO but never seen before'; so Apple has its view that you shouldn't follow your customers but lead them.

In an era of increased openness both have provided their fans with platforms with which to create their own products and realize their ideas. The Apple app store and LEGODesignbyME are the most popular routes through which millions of people share their ideas. At the same time both LEGO and Apple largely monetize these ideas – and their fans don't mind. While these platforms do provide open interaction, the majority of the companies' new innovation is, however, undertaken internally and largely behind closed doors. While some criticize this, others ask 'wouldn't you do the same in their situation?' LEGO and Apple have attracted some of the best talent in the world to work for them, they have competitors desperate to catch them up, and they have the culture and processes internally that consistently deliver game-changing experiences. They don't need to engage the outside world. Yes, LEGO invites kids in to play with new ideas and give feedback, but no longer are they asking externals for ideas like they did with MINDSTORMS NXT. Apple doesn't need to invite consumers in because its design team has 50,000 customers inside the company to use if it so needed. Both organizations therefore seem to have found a balance between internal private innovation and external interaction that, although different, hit the sweet spot for the user.

Lastly, and perhaps most importantly, LEGO and Apple have continuously put products and software in people's hands that are both intuitive and enable creativity. While the technology may not be the absolute best, and there has clearly been a lot of forgiveness from customers along the way, the experiences that users gain from both companies' products is what sets them apart. As well as products that work straight out of the box without the need for any instructions, Apple has also made software like iMovie and Garageband that enable intuitive creativity to a far greater extent than competitors. The way that everything is integrated and works best with other Apple products is in some ways very similar to the way that LEGO works best with LEGO. Both companies have provided the means by which consumers can create new things, but largely as long as they do it within the tent of their products and services.

There is no certainty that in 10 years' time, these two companies will have the leadership positions that they do today. Leadership, competition, regulation, and consumer sentiment are all issues that some see as being in flux. However, from a culture, vision, and confidence point of view, many believe that LEGO and Apple will, for the next few years, continue to be the organizations that bring great products to the world, and products that bring a little bit of magic to the everyday.

LEGO

Growth Impact

The world's best toy company

Distinctive Competence

Deep self-belief in being the only
company in the sector that can
truly invent the future of play

Underlying Capabilities

| Fan-based innovation and product development | Developing and managing communities | Systematic creativity within the organization |

Apple

Growth Impact

The world's most valuable
and iconic company

Distinctive Competence

Consistently delivering great
products that people love,
that they never knew they wanted

Underlying Capabilities

| Self-belief | Control and integration of technology | The best design team in the world |

Part III

The Growth Challenge: Lessons for the Future

The Growth Champions have all outperformed their competition and delivered revenue and margin growth in an impactful and sustainable manner. So what can we learn from looking across these companies, all leaders in their own fields? We know that they have all grown through a mix of strategic intent, innovation focus, and consistent delivery. Equally they all implement rigorous processes, foster talent, and pay close attention to detail.

There is, however, a single approach that is the source of guaranteed success: it is achieved in different ways by different organizations essentially adapting proven techniques to fit individual cultures and strategies. In this third part of the book we first discuss characteristics that are evident in all the companies analyzed and which we think are pivotal to their prolonged success. These are inspirational leadership, clarity of ambition, shared values, organizational confidence, and a focus on innovation. Together these factors help to shape and sustain the unique culture of each of the Growth Champions.

CHAPTER 15

Key Characteristics

Inspirational Leadership

As we undertook the analysis for this book and talked to executives in the varied companies we were able to explore different organizational cultures. As you can imagine these were many and varied. For example the flat structure of Google is very different from the more established, corporate style of the likes of BASF. Equally Apple's tenacious control over its innovation is counter to Procter & Gamble's open approach. That said, one element that we kept encountering, and which permeates throughout each organization, was the role of the leadership teams and particularly the CEO. In nearly all of the companies, the CEO was more than just the top manager or its strategic direction setter; he or she was a catalyst of change, the primary driver of the corporate ambition and its communication to all stakeholders, and a link between the history of the company and its future growth prospects.

Founder CEO's drive

In the companies that are still being, or have recently been, led by their founders, the entrepreneurial spirit that created the varied businesses has not dimmed. As their companies have grown in scale and reach so too has their vision. When Jeff Bezos founded Amazon, he did so with passion and insight: As the company took on the established world of retailing, he kept on coming back to that 'Day 1' perspective in order to drive the business forward. Equally Larry Page and Sergey Brin have been unwavering in taking Google forward. Within Bharti, Sunil Bharti Mittal has been at the heart of the company's every move as it has grown to become a major player in the telecoms sector and in Samsung it has been Chairman Lee who has raised the bar at regular intervals and kept on pushing the organization forward. With Starwood Hotels, Barry Sternlicht had so much drive that he took on the role of chief design officer, creating brands at his kitchen table and making sure that the dreams came true. Equally in Narayana Hrudayalaya, Dr. Shetty has been at the forefront of the organization's development from the start: Not only was it his vision that set the initial direction, he has been the champion of every step forward. In Inditex, Amancio Ortega's role as the entrepreneur who built opportunity from a cancelled order and then made Zara into the world's most effective and dynamic fashion retailer is the subject of many articles, and his position as Spain's richest man is testament to his drive. With ARM, it has been less about an individual and more about the team from Acorn Computers that collectively felt that there was a better way to develop advanced chips and a more effective business model to deploy. Many are still involved in the business, and CEO Warren East was an early joiner and a key part of the initial growth of the company. And of course there was Steve Jobs at Apple. Few would deny his crucial role in not only co-founding the company and setting its initial direction, but also in taking the helm again over the past decade or so and leading its famed rise to number 1 in its field. His departure will be missed.

All these individuals had the original vision but they also have the stamina to keep pace with the organizations they founded as they have grown. As the 'garage start-ups,' such as Google and Apple, became multibillion-dollar global businesses, they were not handed over to other 'professionals.' Experienced talent, such as Eric Schmidt at Google, has been brought in, but the founders have stayed and kept delivering their ambitions. They are far from one stereotypical view of the serial entrepreneur who has a great idea, builds it to scale, and then sells and moves on to the next thing. While few of them probably expected to be where they are today, they have all developed in tandem with their organizations.

One obvious concern often expressed about such individuals and their companies is the long-term sustainability of the business after the founder has moved on. Whether talking about any of those above or Richard Branson and Virgin, Bill Gates and Microsoft, Larry Ellison and Oracle, or Warren Buffet and Berkshire Hathaway, commentators love to question how well companies will do after the founders are no longer there. While nothing is guaranteed, many who contributed to *Growth Champions* are confident that as succession planning and business continuity has been a top priority the right future leaders are already in place. As Steve Jobs, Barry Sternlicht, and Amancio Ortega handed over the running of their companies to others, this is clearly a pertinent issue.

Catalyst of change

While founder CEOs have implicitly been catalysts of change in their industries as their businesses have grown and variously reinvented the market, there are also a number of companies whose CEOs have taken the helm in order to change the organization. Most notable of these is A. G. Lafley at Procter & Gamble who in 2000 was handed the responsibility for a company whose share price had nearly halved in the preceding quarter. Under massive media and investor scrutiny he had to turn the world's largest FMCG company around. His focus on margin improvement, building the core, and growing twice as fast as the sector led to organizational shifts to open innovation, integrated design, and greater customer focus. When he left the business a decade later, it was re-energized and rebuilt. Of course this success was not 100% down to Lafley but he led the team so his role as the chief catalyst of this change is clear. Equally but less publicized has been the role of Jørgen Vig Knudstorp at LEGO. He took the helm of a family-owned business and quickly saw what needed fixing: With the decisions to simplify the supply chain, sell the majority of LEGOLAND, and support the digital move to www.LEGOfactory.com, he enabled the changes that first saved the company and then put it on its growth trajectory.

Although not under the same crisis situations, other CEOs have taken the lead at critical stages in the past few years. In Reckitt Benckiser, Bart Becht took the helm of the merged entity after 10 years in the Benckiser business. Knowing that Reckitt & Colman and Benckiser were different beasts with different cultures, he restarted the corporate timeline from the point of merger and led the new entity almost as if he was the founder of a new company. With the clarity of focus that he brought to the company and its culture, he too acted as a catalyst of change. In Rolls-Royce, Sir John Rose's time at the top saw changes from realigning its portfolio with an acquisition of Vickers to the introduction of the TotalCare business model and the redefinition of the company's approach to

Introduction

The Growth Agenda

Nestlé
PepsiCo

Audi
Samsung

Reckitt
Benckiser
P&G

Starwood
Inditex

Amazon
Google

Narayana
Novo
Nordisk

Rolls-Royce
ARM

BASF
Shell

Tata
Bharti

LEGO
Apple

The Growth
Challenge

technology development. Indra Noori has led with passion and introduced significant change at PepsiCo. In Novo Nordisk, Lars Rebien Sørensen, CEO since 2000, has stated: 'I wish we could solve the problem of diabetes in my lifetime – even if that sounds strange as this is where we make our living. But if it can be done, we must be the ones to do it.'

At Nestlé, chairman Peter Brabeck and CEO Paul Bulke have led the company through a major period of redefinition of purpose. They steered Nestlé away from past reputational problems to be a leader in shared value. Rajan Tata is clearly the dynamo behind the Tata group of companies, while in Shell, Jeroen van der Veer was pivotal in re-setting the company compass to focus on energy rather than on oil alone, as well as integrating what had been two separate businesses into one. Jürgen Hambrecht, BASF CEO from 2003 to 2007, was a dynamic leader well known in Germany for his passion; and at Audi, the chief design-trio of Walter de'Silva, Wolfgang Egger, and Stefan Sielaff have been pivotal in setting the company's products' strategic direction within the Volkswagen Group and making it the profit engine.

As with the founder CEOs, succession of many of these individuals is also an issue. Especially for those that have taken the reins in a time of crisis or other organizational challenge; how well the successors maintain performance is a concern to some. However, as with Steve Jobs handing over to former COO Tim Cook, what we see is very much a passing of the baton to people from within the organization who have been within the growth journey for many years, know it well, are already embedded in the culture, and so have been understudy to the CEO for some time. Bob McDonald in Procter & Gamble was previously COO, Rakesh Kapoor was EVP, category development at Reckitt Benckiser, and Kurt Bock was CFO at BASF, as was Peter Voser at Shell. Only John Rishton at Rolls-Royce moved from another company, but he had been a non-executive director at Rolls-Royce since 2007 and had history in the aviation business. All these individuals have been part of the growth successes of their companies over the past decade and, as they have taken the leadership role, they have been able to ensure continuity as well as a desire for continued progress.

Without exception, the Growth Champions have had leaders that have all brought about change and done it with clear direction and impact. Whether prominent in the public eye or acting as an internal agent of change, all 20 companies have had their direction, their culture, and their growth strategies significantly impacted by the varied individuals at the top of the organization. In an era when some see that professional managers are best equipped to run large businesses, it is notable how these high-performing companies have been led from the front by characters that, whether the original founder or a new standard bearer, have made their mark.

Key lessons

- *Passionate leadership really matters, even in a mature business. A leader who is prepared to challenge conventional wisdoms, internally and externally, and put an aspirational stake in the ground gives the organization focus.*
- *Having the CEO as champion and lead, not just sponsor, the growth agenda engages everyone and can bring about fundamental change in the business and its performance.*
- *Succession planning is important and promoting from within provides continuity and a leadership who understands the culture and shares the values of the organization.*

Clarity of Ambition

The Growth Champions all have a clear ambition around which to align the organization, and the ambition is more defined than in many other companies.

Although vision and mission has been part of the corporate 'must do' list for many years, often the results are a bit generic or even banal. Sampling from the *Fortune 500*, statements like 'to deliver operational excellence in every corner of the company and meet or exceed our commitments to the many constituencies we serve,' 'to achieve profitable growth through superior customer service, innovation, quality and commitment,' 'to be the best in the eyes of our customers, employees and shareholders,' and 'to build a unique portfolio of brands, striving to surpass our competitors in quality, innovation and value,' are all cases in point.

They say nothing significant and hence really have no significant value to their organizations.

What is evident from the Growth Champions is that they have articulated an ambition that actually means something and, as such, provides real focus and drive for the organization. Although none has an identical approach, the mix of ambitions can be clustered into two clear groups – those that provide clear business targets and those that speak to core values or the raison d'être of the company.

Of all the companies, Reckitt Benckiser is probably the most target-focused with the ambition to drive organic growth accompanied by clear numeric targets. Sustainability issues have been added in recent years but foremost the organization is really all about hitting the numbers and that is evident in its culture. While its counterpart in the FMCG sector Procter & Gamble also has business performance targets such as to 'grow twice as fast as the industry; grow by one-and-a-half to two times GDP,' these are accompanied by a values-based ambition – 'to improve the lives of the world's consumers, now and for generations to come.' Employees of Procter & Gamble are engaged just as much by the latter as the former. Equally in BASF, PepsiCo, Shell, Tata, and Nestlé, with its desire to 'create shared value,' you can see evidence of focus on purpose that combines both business performance and societal impact.

In other companies the ambition is very much an aspiration for what the organization wants to achieve, often set within a wider societal context. This is true whether it be to 'put a smile on a kid's face' for LEGO; to 'organize the world's information and make it universally accessible and useful' for Google; to 'enable every man, woman and child to have access to high-tech healthcare within the next 10 to 15 years including in the poorest regions of the world' for Narayana Hrudayalaya; or to 'defeat diabetes' for Novo Nordisk. But in these cases, the impact is the same – to set a clear direction of intent and outcome for the company, one that may be independent of financial targets, but that nevertheless inspires people to help in its achievement. While other companies have lame mission statements, the Growth Champions are succinct about their aspirations and it is this clarity of purpose that helps the organizations to focus on delivering success. The desire for growth is anchored in the ambition that is, in turn, embodied in the company's business strategy. It provides context and clarity for all, it is shared and, even in the high-stretch cases, it is felt to be achievable.

Key lessons

- *Growth aspirations need to both inspire and be specific enough to create focus – ideally they engage the rational and the emotional side in a coherent mix.*
- *Ambition needs to be reflected in the day-to-day business activities and made tangible though clear targets and believable principles.*

Shared Values

The Growth Champions also have core values that shape and steer what they do and how they behave. These values are, like the ambitions, more than just a set of words on a website – they truly reflect the views of all employees and influence the decisions from top to bottom of the organization, every day. Notably, the ways that the Champions express their values also reflect the nature of each unique culture. From Google's 'don't be evil' and Nestlé's 'creating shared value' to Procter & Gamble's 'improve the lives of the world's consumers, now and for generations to come,' and Shell's 'honesty, integrity and respect for people,' the values both summarize the goals and standards of behavior that are embedded in the culture and act as simple litmus tests against which to judge all that is done. The Growth Champions all have in place three key reinforcing ingredients for strong cultures: leadership, ambition, and shared values.

Key lessons

- *Aligned leadership, ambition, and values driven from the top are key to inspiring exceptional performance from within the organization and forming deep relationships with external stakeholders.*
- *Clear ambitions that fit with the organizational values enable all employees to believe that they are doing something worthwhile.*

Organizational Confidence

In the discussion around Apple we highlighted how it had evident self-belief. It is an organization that is not only confident that it can see where its sector is heading, but it can also get there ahead of its peers. All of the companies we analyzed truly believe that they can do what they have set out to achieve. In some this hits you as soon as you start talking to people. For example, most in Reckitt Benckiser, Inditex, and Amazon exude supreme inner belief that they can do things better than the competition. Whether this is faster, cheaper, or more effectively, they all feel that their distinctive competences and culture enable them to win.

For Audi, its design prowess clearly puts it in the top rank of car brands along-side BMW and Mercedes, but its position within Volkswagen gives it the reassurance that it can leverage scale and platforms so effectively that it can launch new products that are both better and more profitable than most of the competition. For ARM its chip design capability and the accompanying business model give it both the will to beat larger rival Intel and the belief that it can do this. Samsung is confident that it can build the world's leading design capability to accompany its technological prowess and take a leadership, rather than imitative, role, in all the categories in which it plays. Bharti is very confident in its business model while Tata believes that its people, its technological capabilities, and its deep financial muscle will make it a success within the sectors in which it chooses to operate. Notably both Bharti and Tata place great significance on their social activities and consider that, as well as doing the right thing for their organizations, they are also doing the right thing for their home society.

Although operating in a difficult landscape, Shell's confidence that it can deliver large-scale, technology-based, complex projects enables it to pursue growth opportunities that many of its peers would shy away from. Equally BASF believes that its highly efficient process mindset will, if aligned with clear direction, enable it to be successful in the short and long term. At Rolls-Royce the faith in technological leadership and access to the best research is accompanied by a strong business model to give it the confidence that it can be number 1. And in Starwood Hotels you find a company that builds on its proven track record with new brand development to give it the conviction that it can continue to create and scale high-impact experiences across the hospitality sector.

None of these companies' self-assurance is based on blind belief. Far more than many of their competitors they are well aware of their weaknesses. As many have either come from behind to lead in their sectors, or overcome major challenges, they know that their leadership positions have not come easy. But having achieved what they have, and learnt what they now know, they are determined to continuously improve their ways of working. Influenced by the direction of their leadership, these organizations simply engender a feeling that they know what they are doing, why they are doing it, and how it will help make them a success in the broadest possible way.

Key lessons

- *Companies need to have an acute understanding of their distinctive competences and areas of weakness and then build an organization that amplifies those competences and addresses the weaknesses.*
- *A clear ambition grounded in proven capability and genuine aspiration builds the confidence that an organization is making the right decisions and moving forward with its eyes open.*

Innovation in the DNA

As expected, innovation has a clear role to play in all these organizations. In one way this is a self-fulfilling insight driven by how we selected the companies to profile in the first place. However, while the selection was based largely on analysis of external data, what is apparent from the internal discussions is the critical dependency of sustained growth based upon innovation. Innovation is very much at the heart of everything our Champions say and do.

In most of the Growth Champions we found specific reference to innovation via organic growth. In some, such as Apple, ARM, and Amazon, it is virtually the sole route to growth and is a proven approach. Take for example, the view that Apple's design team 'has done more innovation than the rest of the computer industry put together.' The same could be said of the respective teams in LEGO, Narayana Hrudayalaya, and Inditex.

Innovation Communication

In all the companies not only is innovation clearly aligned, as Peter Drucker proposed, to 'changes that create a new dimension of performance' but is also focused on delivering a tangible competitive advantage and creating increased value for the businesses and their customers. Many also explicitly place innovation center-stage in their communication with the outside world and the stakeholder communities. They talk about innovation not only in terms of what they do, but also through the perspective of how they are organized. In Reckitt Benckiser every investor interaction is based around announcement of product introductions; while Apple's primary public interaction at MacWorld events is about its new launches. For Samsung, innovation, design, and technology are the words used most often in its external communications; Tata talks about innovation across its portfolio; Audi's communication platform is based around innovation and 'Vorsprung durch Technik'; Novo Nordisk declares that 'innovation is at the core of our business'; while Starwood Hotels promotes its 'commitment to pacesetting innovation.'

In fact, if you, as we did, review the press releases of most of these companies over the past decade, many of the stories they are telling are either about business performance and innovation or the partnerships, organizational changes, or acquisitions that they have made to enhance these two. Yes, innovation has become a buzzword for many companies and is found liberally sprinkled across annual reports and CEO speeches alike, but many do not deliver the goods. In all the Growth Champions, innovation is in the DNA, it is what they do best to drive their business performance and hence it forms a majority of what they talk about.

Innovation beyond the core

In many of the Growth Champions innovation has now moved well beyond the core products and technologies. While Narayana Hrudayalaya and Inditex exemplify process innovation to optimize operational efficiency, Audi also gains massively from Volkswagen's process innovation. Process innovation as a distinct capability can also be found within Samsung, Tata, Apple, and Reckitt Benckiser. Service innovation for Starwood Hotels is also very much based on new process innovation that enables it to deliver great customer experiences without major cost – the same is true in Amazon and Google. From these innovation activities some of our companies discover or create new market niches – from Starwood Hotels with its Heavenly bed, Amazon with its Kindle e-book, and Inditex with fast fashion – all products wrapped in an exceptional customer experience.

However, we also see the rising influence of business model innovation. ARM and Bharti are two organizations whose competitive advantages are based on their unique business models within their sectors. 'Designing once and licensing many times' is what makes ARM so successful and so attractive; while the multiple partnerships that Bharti has established and manages give it the unique ability in the mobile telecoms sector to scale rapidly without bearing major infrastructure investment costs and so open up low-cost telecoms to millions of new customers. From Rolls-Royce's 'power by the hour' TotalCare service to Apple's iTunes and Amazon's Marketplace we also have high-impact, high-margin business model innovation taking place. And let's not forget that Google has been a platform business model pioneer. From Adwords to Gmail to Android, Google is the company that has perhaps most effectively embraced business model innovation as the primary means of value creation and business success.

Many of the Growth Champions also go outside their four walls and embrace variants of 'open innovation' – active programs to engage with and leverage the broader business ecosystem to drive innovation often at the same time reducing their own R&D investment. BASF's Future Business, Procter & Gamble's Connect & Develop, Shell's GameChanger activity, LEGO through its crowd sourcing, and Rolls-Royce through its university programs all provide contrasting and successful examples. As companies ramp up these external programs they are increasing the level of activity without necessarily increasing internal R&D spend. ARM provides a great example of how by designing once and licensing many times, the R&D cost is spread over the whole industry saving an estimated $32 billion when compared to the traditional model of all companies doing in-house R&D.

Introduction

The Growth Agenda

Nestlé
PepsiCo

Audi
Samsung

Reckitt Benckiser
P&G

Starwood
Inditex

Amazon
Google

Narayana
Novo Nordisk

Rolls-Royce
ARM

BASF
Shell

Tata
Bharti

LEGO
Apple

The Growth Challenge

Disruptive innovation

Many companies also clearly understand the need to both distinguish between and balance disruptive and incremental innovation. While some such as Audi, Reckitt Benckiser, BASF, and Tata are largely focused on incremental innovation; those that have embraced disruptive innovation have done so in a coherent rather than reactionary manner. As well as evolving its legacy brands, Starwood Hotels has used new brand creation specifically to create new market niches and customer experiences that disrupt the status quo. Procter & Gamble has explicitly established new organizational responsibilities and teams to focus on disruptive innovation in parallel to ongoing incremental innovation within its core brand teams. ARM's business model has changed the world of semiconductor chip design. Amazon keeps on disrupting the retail industry; a mainstay of much of Google's innovation activity is to disrupt adjacent sectors; with its buildable games products, LEGO is similarly causing commotion for others as it seeks to 'invent the future of play'; and Inditex has changed the way the industry looks at stock levels and time to market. Disruption has moved from being the sole province of challenger start-ups to be part of the innovation mainstream. These companies clearly show how it can be part of the innovation mix, balanced with incremental innovation and integral to the wider growth strategy.

Innovation acquisitions

In most, organic growth is the preferred option. In Procter & Gamble the stated aim is to 'focus on organic growth first, then acquisition for long-term strategic growth.' Equally the CEO of Reckitt Benckiser shared that 'our primary focus is on growing the business organically. That does not mean we do not like to do acquisitions, but we are only doing them if they make sense for us because they fit strategically.' Where growth is achieved through buying another company, it is clearly linked to filling a gap in the product, brand, or technology portfolio and is not just about buying market share. The same approach is taken in organizations as different as Google and Rolls-Royce. Google's acquisitions over the years have very much been small ones focused on bringing a new technology into the mix. When it has bought big, as in the case of YouTube and Motorola, there are clear synergies with the internal growth strategy within Google, whether it be about customer engagement, the integration of services, or bulking up the intellectual property portfolio. In Rolls-Royce acquisitions have similarly been very focused. In recent years, it has bought relatively small technology-based companies to develop its solid oxide fuel cell capability, add to its marine energy automation services, or build its TotalCare portfolio. Even in the cases where major M&A activity has been part of the growth mix, it has been done in the content of supporting, or being supported by, a strong innovation motivation.

Tata's acquisitions of both Corus and Jaguar Land Rover have complemented the organization's market presence and technological competences rather than taking it into totally new territory. Equally Bharti has used acquisition to enable it to migrate its innovative business model into new markets. While in Shell, the 2010 joint acquisition with PetroChina of Australian coal seam gas company Arrow Energy Limited shows how it uses acquisitions to bring in-house the technologies needed for accessing gas from coal seams and then combines this with Shell technologies and its partners' ability to access the Chinese market. Although they are making acquisitions, these companies are all doing so in a focused manner to support their organic growth strategies. Innovation is a major factor in these companies' growth agendas just as much as it is in the likes of Inditex, Apple, and BASF.

Key lessons

- *Successful growth comes from relentless focus on innovation across the board. From core products and services to internal processes and new business models, multifaceted innovation is critical.*
- *Innovation should be anchored in the company's ambition, so it has both context and is a sustainable part of the corporate fabric.*
- *Talking about innovation is easy but you must support what you say with what you can see in the organization – the structures and systems that*

support and reward innovation are balanced with creativity and autonomy – and this translates into what you do and how you do things.

- *Neither R&D investment nor media messaging can be taken as the sole indicators of how innovative a company is. Growth does not come from a single activity but rather from a flexible combination of many factors.*

CHAPTER 16

Further Common Traits

If inspirational leadership, clarity of ambition, shared values, organizational confidence, and having innovation in the DNA are the factors of which we can see evidence in all of the 20 Growth Champions, there are two other commonalities that we can observe in a subset of these. Although not present in all, they are significant because they are clearly having impact in several cases. They are 'Foresight and Insight' and the 'Return of the Conglomerate.'

Foresight and Insight

Doing the wrong thing exceptionally well is for some companies a fast track to failure. From Readers Digest, Encyclopaedia Britannica, and Borders to Woolworths and TWA we can see examples of companies that continued pursuing activities when the market had moved on. In other examples, such as the launch of New Coke or the GM EV1 electric car, significant investment was made in trying to shift the market before it was ready, although luckily for Coca-Cola and General Motors, the realization that they were doing the wrong thing came early enough to prevent them from losing the farm. When faced with reducing business performance many organizations seek operational improvements rather than recognize that the market or society has evolved. Equally when presented with an unexpected opportunity, many fail to capitalize on it due to either lack of context or depth of understanding into the customer, technology, and market implications.

Many of the Growth Champions have shown the ability to meet major challenges and exploit opportunities and this is because they have well-developed foresight or deep insight, or a combination of both. Most importantly, these are not hidden in some research group but are directly connected to decision making to enable strategic moves to be made ahead of the pack. Foresight and insight are highly valued, well resourced, and the outputs have currency within the organization.

Shell has built a reputation on being an exemplar in using scenarios and other foresight techniques to give it a view on changes over the next 20 to 50 years. More than most other organizations, it understands what changes may occur within both the world and its industry and the business, regulatory, customer, technological, and financial implications. However, the company also has very good insight on the world of today. As well as the dynamics of supply and demand within the energy sector, it also has an excellent reading on how governments and the motivations of multinational organizations align and conflict. It understands the ecosystems within which it currently operates and the way they are likely to unfold in the future. The same can be said of Rolls-Royce, ARM, Narayana Hrudayalaya, Novo Nordisk, Tata, and BASF. They all have a clear view of the forces shaping their markets, the implications for their industry, and the opportunities and risks that arise.

Procter & Gamble has also built up a strong capability that has enriched its insight on current consumer preferences, choice, and behavior while simultaneously gaining better understanding of the longer term view. As the Procter & Gamble horizon has moved from 5 to 10 years, it has used its 'Lighthouse' programs to understand far more about the challenges and opportunities that lie ahead. Whether this is about the convergence of cosmetics and healthcare or the environmental constraints that may apply to its product supply, Procter & Gamble today is more aware of the world in which it could be operating in the future. When this is combined with its world-leading insights on consumer behavior gleaned from its ethnographic, semiotic, and other research, it provides the organization with an overview of where and how it might play in the future, what will be the key implications, and how best it can prepare itself for future growth. Again the same can be said for other Growth Champions. Nestlé and PepsiCo in the food sector match deep insight with good foresight, just as much as Amazon, Apple, and Google do in the online world.

As well as differences in time horizon and focus areas, the different cultures and competences of our Champions determine how they take advantage of foresight. Shell seeks technological solutions; Nestlé looks for what is technically possible, commercially viable, and needed by society; while Samsung increasingly starts with design principles in order to develop new solutions to address new insights.

There are some for whom foresight is less significant as they are focused far more either on the here and now or in areas where the future is a natural extension of today. While they variously have very good insight into the present, none of LEGO, Reckitt Benckiser, Starwood Hotels, Bharti, or Inditex would claim great foresight capability. However, for others, where the need to understand the future context is as important as their short-term perspective, this close integration of foresight and insight is paramount. They have shifted from a singular view driven either by foresight OR insight to a combination of foresight AND insight.

Key lessons

- *Growth Champions have demonstrated the ability to understand the insights and implications for their industry and business and turn that into actions that result in innovation and exceptional growth.*
- *Companies that understand the forces and trends shaping their markets and the implications combined with the insights from today are better positioned to lead in emerging opportunities. In an increasingly turbulent world this capability will become more valuable and will often distinguish winners from losers.*
- *This capability must be an integral part of a company's strategic planning: foresight and insight alone do not deliver growth – they have to inform and drive action.*

Return of the Conglomerate

In the past, some of the more established Growth Champions have had periods where they have diversified – PepsiCo used to run restaurants; Shell has been in nuclear, coal, forestry, mining, and solar power; while LEGO has owned theme parks. These companies have prospered because they have now 'returned to the core,' achieving success by focusing and trimming diverse operations from their portfolios. Others such as BASF, Nestlé, Procter & Gamble, and Reckitt Benckiser have diversified portfolios of brands and products but they operate within clearly defined spaces such as chemicals, beauty, grooming, or household care. Beyond our select group we see a similar trend with companies such as ABB, AEG, Diageo, Caterpillar, Boeing, Unilever, and United Technologies – all having relatively narrow but highly focused ranges of activities. General Electric provides perhaps the only major exception to this concept of 'narrow conglomeracy.' It is a highly successful organization that describes itself as an 'advanced technology, services and finance company . . . dedicated to innovation in energy, health, transportation and infrastructure.'

Whilst in the West, diverse conglomerates are therefore in the minority, in Asia they are very much in evidence. In India, where the 'Licence Raj' supported the growth of such organizations as Reliance, ITC, Essar, and Mahindra; and in South Korea, where the *chaebols* such as LG and Hyundai are dominant, conglomerates are the order of the day. Equally in China where the likes of Fosun International, Guotai International, HNA Group, and their peers practice multi-industry activities and especially in Hong Kong where Hutchinson Whampoa, Swire Group, and Jardine Matheson remain strong, conglomerates are increasing their influence. Even in Japan, where *keiretsu* such as Mitsubishi are still very much multi-industry in nature, we can see an approach to running diverse businesses in a way that many management thinkers in the West had, evidently mistakenly, dismissed for its inefficiency and lack of focus.

It is notable that three of the Growth Champions are Asian conglomerates. Tata is one of the largest companies in India with activities stretching from tea, steel, and cars to hotels, consulting, and telecoms; Bharti, although having a strong telecommunications core, is also involved in retail, real estate, insurance, and food production; while Samsung Group is Korea's largest *chaebol*, and, as well as electronics, is active in shipbuilding, retail, theme parks, IT consulting, and insurance: if it were a country, Samsung would be in the world's top 50 by GDP.

At a time when Western management thinking has veered toward clarity of focus on excellence in one or two sectors, it is telling that these three Asian conglomerates are outperforming more concentrated peers in many industries. What is more they have used highly effective M&A activity as a successful part of their growth strategies at a time when most Western acquisitions have failed to deliver value. How they achieve this is due to a combination of unified culture across each group of companies, mutually supporting finance, and very good sharing of knowhow. Just as Tata learned the art of how to integrate an acquisition effectively across its tea, steel, and automotive businesses, so Bharti has excelled at joint ventures, and Samsung has mastered process innovation across its many sectors of activity. Whether we see a resurgence of conglomerates in the West or further growth in Asian groups, time will tell. But for now, it seems that these organizations are running their varied collection of companies across multiple sectors in a different and far more effective way than many Western counterparts achieved 50 or so years ago.

Key lessons

- *Diversified and somewhat integrated conglomerates can work and be highly competitive against more focused peers.*
- *No single conglomerate model guarantees success but the chosen model should be aligned with the organizational culture, capabilities, and leadership's ambition.*
- *Conglomerates enable in-house knowledge transfer and capability building across different sectors.*

The Unifying View

Reviewing the above, we can see two different influences at play. Culture and strategy are interwoven in many of these issues. There are elements that are unique to organizations such as the people, the CEO in particular, the values, and the associated ambition that very much influence the specific culture of each company. While others may seek to replicate some of these, the reality is that they cannot be fully duplicated. They define the nature of the organization. Equally there are many elements that are not specifically unique to each firm. The targets for growth, the scope of innovation activities, the use of foresight and insight, and even the structure and diversity of the organization's activities are all things that can be specifically chosen, changed, and hence imitated. These are strategic choices. From the Growth Champions we have examined, it is apparent that success is not just down to the nature of the firm, nor is it due to the decisions that are taken in terms of how, where, and why to play in different fields. Success is driven by the unification of culture and strategy around the growth ambition and then linked to the competences and capabilities available to the company. The profiles and the above analysis all point to sustained growth being an integrated outcome of these two very different issues into a coherent and well-focused whole.

CHAPTER 17

Future Challenges

While the companies profiled have successfully developed new approaches from which sustained growth has been achieved over the last decade, it has not been plain sailing. Indeed there have been significant challenges along the way that have had to be overcome. Think for example of business continuity for LEGO and Procter & Gamble to the negative PR around obesity for Nestlé and PepsiCo and the increasing environmental impacts of the industries within which Audi, BASF, Shell, and Tata operate. Rather than bury their heads in the sand hoping that the challenges will disappear, our Champions have already proven adept at rising to the challenge by taking clear decisions, resetting the organization, and delivering new sustained growth platforms.

As highlighted earlier there are a number of issues that organizations seeking to prosper in the future need to address. There also seems to be common agreement around some of the future challenges that they, and other companies, will need to confront if they are to achieve or maintain ongoing growth over the next decade.

China

Foremost is the influence of China. With one out of five people on the planet living in China, it is the world's most populated country and within the next decade it will be, on most measures, the most powerful economy. Current estimates put China's foreign exchange reserves at more than $2 trillion and in 2009/2010 it loaned $110 billion to developing countries – greater than that provided by the World Bank. So the combination of a huge and growing population queuing up to be 21st-century consumers, global economic influence, an educated workforce, and a host of significant Chinese companies means that China provides multiple levels of future challenge and opportunity, from accessing it as a market and satisfying its surging demand to the rise of Chinese companies and their potential leadership on the global stage.

Accessing China

Many of the companies profiled have identified China as the priority emerging market for their products and services. To date there are differences in the degree of success that has been achieved. For Samsung, China is very much its closest and largest market; for Audi it is the brand's highest growth market; for Starwood Hotels it is the country where it is opening more hotels than anywhere else; and for Tata it is the primary market for its steel and probably for its cars. For Procter & Gamble, Reckitt Benckiser, PepsiCo, Nestlé, Apple, BASF, and Inditex, it is already the number 1 geographical source of future growth; while for others, like Google and Amazon, it has been the place of a few false starts. For LEGO and Narayana Hrudayalaya it is yet to be a major market but it is certainly on the radar.

The challenge is that, for many, China is completely different from the known markets in which previous growth has been achieved. While so far many companies have been able to sell their products to Chinese customers through joint ventures and affiliates, as things scale up and local competition intensifies these may not be the winning models. While brands such as Apple and Audi may well be able to develop the long-term retail partnerships that enable their premium products to be offered to an ever-wider consumer base, for others accessing the Chinese customer is going to be more problematic.

Organizations such as Reckitt Benckiser already recognize that their models need to be adapted. The local pull for the global 'powerbrands' approach that has done so well in the West may need modifying for China. New-for-China-only brands is an obvious step, but product promotion and distribution may also have to be different. The same holds true for PepsiCo and Nestlé even though they have already established bigger footprints. When the new competitors are homegrown China-only domestic brands, the global/local strategy may not suffice. Likewise, for Starwood Hotels, it has so far been about taking established brands into China – but how much of this has been the international traveler and the internationally experienced domestic businessman? The Chinese use of hotels is completely different to that of the West not just from the purpose of stay but also the expected experience. So, given its U.S. heartland, how does Starwood Hotels deliver the winning combination that gives the Chinese consumers what they want? Equally how do companies such as Audi, BASF, LEGO, and Shell with European-dominated management teams really understand the workings of the Chinese business world?

Accommodating China's demand

China is already the world's number 1 consumer of major resources such as steel, aluminum, and concrete. Pretty soon it will have eclipsed the United States to be the biggest user of energy, chemicals, and food. As its economy continues to grow and healthcare becomes more accessible, many see that China will also at some point become the world's leading pharmaceutical market. For some, such as Novo Nordisk, China's demand provides a specific set of challenges. Given the shifts taking place in diet and wealth, there will soon be more diabetics in China than anywhere else. Will the prices for insulin be the same as found in today's main markets? How will Novo Nordisk's educational programs best be adapted to a market with escalating protein and fast-food consumption within a completely different culture?

For Shell and BASF, China is a major source of immediate demand for fossil fuels and oil-based chemicals, but this is also increasing the magnitude of meeting the environmental challenges associated with their industries. From a carbon perspective alone, the world cannot cope if China's demand for fossil fuels goes anywhere near Western levels of use. China needs different solutions, but what will those be and how will they be delivered? Will this initially mean gas and nuclear rather than coal then hydrogen, wind, or solar energy? Will it mean more white biotech-based chemicals and will these companies want to give the very latest technology to China first? What will China's escalating demand do to global raw material prices and what will be the corresponding impacts on established markets? This is as significant for Tata in the steel industry as it is for Nestlé in the food sector.

Chinese champions

Whilst no Chinese company made the final list of Growth Champions there are already a good number of Chinese companies growing well, some of which have already started to show major global success – Huawei in the telecommunications sector is already challenging the likes of Ericsson and is the preferred partner for many of the world's largest mobile operators. Lenovo is growing its PC market as quickly as Haier is expanding its presence in domestic appliances. Right now, whilst none of the Chinese companies that you can see in the top 100 lists are seen as number 1 Growth Champions in different sectors it won't be long. Just as Tata and Bharti have already broken into the top echelon from India, within the next few years expect a host of Chinese companies to make similar progress.

This provides a challenge to the current incumbents to up their game. It will not be easy as new entrants will arrive with a billion or so customers already in the bag; they will have financial advantage from being supported by the Chinese state and gaining from its currency exchange policy; and they will increasingly be quality as well as cost competitive. They will also be active in many sectors – from cars, consumer electronics, and banking to food and fashion. If you talk to Procter & Gamble, Reckitt Benckiser, Nestlé, and PepsiCo about the 10-year global landscape they see new China-based brands as their biggest future competitors. Just as many banks are worried about their Chinese counterparts, Shell is concerned about CNOOC, and Google is keeping an eye on Baidu.

With the large Chinese Diaspora in concentrated markets around the world and the economic influence that the Chinese government has achieved through its foreign investment policy, maybe the bridgeheads for Chinese companies are already established? As the world's center of economic power accelerates East, fast-growing Chinese companies will increasingly be the sources of competition and, given the structure of China's economy, they will be playing by different rules. And as China moves from a stage 2 efficiency-driven economy to a stage 3 innovation economy maybe we should be looking to China as the next source of disruption.

Key lessons

- *Many of the Growth Champions of the next decade are likely to be Chinese companies with deep pockets and different approaches.*
- *Many business leaders today are now looking at Chinese companies as a source of potential disruption rather than as low-cost suppliers.*

Open Network Collaboration

Many Growth Champions are excelling at strategic partnerships and collaboration. They are growing by playing the collaborative game and have cultures that support this internally and externally. They recognize that they cannot be masters of everything, have a deep appreciation for their own core competences, but are also able to better collaborate where they need to – often outside their own industry.

Whether you look at PepsiCo and Cargill working together on new sources of natural sweeteners; LEGO's production with Flextronics and distribution with DHL; Nestlé's partnerships with General Mills and Coca-Cola; Shell's joint venture in Brazil; Bharti's partnered business model; or Samsung's technology supply relationships with its competitors, effective bilateral collaborations are very much in evidence. Many already do collaboration well without losing sight of the need to continually focus on performance delivery, cost control, and efficiency. Indeed many achieve lower cost through their collaborations and partnerships. As they succeed they create scale and sources of competitive advantage that make it harder for others to do anything but join in.

Such collaboration requires shared ambitions and the win/win of shared value creation. Historically this has been hard to deliver as coordination costs are high and information is not equally and freely shared. As a result delivering value at scale from networks has been highly challenging. However, when combined with the appropriate culture and shared ambition, recent innovations in technology are enabling coordination costs to be lowered and information to be equally shared: Inditex is running a highly efficient supply chain network with multiple partners in order to deliver fast fashion; Rolls-Royce's UTC network with over 30 universities is proving the value of a choreographed approach where all have clear inputs, areas of focus, and hence skin in the game. As ARM's business model highlights, collaboration across networks is an elemental shift in some sectors and one where the capabilities for companies are fast moving from partnership management to ecosystem choreography. These are more than bilateral partnerships but they are nevertheless still bounded in terms of limited membership and hence ability to manage.

In the future the nature of collaboration will change as increasingly open networks replace strategic partnerships, intellectual property becomes a shared commodity, and knowhow is transferred globally. This helps drive collaboration, fosters higher levels of innovation, and goes further than open innovation. Some of the companies profiled already demonstrate a shift from direct control over resources to one where resources are accessed through open network collaboration. For example, Google has already started to share the intellectual property it acquired from the Motorola purchase with other mobile device firms within the Android network. What is changing is the size of the networks and the permeability of membership: Open networks are not about 'in' vs. 'out' but multiple, flexible memberships of clubs having a host of interactions around issues, technologies, and opportunities. Business relationships and collaborative networks are increasingly resembling the social networks.

Open network collaborations are springing up as discrete positions in the value chain: ARM, Rolls-Royce, Inditex, Amazon, Google, and apps for the iPad are cases in point. Companies are choosing where to collaborate and where to control – whilst Apple may seek to go alone for product development, for its business model to continue to scale, broader network activities around apps, iTunes, and whatever comes next are probable. For the majority, leading new open networks will be a major source of future competitive advantage. Some are already creating marketplaces – for shopping, information, entertainment, research, and healthcare. These 21st-century marketplaces are where the greatest prospects for growth and disruption may lie.

A significant challenge is to develop the competences needed to successfully leverage the power of networks – the Rolls-Royce experience highlights the importance of focusing on both the partnership relationships and the content created by the partnership. And this requires two different sets of competence – relationship management and content expertise – that most likely reside in different people, often in different parts of the organization. So there is also a need to have the competence to manage and align these internal activities that enable external open networks to succeed.

Key lessons

- *Collaboration is an increasingly significant growth driver – but it can be difficult for many to make the leap, as it needs a fundamental change in mindset and management skills.*
- *Companies need to be clear where in the value chain they are collaborating and why – and this requires a deep appreciation of the distinctive competences that they have and the gaps that could be filled through collaboration.*
- *External collaboration is rooted in an understanding of the organization's place within society as a whole and the communities that it touches. Collaborative thinking has to start at the top and be embedded into the culture and values of an organization.*
- *Open network collaborations may create a shift in strategy to participation in emergent and adaptive ecosystems. To be successful requires focus on maintaining relationships and on the content created by the network – which requires different sets of skills.*

Sustainability

Although a number of the Growth Champions highlight sustainability as a current battlefield, for the majority they are actually talking about eco-efficiency. As the world faces increasing resource constraints and new regulations around carbon, energy, water, and land use start to be enforced, many will have to move from accommodating environmental sustainability issues to placing both environmental and social concerns center-stage.

As discussed in Part I, sustainable growth is the aspiration for many today, but it is also an ambition that few are yet to fully achieve. Although the topic has become a buzzword and has moved into many corporate boardrooms, how to make the green economy work is enough of a challenge for most without extending the wider sustainability agenda. The One-Planet view of growth within our resources is gaining momentum and a more balanced view of economic growth is beginning to appear in some quarters. However, with the West still struggling to extract itself from recession and the East just growing, some see that few are able or keen to focus on the sustainability challenge as much as they either could or should.

Within the Growth Champions we see organizations like BASF and Shell tackling the challenges of resource sustainability. Equally Nestlé, PepsiCo, and Procter & Gamble are paying more attention to water. Tata is not alone in looking for lower carbon production and Audi is seeking to make a strong play in electric mobility. The achievements of these and other companies are all to be recognized, but they may not be enough.

Over the next decade, expect a shift to a broader view of sustainability beyond eco-efficiency. Whilst we can see the beginnings of a shift away from purely shareholder value to a wider stakeholder value and ambitions being set that incorporate a higher social purpose, there is still a long way to go. As the social side of sustainability becomes as important as the environmental side, the activities that Tata and Bharti support with their foundations and the varied initiatives already underway from those such as Google and Nestlé may not be enough.

Local supply

For example, if all resources had to be locally sourced, an increasing focus on closer supply could challenge Amazon's long distance, centralized, regional distribution model just as much as it will cause issues for how the likes of BASF, PepsiCo, Procter & Gamble, Reckitt Benckiser, and Tata operate their businesses. Equally how will Nestlé and PepsiCo cope with further constrained local supply for key ingredients such as wheat, chocolate, and water?

Resource use

How will LEGO deal with being a manufacturer that uses primarily oil-based plastics? Emission targets, carbon prices, and fuel constraints could accelerate the shift away from kerosene to bio-fuels and alternative propulsion systems for airlines. Will Rolls-Royce's current technology leadership be usurped by a new development coming from left-field? In a world of silent electric mobility, will Audi's sporty performance brand still be a premium? As waste recycling regulations enforce manufacturers to take back their products at the end of lifecycles, how will a probable shift to leasing impact Samsung's profitability and business processes? How will Shell halve its carbon footprint and what will be the impact of a doubling of the price of carbon on Tata's steel production and profitability?

Choice

There will also be the challenge of responding to changes in societal attitudes to sustainability and the resultant choices that are made by consumers and regulators. Will, for instance, a backlash against genetically modified crops impact BASF's supply chain as well as that of Nestlé and PepsiCo? And, if we start to travel less, what will be the impact not only on Rolls-Royce's order book, but also on the revenues for Starwood Hotels and Narayana Hrudayalaya – how will more expensive flights impact medical tourism? On the social side, if there is a major public backlash against privacy invasion, what will be the implications for Amazon and Google as well as Apple? How will proactive regulation in this and other areas constrain business activity or make certain markets less attractive?

Key lessons

- *Most companies focus on a subset of sustainability – but meeting the full challenge of sustainability is some way off.*
- *Addressing sustainability can drive growth – it has gone beyond corporate social responsibility – and boardrooms, like it or not, will have to take note.*

Further Challenges

Whereas in the past, companies could choose to grow by being highly efficient and following a low-cost strategy or by pursuing a differentiating strategy supported by high levels of innovation, the challenge for the 21st century is to do both – to continually provide exceptional performance whilst developing new growth pathways.

The end of intellectual property?

In doing this, a potential challenge is in the arena of knowhow and IP. Currently things like the impact of crowd sourcing on Amazon's recommendation-based system; Intel's fight back against ARM; and even global sharing of pharmaceutical patents for drugs that did not make it through their clinical trials but could have benefit in other areas are all potentially questioning the ownership of knowledge. Indeed, in several sectors, many see that intellectual property itself will cease to have relevance in its current form. Open innovation and bilateral technology partnerships have been very much focused on having tradable intellectual property. As business model innovation comes more to the fore, it will be less about patents and copyright and more about knowhow – something which in a connected world can often pass from one to another at Twitter speed.

The war for talent

Equally, and perhaps more fundamentally, in an increasingly flattened world the competition for access to talent for global companies will increase. Not only is this about the challenge of growing organizations that increasingly have fewer full-time employees and more temporary free agents working with them on a project-by-project basis. It is also about attracting the right talent and 'the people worth employing.' This applies as much for Samsung, BASF, and Tata securing access to the best engineers in the world at a time when there are fewer of them graduating from many institutions as it does for PepsiCo, Starwood Hotels, and LEGO attracting the top consumer insight talent.

Seeing Emerging Challenges Clearer

The chances of all these future challenges emerging concurrently and with equally high impact are relatively low, but it would be foolish to think that the likelihood of none occurring is also slim. One or more of these shifts is highly probable and will therefore have some impact over the next decade. As well as undertaking foresight for highlighting potential innovation opportunities, as we have seen, more companies are also using similar techniques for identifying and assessing emerging threats. This is happening not only within individual organizations but also across open collaborative networks of companies as programs like the Future Agenda develop and share more insights into these and their potential implications. In developing and executing effective growth strategies, we clearly need to keep an eye out for the 'known-knowns' – the predictable events that will occur. However, we also need to look beyond the less certain inevitable surprises and also explore and act upon the possible implications of the wild cards.

CHAPTER 18

The Growth Agenda – The Essential Implications

At the end of this project, it is clear that not only is growth still a universally attractive ambition, but also that its manifestation is highly varied. From the insights it is evident that any company wishing to successfully grow needs to pay attention to a number of core points. Although there is no master to-do list for growth, from all the analysis and discussions, we can see the unmistakable ingredients that support success, not only in the companies profiled, but also in others that were part of the wider analysis that informed this project.

From all that has gone before, boiling everything down to a conclusion, we see 10 core implications for the future of successful and sustained growth.

1 Clear Ambition

Growth Champions know what and where is the prize. They know whether there is a 'gap in the market and a market in the gap' and also have a clear view on how to create a new market that will be a sustained growth platform. The leaders in their fields know what will differentiate a company from tomorrow's competition just as much as today's and in making full use of this have a clear, succinct, and individual ambition that employees, customers, and wider stakeholders all understand.

2 Distinctive Competence

While many organizations have identified capabilities and competences that enable them to operate and deliver products and services to their customers, few seem to have distinctive competences. Although the associated thinking has been around for many years, surprisingly few firms are yet to be clear about their real and defendable USP, what advantage it gives, and for how long. The Growth Champions by contrast do know, and even those that don't yet possess a truly future-proof distinctive competence, recognize what it should be and how they can most effectively build and develop it.

3 Innovation Priority

Successful companies not only innovate better than their peers, but they also have clear priority. They know where to most effectively innovate to put clear blue water between themselves and the competition. They use multiple innovations across product, service, and business models to create a complete innovation ecosystem, and they recognize what will be the future priority and why.

4 Unique Insight

While many organizations have access to ever better insights, many are buying them off the shelf using the same suppliers as their peers. The Growth Champions really know what it is that is needed ahead of their peers. They have experience and informed gut feel, but they also have evidence from bespoke research. The organizations that win by placing informed bets do so because they have unique insight.

5 Organizational Confidence

All the companies profiled have self-belief in what they are doing and why. They are all confident that they can deliver their respective ambitions. Partly this is based on a track record of exceptional delivery and both understanding and nurturing their distinctive competences. However, it is also very much seeding in a conviction that they are sure that they are doing the right thing and that they can do it well – and better than anyone else.

Introduction

The Growth Agenda

Nestlé PepsiCo

Audi Samsung

Reckitt Benckiser P&G

Starwood Inditex

Amazon Google

Narayana Novo Nordisk

Rolls-Royce ARM

BASF Shell

Tata Bharti

LEGO Apple

The Growth Challenge

6 Risk Appetite

The interplay between success and failure is a well-debated issue. While some companies favor processes to reduce failure, others permit creativity and experimentation. However, the Growth Champions all have a proportionate appetite for risk. Some will gives things a go, even before they are 100% defined, and are confident that they can learn quickly from mistakes and manage the upside. Others keep everything internal and obsessively experiment within the tent so that what gets delivered is as close to perfect as they can make it. However, both extremes are comfortable with risk and see it as an essential ingredient.

7 Innovation Balance

Linked to but distinct from the above, the successful growth companies of the past few years have the right balance between systematic innovation and creativity. Within their organizations, the culture and structure is in place to enable both to coexist and work together. Whether as part of a planned portfolio of activities or as a core element for every growth platform, they balance the level of innovation as much as the type. Incremental and disruptive product, service, and business models are emerging simultaneously from within single organizations as part of a coherent strategy.

8 Disruptive Innovation

Conventional thinking has it that disruption usually happens when small companies want to take on big ones and introduce change into a market. What is clear from many of the companies profiled is that disruption is no longer the sole property of start-ups – the Growth Champions clearly show that disruptive innovation can be nurtured and thrive within large corporations to deliver transformational growth. Some have done it, some are doing it, and others are getting ready to do it. But for all, disruptive innovation is no longer something just done to them but can also be a source of major growth as well.

9 Aligned Investment

After years of analysis, it is clear to the majority that innovation pays dividends but requires support. Whether solely focused on organic growth or including the targeted acquisition of new capabilities, the investment being made on delivering the future growth platforms is evidently aligned with the growth strategy. Access to lower cost capital than peers is critical for many and, whether from internal or external sources, is increasingly being well used. The high returns on innovation achieved by the Growth Champions rely equally on innovation impact as they do on well-focused investment where it matters most.

10 Acting at Speed

Lastly, we come to speed. Across virtually all of the examples, being fast to market – either as a leader or a follower – has been a critical commonality. Whether exploiting new technologies and business models ahead of peers, or doing a better job soon after their first move, Growth Champions operate at a speed that eclipses the competition. These companies have accelerated cycle times and in many cases halved their industry's established clock speed. They deliver the core incremental changes better and faster than the competition while also creating the next big thing that disrupts the market.

Whether using all or parts of this book, we hope that the views, insights, and lessons from the varied sections prove beneficial. These 10 implications will hopefully serve as a practical and succinct aide memoire of what has been covered. The world is clearly changing quicker than ever before as new challenges and opportunities emerge: growth in its many forms is evidently a priority for many. In the ambition to help inform and preferably stimulate those keen to deliver sustained growth, we hope that you find the stories and perspectives contained herein of use.

Introduction

The Growth Agenda

Nestlé PepsiCo

Audi Samsung

Reckitt Benckiser P&G

Starwood Inditex

Amazon Google

Narayana Novo Nordisk

Rolls-Royce ARM

BASF Shell

Tata Bharti

LEGO Apple

The Growth Challenge

Resources and References

In this section we provide information on the publications we have used in the research for Growth Champions that may be useful resources for further reading.

Part I: The Growth Agenda

- Accenture, *The Rise of the Emerging-Market Multinational*, Accenture, 2010
- Allan, Dave, Kingdon, Matt, Murrin, Kris and Rudkin, Daz, *Sticky Wisdom: How to Start a Creative Revolution at Work*, Capstone, 2002
- Andrews, Kenneth, *The Concept of Corporate Strategy*, Richard D. Irwin, 1971
- Barney, J. B., 'Firm Resources and Sustained Competitive Advantage', *Journal of Management*, Vol. 17: 1, pp. 99–120, 1991
- Birkinshaw, Julian, Bouquet, Cyril and Barsoux, J.-L., 'The 5 Myths of Innovation', *MIT Sloan Management Review*, December 16, 2010
- Chesbrough, Henry, *Open Innovation*, Harvard Business School Press, 2003
- Collins, David and Montgomery, Cynthia A., 'Competing on Resources: Strategy in the 1990s', *Harvard Business Review*, Issue 73 (July–August), pp. 118–128, 1995
- Department for Business Enterprise & Regulatory Reform, High Growth Firms in the UK: Lessons from an Analysis of Comparative UK Performance, 2008 www.bis.gov.uk/files/file49042.pdf
- Economist Intelligence Unit, Brazil Finance: Stepping into Africa 2010 http://viewswire.eiu.com/index.asp?layout=VWArticleVW3&article_id=107358795&ec=true&rf=0
- Fast Company, The World's Most Innovative Companies 2011 www.fastcompany.com/most-innovative-companies/2011/
- Gutmann, Peter, 'Strategies for Growth', *California Management Review*, Vol. 6: 3, pp. 31–36, 1964
- Harreld, J. B., O'Reilly, C. A. and Tushman, M. L., 'Dynamic Capabilities at IBM: Driving Strategy into Action', *California Management Review*, Vol. 49: 4, pp. 21–43, 2007
- Huston, Larry and Sakkab, Nabil, 'Connect + Develop: Inside Procter & Gamble's New Model for Innovation', *Harvard Business Review*, Vol. 84: 3, March 2006
- Jackson, Tim, *Prosperity without Growth*, Routledge, 2009
- Jones, Tim, *Innovation Leaders*, Infinite Ideas 2008 www.innovationleaders.org

- Jones, Tim and Dewing, Caroline, *Future Agenda: The World in 2020*, Infinite Ideas 2010 www.futureagenda.org
- Kao, John, *Innovation Nation*, Free Press, 2007
- Kelley, Tom, *The Art of Innovation: Lessons in Creativity from IDEO, America's Leading Design Firm*, Crown Business, 2001
- Kim, W. Chan and Mauborgne, Renée, *Blue Ocean Strategy*, Harvard Business School Press, 2005 www.blueoceanstrategy.com
- Leadbeater, Charles and Meadway, James, *Attacking the Recession: How Innovation Can Fight the Downturn*, NESTA, 2008
- Lee, Anne C., Ten Most Innovative Companies in China 2010 www.fastcompany.com/mic/2010/industry/most-innovative-china-companies
- 'Nicolas Sarkozy Wants to Measure Economic Success in "Happiness"', *The Telegraph*, 2009 www.telegraph.co.uk/news/worldnews/europe/france/6189530/Nicolas-Sarkozy-wants-to-measure-economic-success-in-happiness.html
- OECD Innovation Strategy 2011 www.oecd.org/innovation/strategy
- Porter, Michael, *The Competitive Advantage of Nations*, Free Press, 1990
- Prahalad, C. K. and Hamel, Gary, *Competing for the Future*, Harvard Business School Press, 1996
- Prosperity without Growth Report, Sustainability Commission 2009 www.sd-commission.org.uk/data/files/publications/prosperity_without_growth_report.pdf
- Ricardo, David, *On the Principles of Political Economy and Taxation*, John Murray, 1817
- Schumpeter, Joseph A., *Capitalism, Socialism, and Democracy*, Harper & Row, 1942
- Schwab, Klaus, 'The Global Competitiveness Report 2011–2012', *World Economic Forum* http://reports.weforum.org/global-competitiveness-2011-2012/
- Selznick, Peter, *Leadership in Administration*, Row Peterson, 1957
- Smith, Adam, *An Inquiry into the Nature and Causes of the Wealth of Nations*, W. Strahan and T. Cadell, 1776
- Snyder, Nancy Tennant, *Unleashing Innovation: How Whirlpool Transformed an Industry*, Jossey-Bass, 2008
- Solow, Robert M., 'A Contribution to the Theory of Economic Growth', *Quarterly Journal of Economics*, Vol. 70: 1, pp. 65–94, 1956
- Stevenson, Howard H., 'Defining Corporate Strengths and Weaknesses', *Sloan Management Review*, Vol. 17: 3, pp. 51–68, 1976
- Swan, Trevor, 'Economic Growth and Capital Accumulation', *Economic Record*, Vol. 32: 2, pp. 334–361, 1956
- Teece, D., Pisano, G. and Shuen, A., 'Dynamic Capabilities and Strategic Management', *Strategic Management Journal*, Vol. 18: 7, pp. 509–533, 1997

- The Lisbon Treaty, *Europa.eu* 2007 http://europa.eu/legislation_summaries/institutional_affairs/treaties/lisbon_treaty/index_en.htm
- Tidd, Joe and Bessant, John, *Managing Innovation: Integrating Technological, Market and Organizational Change*, John Wiley & Sons, 2009
- Tushman, Michael L. and Anderson, Philip, *Managing Strategic Innovation and Change*, Oxford University Press, 1997
- Ulwick, Anthony, *What Customers Want: Using Outcome-Driven Innovation to Create Breakthrough Products and Services*, McGraw-Hill, 2005
- UN News Centre, 'Happiness Should Have Greater Role in Development Policy – UN Member States', 2011 http://www.un.org/apps/news/story.asp?NewsID=39084&Cr=general+assembly&Cr1=
- Von Hippel, Eric, *Democratizing Innovation*, MIT Press, 2005
- World Bank, Migration and Remittances Factbook 2011 http://siteresources.worldbank.org/INTPROSPECTS/Resources/334934-1199807908806/Top10.pdf
- World Economic Forum (WEF), 'Summer Davos in Asia' 2010 http://www.weforum.org/pdf/summitreports/newchampions2010.pdf

Part II: The Growth Champions

As well as background analysis and research, we interviewed a wide range of individuals for these case studies: some on the record and others off. Rather than reference every quote, within the core text we have highlighted the views that have come from specific individuals. Other quotes in each chapter are taken either 'off the record' or from the publications and media coverage that we have identified below against each company. For further reading on these organizations and their growth activities, alongside the respective company websites and annual reports, we would therefore recommend the following resources:

Amazon

- 'Amazon: The Wal-Mart of the Web', *The Economist*, 1 October 2011 www.economist.com/node/21530980
- Donkin, Richard, 'The Death of Management as We Know It', *Financial Times*, 10 October 2011 www.ft.com/cms/s/2/dc03b33e-f100-11e0-b56f-00144feab49a.html#axzz1alpk3Wcb
- Hamilton, James, 'Cloud Computing is Driving Infrastructure Innovation', Amazon Technology Open House, 2011 http://mvdirona.com/jrh/TalksAndPapers/JamesHamilton_AmazonOpenHouse20110607.pdf

– 'Interstate sales taxes: The Amazon War', *The Economist*, 21 July 2011 www.economist.com/node/18988624

– Rose, Charlie, 'A Conversation with Amazon.com CEO Jeff Bezos', *charlierose.com*, 19 November 2007 www.charlierose.com/view/interview/8784

– Routson, Joyce, 'Jeff Bezos Makes Magic Out of Online Retailing', *business.in.com*, 17 February 2011 http://business.in.com/article/stanford/jeff-bezos-makes-magic-out-of-online-retailing/22472/1

Apple

– 'American Business: Big Apple vs. Big Oil', *The Economist*, 11 August 2011 www.economist.com/node/21525937

– Esslinger, Hartmut, *A Fine Line: How Design Strategies are Shaping the Future of Business*, Jossey Bass, 2009

– Hertzfeld, Andy, 'Pirate Flag', *folklore.org*, August 1983 www.folklore.org/StoryView.py?story=Pirate_Flag.txt

– Isaacson, Walter, 'Steve Jobs: A Biography', Simon & Schuster, 2011

– Kahney, Leander, 'Our Bad. *Wired* Had Some Tips For Apple – We Were Wrong', *Wired*, 18 March 2008

– Kirkpatrick, David, 'The Second Coming of Apple Through a Magical Fusion Of Man – Steve Jobs – and Company, Apple is Becoming Itself Again: The Little Anticompany That Could', *Fortune Magazine*, 9 November 1998 http://money.cnn.com/magazines/fortune/fortune_archive/1998/11/09/250834/index.htm

– Lashinsky, Adam, 'How Apple Works: Inside the World's Biggest Startup', *Fortune Magazine*, 23 May 2011 http://tech.fortune.cnn.com/2011/08/25/how-apple-works-inside-the-worlds-biggest-startup/

– Naughton, John, 'What Made Steve Jobs a Giant among the World's Greatest Communicators?' *The Observer*, 28 August 2011 www.guardian.co.uk/technology/2011/aug/27/steve-jobs-apple-ipod-ipad

– 'Steve Jobs' 2005 Stanford Commencement Address, Stanford University', *YouTube*, 2005 http://www.youtube.com/watch?v=UF8uR6Z6KLc

– 'Steve Jobs Introduces the "Digital Hub" Strategy at Macworld 2001', *YouTube*, 2001 www.youtube.com/watch?v=9046oXrm7f8

– 'Steve Jobs' Legacy: With Apple, the Medium Made the Message', *The Economist*, 11 October 2011 www.economist.com/blogs/prospero/2011/10/steve-jobss-legacy

– 'Steve Jobs Resigns: The Minister of Magic Steps Down', *The Economist*, 27 August 2011 www.economist.com/node/21526948

– 'Steve Jobs: The Magician', *The Economist*, 11 October 2011 www.economist.com/node/21531529

– Walters, Helen, 'Apple's Design Process', *Business Week*, 8 March 2008 www. businessweek.com/the_thread/techbeat/archives/2008/03/apples_design_p.html
– Wolff, Martin, 'In Memoriam: Steve Jobs', *Financial Times*, 10 October 2011 http://blogs.ft.com/martin-wolf-exchange/2011/10/10/in-memoriam-steve-jobs-2/#axzz1arCzNLes
– www.wired.com/techbiz/it/magazine/16-04/bz_apple_ourbad
– www.youtube.com/watch?v=UF8uR6Z6KLc

ARM

– Fern, M. J., 'ARM Disrupting Intel with its Business Model', *Fern Strategy*, 10 March 2011 http://fernstrategy.com/2011/03/10/arm-disrupting-intel-with-its-business-model/
– Watkins, Mary, 'Microsoft Strengthens the Outlook for ARM', *Financial Times*, 6 January 2011 www.ft.com/cms/s/0/6070eea6-19cb-11e0-b921-00144feab49a.html# axzz1alpk3Wcb

Audi

– 'Audi's Design Drive', *Business Week*, 26 November 2007 www.businessweek.com/ innovate/content/nov2007/id20071119_404008.htm
– Pollard, Tom, 'CAR Video Interview: Audi Design Chief Wolfgang Egger', 2010 www. carmagazine.co.uk/News/Search-Results/Industry-News/CAR-video-interview-Audi-design-chief-Wolfgang-Egger/

BASF

– Schäfe, Daniel, 'BASF Boosted by Rising Demand and Stake Sale', *Financial Times*, 6 May 2011 www.ft.com/cms/s/0/d5e759b4-77c6-11e0-ab46-00144feabdc0.html# axzz1alpk3Wcb
– 'The Chemical Industry: BASF Seeks a Stable Formula', *The Economist*, 23 June 2010 www.economist.com/blogs/newsbook/2010/06/chemical_industry

Bharti

– 'India in Africa: Catching Up', *The Economist*, 26 May 2011 www.economist.com/ node/18745335

– 'Indian Mobile Telecoms: Happy Customers, No Profits', *The Economist*, 16 June 2011 www.economist.com/node/18836120
– 'Interview: Manoj Kohli of Bharti Airtel', 1 April 2008, www.globaltelecomsbusiness. com/Article/2199376/Regions/25189/Interview-Manoj-Kohli-of-Bharti-Airtel.html?Articl eID=2199376&Type=Regions&ID=25189

Google

– 'A Gamble for Google', *The Economist*, 17 August 2011 www.economist.com/blogs/ babbage/2011/08/babbage-august-17th-2011
– Crawford, James, 'On the Future of Books', *Inside Google Books*, 14 October 2010 http://booksearch.blogspot.com/2010/10/on-future-of-books.html
– 'Google's CEO: "The Laws Are Written by Lobbyists"', 1 October 2010 www.theatlantic. com/technology/archive/2010/10/googles-ceo-the-laws-are-written-by-lobbyists/ 63908/#video
– 'Google Reaches 1 Billion Global Visitors', *comScoreDataMine.com*, 22 June 2011 www.comscoredatamine.com/2011/06/google-reaches-1-billion-global-visitors/
– 'In US, Smartphones Now Majority of New Cellphone Purchases', 30 June 2011 http:// blog.nielsen.com/nielsenwire/online_mobile/in-us-smartphones-now-majority- of-new-cellphone-purchases/
– 'Inside Google+ – How the Search Giant Plans to Go Social', 28 June 2011 www.wired. com/epicenter/2011/06/inside-google-plus-social
– Jenkins, Holman, W., 'Google and the Search for the Future', *Wall Street Journal*, August 14 2010 http://online.wsj.com/article/SB100014240527487049011045754232 94099527212.html
– Levy, Stephen, *In the Plex: How Google Thinks, Works, and Shapes Our Lives*, Simon & Schuster, 2011
– Manyika, James, 'Google's View on the Future of Business: An Interview with CEO Eric Schmidt', *McKinsey Quarterly*, September 2008 www.mckinseyquarterly.com/ Googles_view_on_the_future_of_business_An_interview_with_CEO_Eric_Schmidt_ 2229?pagenum=1
– 'Marissa Mayer Talking to Stanford University Students', *YouTube*, 30 June 2006 www. youtube.com/watch?v=soYKFWqVVzg
– Merrill, Douglas, 'Innovation at Google', *YouTube*, 2 August 2007 www.youtube.com/ watch?v=2GtgSkmDnbQ
– Rubin, Andy, @arubin, *Twitter*, 28 June 2011 https://twitter.com/#!/Arubin/status/ 85660213478309888

– Sims, Peter, 'The Montessori Mafia', *Wall Street Journal*, 5 April 2011 http://blogs.wsj.com/ideas-market/2011/04/05/the-montessori-mafia/
– Taycher, Leonid, 'Books of the World, Stand Up and Be Counted! All 129,864,880 of You', *Inside Google Books*, 5 August 2010 http://booksearch.blogspot.com/2010/08/books-of-world-stand-up-and-be-counted.html

Inditex

– Badia, Enrique, *Zara and Her Sisters*, Palgrave Macmillan, 2010
– Jones, Tim and Dewing, Caroline, *Future Agenda: The World in 2020*, Infinite Ideas 2010 www.futureagenda.org
– Nueno, Jose Luis and Ghemawat, Pankaj, 'Zara: Fast Fashion', *Harvard Business School*, Vol. 9, 21 December 2006, pp. 703–797
– Ton, Zeumetp, Corsi, Elena and Dessain, Vincent, 'Zara: Managing Stores for Fast Fashion', HBS Case 9-610-042, 19 January 2010

LEGO

– Koerner, Brendan I., 'Geeks in Toyland', Wired, Issue 14.02 (February), 2006 www.wired.com/wired/archive/14.02/lego.html
– Oliver, Keith, Samakh, Edouard and Heckmann, Peter, 'Rebuilding LEGO, Brick by Brick – Strategy + Business', Autumn 2007 www.strategy-business.com/article/07306?gko=99ab7
– Tidd, Joe and Bessant, John, 'Managing Innovation – LEGO Case Study', 2009 www.managing-innovation.com/case_studies/Lego.pdf

Narayana Hrudayalaya

– Anand, Geeta, 'The Henry Ford of Heart Surgery', *Wall Street Journal*, 25 November 2009 http://online.wsj.com/article/SB125875892887958111.html
– IBEF, 'Indian Health Care Market Facts', 2011 www.ibef.org/industry/healthcare.aspx
– Khanna, Tarun, Rangan, Kasturi and Manocaran, Melina, 'Narayana Hrudayalaya Heart Hospital: Cardiac Care for the Poor', Harvard Business School Case N9-505-078, 14 June 2005
– Lange, Roy, 'The Wal-Mart Effect Makes Good Hearts', *Indian Newslink*, March 2011 www.indiannewslink.co.nz/index.php/archives_2011/feb_15_2011/%E2%80%98the-wal-mart-effect%E2%80%99-makes-good-hearts.html

- 'Now, Narayana Eyes Local Expansion', *The Economic Times*, 19 July 2010 http://articles.economictimes.indiatimes.com/2010-07-29/news/27599916_1_beds-hospital-trust-narayana-hrudayalaya
- 'Shetty Health to Bring Medical Tourism to Cayman Islands', *International Medical Travel Journal*, 20 April 2010 www.imtj.com/news/?EntryId82=196131

Nestlé

- Bauer, Werner, 'Innovation and Renovation Consumers at the heart of Nestlé's R&D', *Nestlé Research Center*, November 2006, www.research.nestle.com/NR/rdonlyres/A0B6A926-179C-439E-906F-AC1E996D44E6/0/WernerBauerPresentation.pdf
- Edgar, Richard, 'Paul Bulcke Interview', *FT.com*, 31 March 2011 http://video.ft.com/v/873046492001/Paul-Bulcke-of-Nestl-Full-interview
- Lucas, Louise, 'Emerging Markets Fuel Nestlé's Growth', *Financial Times*, 17 February 2011 www.ft.com/cms/s/0/420bac2e-3a8e-11e0-9c65-00144feabdc0.html#axzz1PMHKVSZj
- Nestlé, 'Creating Shared Value', 2011 www.nestle.com/csv
- Porter, Michael and Kramer, Mark, 'The Big Idea: Creating Shared Value', *Harvard Business Review*, January 2011 http://hbr.org/2011/01/the-big-idea-creating-shared-value

Novo Nordisk

- 'Chronic Diseases in Developing Countries: Growing Pains', *The Economist*, 24 September 2011 www.economist.com/node/21530099
- 'Novo Nordisk', *Financial Times*, 29 October 2009 www.ft.com/cms/s/3/73f5a600-c46e-11de-912e-00144feab49a.html#axzz1alpk3Wcb
- 'Novo Nordisk', *Financial Times*, 11 September 2011 www.ft.com/cms/s/3/433d2834-d96c-11e0-b52f-00144feabdc0.html#axzz1alpk3Wcb

PepsiCo

- Gilligan, Tom, 'Indra Nooyi Interview with Dean of the McCombs School of Business', *YouTube*, 16 September 2010 www.youtube.com/watch?v=Ft7G549GF3Y
- 'Pepsi Gets a Makeover' *The Economist*, 25 March 2010 www.economist.com/node/15772138
- 'PepsiCo: Reasons to be Bubbly', *Financial Times*, 21 July 2011 www.ft.com/cms/s/3/55c18808-b3d1-11e0-855b-00144feabdc0.html#axzz1alpk3Wcb
- 'PepsiCo UK Health Report', 2010 www.pepsico.co.uk/purpose/health/health-report-2010

Procter & Gamble

- Brown, Bruce and Anthony, Scott D., 'How P&G Tripled its Innovation Rate', *Harvard Business Review*, June 2011 http://hbr.org/2011/06/how-pg-tripled-its-innovation-success-rate/ar/
- 'Consumer Goods: Basket Cases', *The Economist*, 14 October 2010 www.economist.com/node/17258888
- Dhar, Ravi, 'Interview with P&G CEO Bob McDonald, Yale School of Management', *YouTube*, 2011 www.youtube.com/watch?v=mGnc-rquSpI
- Huston, Larry and Sakkab, Nabil, 'Connect + Develop: Inside Procter & Gamble's New Model for Innovation', *Harvard Business Review*, Vol. 84: 3, 2006 http://hbr.org/2006/03/connect-and-develop-inside-procter-gambles-new-model-for-innovation/ar/1
- Lafley, A. G. and Charan, Ram, *The Game-Changer: How You Can Drive Revenue and Profit Growth with Innovation*, Crown Business, 2008 www.amazon.com/Game-Changer-Revenue-Profit-Growth-Innovation/dp/0307381730
- Management Lab, 'MLab Case on P&G', 2010 www.managementlab.org/publications/casestudies/procter-gamble
- Sellers, Patricia, 'P&G's Lafley: Lessons in Leadership', *Fortune Magazine*, 9 June 2009 http://postcards.blogs.fortune.cnn.com/2009/06/09/pgs-lafley-lessons-in-leadership/

Reckitt Benckiser

- Becht, Bart, 'Building a Company without Borders', *Harvard Business Review*, April 2010 http://hbr.org/2010/04/how-i-did-it-building-a-company-without-borders/ar/1
- Moulds, Josephine, 'Consumer Champion', *CNBC Magazine*, April 2009 www.cnbcmagazine.com/story/consumer-champion/924/1/
- 'Reckitt Benckiser: Robust Results', *Financial Times*, 25 July 2011 www.ft.com/cms/s/3/3ab6b426-b6c8-11e0-ae1f-00144feabdc0.html#axzz1alpk3Wcb
- Urry, Maggie, 'Reckitt's Strongly Flavoured Essence', *Financial Times*, 21 January 2008 www.ft.com/intl/cms/s/0/0dc91f26-c842-11dc-94a6-0000779fd2ac.html#axzz1YMef2Umv
- Wilson, Amy, 'Reckitt Benckiser's Bart Becht: A Lean, Clean Sales Machine', *The Telegraph*, 21 July 2010 www.telegraph.co.uk/finance/newsbysector/retailandconsumer/7902281/Reckitt-Benckisers-Bart-Becht-a-lean-clean-sales-machine.html

Rolls-Royce

- 'Manufacturing: A Tale of Two Industries', *The Economist*, 30 July 2011 www.economist.com/node/21524937

– 'Rolls-Royce: Per Ardua', *The Economist*, 3 February 2011 www.economist.com/node/18073351

Samsung Electronics

– 'Camp Samsung', *Business Week*, June 2006 www.businessweek.com/globalbiz/content/jun2006/gb20060622_914971.htm
– Freeze, Karen J. and Chung, Kyung-won, *Design Strategy at Samsung Electronics: Becoming a Top-Tier Company*, Design Management Institute, 2008
– Kharif, Olga, 'Samsung, LG Take Aim at Whirlpool with Smart Appliances', *Business Week*, January 2011 www.businessweek.com/technology/content/jan2011/tc20110126_265727.htm
– 'Research and Development: Rising in the East', *The Economist*, 30 December 2008 www.economist.com/node/12863581
– 'Samsung and its Attractions: Asia's New Model Company', *The Economist*, 1 October 2011 www.economist.com/node/21530984
– 'Samsung Design', *Business Week*, November 2004 www.businessweek.com/magazine/content/04_48/b3910003.htm

Shell

– Colvin, Geoff, 'Harry Brekelmans on the Future of Shell', *Fortune Magazine*, October 2011 http://money.cnn.com/2011/10/05/news/companies/shell_harry_brekelmans.fortune/index.htm
– Reed, Stanley and Tuttle, Robert, 'Gas into Oil: Shell's Water-into-Wine Project', *Business Week*, 11 March 2011 www.businessweek.com/magazine/content/10_12/b4171054613987.htm
– 'The Future of Natural Gas: Coming Soon to a Terminal Near You', *The Economist*, 6 August 2011 www.economist.com/node/21525381

Starwood Hotels

– Center for Hospitality Research, 'Starwood Hotels and Resorts – A Case Study', Cornell University, 2003 www.hotelschool.cornell.edu/research/chr/pubs/register/login.html?url=%2Fchr%2Fpdf%2Fshowpdf%2Fchr%2Fresearch%2Fcasestudies%2Fstarwood.pdf%3Fmy_path_info%3Dchr%2Fresearch%2Fcasestudies%2Fstarwood.pdf
– Davidson, Andrew, 'Frits van Paasschen Interview', *The Sunday Times*, 20 December 2009 www.thesundaytimes.co.uk/sto/business/article193145.ece

- 'Hotels 325: Special Report', *Hotels Magazine*, October 2010 www.marketingandtechnology.com/repository/webFeatures/HOTELS/2010giants.pdf
- Palmeri, Christopher and Balfour, Frederik, 'Behind Starwood's Hotel Expansion in China', *Business Week*, 27 August 2009 www.businessweek.com/magazine/content/09_36/b4145056702173.htm
- 'Starwood: Fashion House', *The Economist*, 16 March 2011 www.economist.com/blogs/gulliver/2011/03/starwood

Tata

- Dobbs, Richard and Gupta, Rajat, 'An Indian Approach to Global M&A: An Interview with the CFO of Tata Steel', *McKinsey Quarterly*, October 2009 www.mckinseyquarterly.com/An_Indian_approach_to_global_MA_An_interview_with_the_CFO_of_Tata_Steel_2441
- 'Emerging-Market Giants: Tata Sauce', *The Economist*, 3 May 2011 www.economist.com/node/18283899
- Krishnan, Rishikesha, 'From Jugaad to Systematic Innovation: The Challenge for India', The Utpreraka Foundation, Bangalore, 2010 http://jugaadtoinnovation.blogspot.com/
- 'The BrandFinance Global 500', 2010 http://brandirectory.com/league_tables/table/global_500
- 'The Tata Group: Out of India', *The Economist*, 3 May 2011 www.economist.com/node/18285497

Part III: The Growth Challenge

- Drucker, Peter, 'A Message from Peter Drucker (1909–2005)', www.cgu.edu/pages/4126.asp

Appendix – Key Data for the Growth Champions

Amazon USA	NASDAQ:AMZN					
	2005	2006	2007	2008	2009	2010
Total sales ($ billion)	8.49	10.71	14.84	19.17	24.51	34.20
Total sales growth (%)	23%	26%	39%	29%	28%	40%
EBIT ($ million)	432	389	660	901	1161	1497
EBIT growth (%)	22%	–10%	70%	37%	29%	29%
Operating margin (EBIT/Revenue)	5.1%	3.6%	4.4%	4.7%	4.7%	4.4%
Net income ($ million)	359	190	476	645	902	1152
Net income growth (%)	–39%	–47%	151%	36%	40%	28%
Total assets ($ million)	3696	4363	6485	8314	13,813	18,797
Research and development ($ million)	–	–	818	1033	1240	1734
Employees	12,000	13,900	17,000	20,700	24,300	33,700
Sales per employee ($ 000)	707.5	770.6	872.6	925.9	1008.6	1015.0
R&D intensity	–	–	5.5%	5.4%	5.1%	5.1%
Share price at end of year ($)	47.15	39.46	92.64	51.28	134.52	180
Share price growth (%)	6%	–16%	135%	–45%	162%	34%

Apple USA	NASDAQ:AAPL					
	2005	**2006**	**2007**	**2008**	**2009**	**2010**
Total sales ($ million)	13,931	19,320	24,578	37,491	42,905	65,225
Total sales growth (%)	68%	39%	27%	53%	14%	52%
EBIT ($ million)	1808	2820	5006	8947	12,066	18,540
EBIT growth (%)	389%	56%	78%	79%	35%	54%
Operating margin (EBIT/Revenue)	13%	15%	20%	24%	28%	28%
Net income ($ million)	1328	1990	3495	6119	8235	14,013
Net income growth (%)	399%	50%	76%	75%	35%	70%
Total assets ($ million)	11,516	17,200	25,347	36,171	47,501	75,183
Research and development ($ million)	535	712	782	1109	1333	1782
Employees	14,800	17,787	21,600	32,010	34,306	46,646
Sales per employee ($ 000)	941	1086	1138	1171	1251	1398
R&D intensity	3.8%	3.7%	3.2%	3.0%	3.1%	2.7%
Share price at end of year ($)	71.89	84.84	198.08	85.35	210.73	322.56
Share price growth (%)	123%	18%	133%	−57%	147%	53%

ARM UK	LON: ARM					
	2005	2006	2007	2008	2009	2010
Total sales (£ million)	232.4	263.254	259.16	298.934	305.022	406.595
Total sales growth (%)	52.0%	13.3%	−1.6%	15.3%	2.0%	33.3%
EBIT (£ million)	40.474	56.006	45.096	63.189	47.259	110.027
EBIT growth (%)	15%	38.4%	−19.5%	40.1%	−25.2%	132.8%
Operating margin (EBIT/Revenue)	17%	21%	17%	21%	15%	27%
Net income (£ million)	29.647	48.156	35.25	43.592	40.439	85.974
Net income growth (%)	14.9%	62.4%	−26.8%	23.7%	−7.2%	112.6%
Total assets (£ million)	817.668	744.256	642.944	848.183	844.433	1084.662
Research and development (£ million)	80.3	84.9	84.0	87.6	112.2	139.8
Employees	1324	1659	1728	1740	1710	1889
Sales per employee (£ 000)	175,528.70	158,682.34	149,976.85	171,801.15	178,375.44	215,243.52
R&D Intensity	35%	32%	32%	29%	37%	34%
Share price at end of year (£)	121	125.75	124	86.5	177.5	423.3
Share price growth	9.5%	3.9%	−1.4%	−30.2%	105.2%	138.5%

Audi Germany	ETR:NSU					
	2005	2006	2007	2008	2009	2010
Total sales (€ million)	26,591	31,142	33,617	34,196	29,840	35,441
Total sales growth (%)	8.5%	17.1%	7.9%	1.7%	−12.7%	18.8%
EBIT (€ million)	1310	1946	2915	3177	1928	3634
EBIT growth (%)	15%	49%	50%	9%	−39%	88%
Operating margin (EBIT/Revenue)	4.9%	6.2%	8.7%	9.3%	6.5%	10.3%
Net income (€ million)	824	1343	1692	2207	1347	2630
Net income growth (%)	−5%	63%	26%	30%	−39%	95%
Total assets (€ million)	16,112	18,910	22,578	26,056	26,550	30,772
Research and development (€ million)	1585	1982	2226	2161	2050	2469
Employees	52,412	52,297	53,347	57,533	57,723	59,221
Sales per employee (€ k)	507	595	630	594	517	598
R&D Intensity	6%	6%	7%	6%	7%	7.0%
Share price at end of year (€)	295.00	543.00	623.00	416.00	502.00	635.00
Share price growth (%)	37.9%	84.1%	14.7%	−33.2%	20.7%	26.5%

BASF Germany	ETR:BAS					
	2005	2006	2007	2008	2009	2010
Total sales (€ billion)	42.7	52.6	58.0	62.3	50.7	63.9
Total sales growth (%)	13.9%	23.1%	10.2%	7.5%	−18.6%	26.0%
EBIT (€ billion)	5.8	6.8	7.3	6.5	3.7	7.8
EBIT growth (%)	12.3%	15.8%	8.4%	−11.7%	−43.1%	111.1%
Operating margin (EBIT/Revenue)	13.6%	12.8%	12.6%	10.4%	7.3%	12.2%
Net income (€ billion)	3.01	3.22	4.07	2.91	1.41	4.56
Net income growth (%)	50%	7%	26%	−28%	−52%	223%
Total assets (€ billion)	35.7	45.3	46.8	50.9	51.3	59.4
Research and development (€ billion)	1.06	1.28	1.38	1.36	1.40	1.49
Employees	80,945	95,247	95,175	96,924	104,779	109,140
Sales per employee (€ 000)	528.1	552.4	608.9	642.8	483.8	585.2
R&D intensity	2.5%	2.4%	2.4%	2.2%	2.8%	2.3%
Share price at end of year (€)	64.7	73.8	101.4	26	43.5	59.60
Share price growth (%)	22%	14%	37%	−74%	67%	37%

Bharti Airtel India

	BSE – 532454					
	2005	**2006**	**2007**	**2008**	**2009**	**2010**
Total sales (INR million)	116,215.453	185,195.992	270,249.348	369,615.517	396,150.229	594,672
Total sales growth (%)	45%	59%	46%	37%	7%	50%
EBIT (INR million)	25,365.717	48,860.411	76,537.043	93,072.956	106,977.983	76,782
EBIT growth (%)	53%	93%	57%	22%	15%	−28%
Operating margin (EBIT/Revenue)	22%	26%	28%	25%	27%	0.1291
Net income (INR million)	22,567	42,572	68,158	86,458	93,019	60,467
Net income growth (%)	35.9%	88.6%	60.1%	26.8%	7.6%	−35.0%
Total assets (INR million)	161,546.985	217,243.161	297,887.765	472,643.612	603,947.465	646,407.747
Employees	7827	10,970	20,314	25,543	24,538	18,354
Sales per employee (INR million)	14.85	16.88	13.30	14.47	16.14	32.40
Share price at end of year (INR)	172.5	314.4	474.10	352.4	328.8	358.40
Share price growth	64%	82.3%	50.8%	−25.7%	−6.7%	9.0%
Number of customers (million)	18	27	40	75	96	220

Google USA	NASDAQ:GOOG					
	2005	2006	2007	2008	2009	2010
Total sales ($ billion)	6.14	10.60	16.59	21.80	23.65	29.32
Total sales growth (%)	92%	73%	56%	31%	9%	24%
EBIT ($ billion)	2.14	4.01	5.67	5.85	8.38	10.80
EBIT growth (%)	23%	87%	41%	3%	43%	29%
Operating margin (EBIT/Revenue)	34.9%	37.8%	34.2%	26.9%	35.4%	36.8%
Net income ($ million)	1.47	3.08	4.20	4.23	6.52	8.51
Net income growth (%)	267%	110%	37%	1%	54%	30%
Total assets ($ billion)	10.27	18.47	23.34	31.77	40.50	57.85
Research and development ($ million)	484.0	1228.6	2120.0	2793.2	2843.0	3762.0
Employees	5680	10,674	16,805	20,222	19,835	24,400
Sales per employee ($ million)	1.08	0.99	0.99	1.08	1.19	1.202
R&D intensity	7.88%	11.59%	12.78%	12.82%	12.02%	12.83%
Share price at end of year ($)	414.86	460.48	691.48	307.65	619.98	593.97
Share price growth (%)	115%	11%	50%	–56%	102%	–4%

Inditex Spain	ITX.MC					
	2005	**2006**	**2007**	**2008**	**2009**	**2010**
Total sales (€ million)	6741	8196	9435	10,407	11,084	12,527
Total sales growth (%)	21%	22%	15%	10%	7%	13%
EBIT (€ million)	1094	1356	1652	1609	1729	2290
EBIT growth (%)	19%	24%	22%	−3%	7%	32%
Operating margin (EBIT/Revenue)	16%	17%	18%	15%	16%	18%
Net income (€ million)	803	1002	1250	1253	1314	1732
Net income growth (%)	26%	25%	25%	0%	5%	32%
Total assets (€ million)	5202.9	5742.2	7105.6	7776.6	8335.4	9826.1
Employees	58,190	69,240	79,517	89,112	92,301	100,138
Sales per employee (€)	115,844.65	118,370.88	118,653.87	116,785.62	120,085.37	125,097.37
Share price at end of year (€)	27.55	40.81	42.02	31.33	43.39	56.03
Share price growth (%)	27%	48%	3%	−25%	38%	29%
Number of stores	2692	3131	3691	4264	4607	5044
Average revenue per store (€ million)	2.5	2.6	2.6	2.4	2.4	2.5

LEGO Denmark	Private Company					
	2005	2006	2007	2008	2009	2010
Total sales (DKK million)	7027	7798	8027	9526	11,661	16,014
Total sales growth (%)	12%	59%	59%	59%	59%	59%
EBIT (DKK million)	329	1281	1414	1852	2887	4889
EBIT growth (%)	–	289%	10%	31%	56%	69%
Operating margin (EBIT/Revenue)	5%	16%	18%	19%	25%	31%
Net income (DKK million)	214	1290	1028	1352	2204	3718
Net income growth (%)	–	503%	−20%	32%	63%	69%
Total assets (DKK million)	7058	6907	6009	6496	7788	10,972
Research and development (DKK million)	–	202	222	248	292	306
Employees	5302	4908	4199	5388	7286	8365
Sales per employee (DKK million)	1.33	1.59	1.91	1.77	1.60	1.91
R&D intensity	–	2.6%	2.8%	2.6%	2.5%	1.9%

Nestlé Group Switzerland	NESN.VX					
	2005	2006	2007	2008	2009	2010
Total sales (CHF billion)	91.08	98.46	107.55	109.91	107.62	109.72
Total sales growth (%)	8%	8%	9%	2%	–2%	2%
EBIT (CHF billion)	11.88	13.30	15.02	15.68	15.70	16.19
EBIT growth (%)	10%	12%	13%	4%	0%	3%
Operating margin (EBIT/Revenue)	13%	14%	14%	14%	15%	15%
Net income (CHF billion)	8.60	9.85	11.38	19.05	11.79	35.38
Net income growth (%)	22%	14%	16%	67%	–38%	200%
Total assets (CHF billion)	103.4	101.8	114.7	106.2	110.9	111.6
Research and development (CHF billion)	1.50	1.73	1.88	1.98	2.02	1.88
Employees	253,000	265,000	276,000	283,000	278,000	281,000
Sales per employee (CHF k)	360.0	371.5	389.7	388.4	387.1	390.5
R&D intensity	1.6%	1.8%	1.7%	1.8%	1.9%	1.7%
Share price at end of year (CHF)	39.3	43.3	52	41.6	50.2	54.75
Share price growth (%)	32%	10%	20%	–20%	21%	9%

Novo Nordisk Denmark	NYSE: NVO					
	2005	2006	2007	2008	2009	2010
Total sales (DKK million)	33,760	38,743	41,831	45,553	51,078	60,766
Total sales growth (%)	16%	15%	8%	9%	12%	19%
EBIT (DKK million)	8234	9164	10,971	12,695	13,988	18,286
EBIT growth (%)	10%	11%	20%	16%	10%	31%
Operating margin (EBIT/Revenue)	24%	24%	26%	28%	27%	30%
Net income (DKK million)	5864	6452	8522	9654	10,768	14,403
Net income growth (%)	17%	10%	32%	13%	12%	34%
Total assets (DKK million)	41,960	44,692	47,731	50,603	54,742	61,402
Research and development (DKK million)	5097.8	6315.11	7194.93	7516.24	6932	9601.03
Employees	22,460	23,613	26,008	27,068	27,985	30,483
Sales per employee (DKK million)	1.50	1.64	1.61	1.68	1.83	1.99
R&D intensity	15.10%	16.30%	17.20%	16.50%	13.57%	15.80%
Share price at end of year ($)	28.14	41.82	64.86	51.39	63.85	112.57
Share price growth (%)	4%	49%	55%	−21%	24%	76%

PepsiCo USA	NYSE:PEP					
	2005	2006	2007	2008	2009	2010
Total sales ($ billion)	32.562	35.137	39.474	43.251	43.232	57.838
Total sales growth (%)	11%	8%	12%	10%	0%	34%
EBIT ($ billion)	6.382	6.989	7.643	7	8	8.232
EBIT growth (%)	15%	10%	9%	−8%	15%	2%
Operating margin (EBIT/Revenue)	20%	20%	19%	16%	19%	14%
Net income ($ billion)	4.078	5.642	5.658	5.142	5.94	6.32
Net income growth (%)	−3%	38%	0%	−9%	16%	6%
Total assets ($ million)	31.727	29.93	35	35.994	39.848	68
Research and development ($ million)	340	282	364	388	414	488
Employees	60,634	62,251	58,532	57,080	58,340	100,415
Sales per employee ($)	537.03	564.44	674.40	757.73	741.04	575.99
R&D intensity	1.0%	0.8%	0.9%	0.9%	1.0%	0.8%
Share price at end of year ($)	59.54	62.55	75.90	54.77	60.8	65.33
Share price growth (%)	14%	5%	21%	−28%	11%	7%

Procter & Gamble USA	NYSE: PG					
	2005	2006	2007	2008	2009	2010
Total sales ($ billion)	56.7	68.2	72.4	79.3	76.7	78.9
Total sales growth (%)	10%	20%	6%	9%	−3%	3%
EBIT ($ billion)	10.0	12.4	13.7	14.9	14.4	15.0
EBIT growth (%)	7%	24%	10%	9%	−3%	4%
Operating margin (EBIT/Revenue)	18%	18%	19%	19%	19%	19%
Net income ($ billion)	6.9	8.7	10.3	12.1	13.4	12.7
Net income growth (%)	12%	25%	19%	17%	11%	−5%
Total assets ($ billion)	20.3	135.7	138.0	144.0	134.8	128.2
Research and development ($ billion)	1.93	2.06	2.21	2.21	2.04	1.95
Employees	107,000	136,000	135,000	135,000	132,000	127,000
Sales per employee ($ 000)	530	502	537	587	581	622
R&D intensity	3.4%	3.0%	3.1%	2.8%	2.7%	2.5%
Share price at end of year ($)	57.6	64.3	72	61.8	60.6	64.3
Share price growth (%)	9%	12%	12%	−14%	−2%	6%

Reckitt Benckiser UK	LON:RB					
	2005	2006	2007	2008	2009	2010
Total sales (£ billion)	4.179	4.922	5.269	6.563	7.753	8.453
Total sales growth (%)	8%	18%	7%	25%	18%	9%
EBIT (£ million)	876	874	1209	1474	1892	2136
EBIT growth (%)	0.1377%	0%	38%	22%	28%	13%
Operating margin (EBIT/Revenue)	21.0%	17.8%	22.9%	22.5%	24.4%	25.3%
Net income (£ million)	669	674	938	1120	1418	1570
Net income growth (%)	16%	1%	39%	19%	27%	11%
Total assets (£ billion)	4.21	5.74	5.87	9.18	8.66	13.34
Research and development (£ million)	63	82	92	109	126	125
Employees	20,300	21,900	23,400	24,300	24,900	27,200
Sales per employee (£ 000)	205.86	224.75	225.17	270.08	311.37	310.77
R&D intensity	1.5%	1.7%	1.7%	1.7%	1.6%	1.5%
Share price at end of year (£)	1920	2334	2914	2578	3356	3525
Share price growth (%)	22%	22%	25%	−12%	30%	5%

Rolls-Royce UK

	LON:RR					
	2005	2006	2007	2008	2009	2010
Total sales (£ million)	6603	7156	7435	9082	10,414	11,085
Total sales growth (%)	11%	8%	4%	22%	15%	6%
EBIT (£ million)	877	700	512	862	1172	1134
EBIT growth (%)	110%	−20%	−27%	68%	36%	−3%
Operating margin (EBIT/Revenue)	13%	10%	7%	9%	11%	10%
Net income (£ million)	347	1140	645	−1342	2217	543
Net income growth (%)	31%	229%	−43%	−308%	265%	−76%
Total assets (£ million)	9563	10,451	11,490	15,227	15,491	16,234
Research and development (£ million)	663	747	824	885	864	923
Employees	36,200	38,000	39,500	39,000	38,500	38,900
Sales per employee (£ 000)	55.39	52.79	50.81	51.49	52.18	51.67
R&D intensity	10.0%	10.4%	11.1%	9.7%	8.3%	8.3%
Share price at end of year (p)	427.5	447.75	546	335.5	483.5	623
Share price growth (%)	68%	5%	22%	−39%	44%	29%

Samsung Electronics South Korea	005935.KS					
	2005	2006	2007	2008	2009	2010
Total sales (KRW billion)	80,630	85,426	98,508	121,294	138,994	154,630
Total sales growth (%)	−2%	6%	15%	23%	15%	11%
EBIT (KRW billion)	7575	9008	8973	5636	11,578	19,328
EBIT growth (%)	−36%	19%	0%	−37%	105%	67%
Operating margin (EBIT/Revenue)	9%	11%	9%	5%	8%	12%
Net income (KRW billion)	7640	7926	7421	5526	9649	16,147
Net income growth (%)	−29%	4%	−6%	−26%	75%	67%
Total assets (KRW billion)	74,462	81,366	93,375	105,301	118,281	134,288
Research and development (KRW billion)	5499.9	5714.8	6074.0	7057.9	7616.2	9099.1
Employees	80,594	138,000	144,000	164,600	187,800	190,500
Sales per employee (KRW million)	1000.45	619.03	684.08	736.90	740.12	811.71
R&D intensity	6.8%	6.7%	6.2%	5.8%	5.5%	5.9%
Share price at end of year	491	480	411	258	525	649
Share price growth (%)	65%	−2%	−14%	−37%	103%	−24%

Shell Netherlands	RDSA.AS					
	2005	2006	2007	2008	2009	2010
Total sales ($ billion)	306.7	318.8	355.8	458.4	278.2	368.1
Total sales growth (%)	15.0%	3.9%	11.6%	28.8%	−39.3%	32.3%
EBIT ($ billion)	44.6	44.6	50.6	50.8	21.0	35.3
EBIT growth (%)	40.8%	0.1%	13.3%	0.5%	−58.6%	68.1%
Operating margin (EBIT/Revenue)	14.5%	14.0%	14.2%	11.1%	7.6%	9.6%
Net income ($ billion)	26.6	26.3	31.9	26.5	12.5	20.1
Net income growth (%)	36.9%	−1.0%	21.3%	−17.1%	−52.7%	60.8%
Total assets ($ billion)	219,516	235,276	269,470	282,401	292,181	322,560
Research and development ($ million)	588	885	1167	1230	1125	1019
Employees	110,500	108,000	104,000	102,000	101,000	97,000
Average sales per employee ($ million)	2.78	2.95	3.42	4.49	2.75	3.79
R&D intensity	0.19%	0.28%	0.33%	0.27%	0.40%	0.28%
Share price at end of year (€)	25.78	26.72	28.81	18.34	21.10	24.73
Share price growth (%)	21.7%	3.6%	7.8%	−36.3%	15.0%	17.2%

Starwood Hotels USA

	NYSE:HOT					
	2005	2006	2007	2008	2009	2010
Total sales ($ million)	5977	5979	6153	5907	4696	5071
Total sales growth (%)	11%	0%	3%	−4%	−21%	8%
EBIT ($ million)	642	682	716	321	−296	335
EBIT growth (%)	6%	6%	5%	−55%	−192%	213%
Operating margin (EBIT/Revenue)	11%	11%	12%	5%	−6%	7%
Net income ($ million)	422	10,403	542	329	73	477
Net income growth (%)	7%	2365%	−95%	−39%	−78%	553%
Total assets ($ million)	12,454	9280	9622	9703	8761	9776
Employees	145,000	145,000	145,000	145,000	145,000	145,000
Sales per employee ($)	13,827.59	13,834.48	13,841.38	13,848.28	13,855.17	13,862.07
Share price at end of year ($)	51.6	62.5	44.03	17.09	36.57	60.78
Share price growth (%)	−12%	21%	−30%	−61%	114%	66%
Number of hotels	864	896	925	968	992	1041
Number of rooms	264,000	272,500	282,000	292,000	298,500	308,000
Average revenue per room per year ($ 000)	23	22	22	20	16	16

Tata Steel India	BOM:500470					
	2005	2006	2007	2008	2009	2010
Total sales (INR crores)	17,399	20,196	134,562	150,250	105,415	122,326
Total sales growth (%)	10%	16%	566%	12%	−170%	16%
EBIT (INR crores)	5239	6261	18,287	18,495	31	12,102
EBIT growth (%)	31%	20%	192%	1%	−100%	38,939%
Operating margin (EBIT/Revenue)	30%	31%	14%	12%	0%	0%
Net income (INR crores)	3506	4222	12,321	4849	−2120	8856
Net income growth (%)	1%	20%	192%	−61%	−144%	518%
Total assets (INR crores)	14,617	255,987	92,193	91,355	64,232	78,555
Research and development (INR crores)	20.84	26.85	36.67	39.70	41.40	75.69
Employees	38,182	37,205	87,598	86,548	81,269	81,251
Sales per employee (INR crores)	0.46	0.54	1.54	1.74	1.30	1.51
R&D intensity	0.12%	0.13%	0.03%	0.03%	0.04%	0.06%
Share price at end of year	380	482	931	211	617	679
Share price growth (%)	−1%	27%	93%	−77%	192%	10%

Contributor Credits

Part I: The Growth Agenda
Tim Jones, Dave McCormick, Palie Smart

Part II: The Growth Champions
Amazon and Google – Stephen Johnston
Audi and Samsung Electronics –Charlie Dawson, Roger Dennis and Tim Jones
BASF and Shell– Tobias Rooney and Dave McCormick
LEGO and Apple– Neal Stone, Lucy Hooberman and Tim Jones
Nestlé and PepsiCo – Cliff Dennett and Tim Jones
Narayana Hrudayalaya and Novo Nordisk– Satish Rao and Tobias Rooney
Reckitt Benckiser and Procter & Gamble– Mariah Hartman, Joss Langford and Tim Jones
Rolls-Royce and ARM – David Coates
Starwood Hotels and Inditex– James Alexander, Lisa McDowell and Tim Jones
Tata and Bharti– Hamsini Shivkumar

Part III: The Growth Challenge
Dave McCormick, Peter Bryant and Tim Jones
Additional Data and Secondary Research
Joanna Roszak – Cranfield School of Management
Nitya Varma – Oxford University/Space Doctors
Louise Tan – The Foundation
Overall Editors
Tim Jones, Dave McCormick and Caroline Dewing

Index